GREAT WRITING 2

Great Paragraphs

FOURTH EDITION

KEITH S. FOLSE
UNIVERSITY OF CENTRAL FLORIDA

APRIL MUCHMORE-VOKOUN
HILLSBOROUGH COMMUNITY COLLEGE

ELENA VESTRI SOLOMON
KHALIFA UNIVERSITY OF SCIENCE, TECHNOLOGY, AND RESEARCH, UAE

Australia • Canada • Mexico • Singapore • Spain • United Kingdom • United States

Great Writing 2: Great Paragraphs
Keith S. Folse, April Muchmore-Vokoun, Elena Vestri Solomon

Publisher: Sherrise Roehr

Executive Editor: Laura Le Dréan

Development Editor: Charlotte Sturdy

Director of Global Marketing: Ian Martin

International Marketing Manager: Caitlin Thomas

Director of Content and Media Production: Michael Burggren

Senior Content Project Manager: Daisy Sosa

Senior Print Buyer: Mary Beth Hennebury

Cover Design: Christopher Roy and Michael Rosenquest

Cover Image: JOEL SARTORE/ National Geographic Stock

Interior Design: Aysling Design

Composition: PreMediaGlobal, Inc.

U.S. Edition

ISBN-13: 978-1-285-19490-5

International Student Edition

ISBN-13: 978-1-285-75060-6

National Geographic Learning
20 Channel Center Street
Boston, MA 02210
USA

Cengage Learning is a leading provider of customized learning solutions with office locations around the globe, including Singapore, the United Kingdom, Australia, Mexico, Brazil, and Japan.

Cengage Learning products are represented in Canada by Nelson Education, Ltd.

Visit National Geographic Learning online at **ngl.cengage.com**

Visit our corporate website at **www.cengage.com**

Printed in the United States of America
2 3 4 5 6 7 18 17 16 15 14

Contents

Scope and Sequence

Unit	Writing	Grammar for Writing	Building Better Vocabulary	Original Student Writing
1 p. 2 **PARAGRAPHS**	• What Is a Paragraph? • Four Features of a Paragraph • Working with Paragraphs	• Using the Simple Present Tense with Facts • Using the Imperative in Process Paragraphs • Using the Simple Past Tense in Narrative Paragraphs • Checking for Verbs and Fragments	• Word Associations • Using Collocations	**Original Student Writing:** Write a paragraph of your choice. **Photo Topic:** Write about something thrilling. **Timed Writing Topic:** Describe the daily life of a police officer.
2 p. 32 **DEVELOPING IDEAS FOR WRITING A PARAGRAPH**	• Brainstorming • How Brainstorming Works	• Subject-Verb Agreement	• Word Associations • Using Collocations	**Original Student Writing:** Write a paragraph of your choice. **Photo Topic:** Write about something very scary. **Timed Writing Topic:** Is English easy or difficult to learn?
3 p. 46 **TOPIC SENTENCES**	• The Topic Sentence • Features of a Good Topic Sentence	• Using Commas in Sentences • Avoiding Three Common Sentence Errors	• Word Associations • Using Collocations	**Original Student Writing:** Brainstorm and write a paragraph about animal communication, international flights, pollution, or smart phones. **Photo Topic:** Write about learning something new. **Timed Writing Topic:** Why do so many people want to learn English?
4 p. 70 **SUPPORTING AND CONCLUDING SENTENCES**	• Supporting Sentences • Concluding Sentences	• Using Pronouns in Place of Key Nouns	• Word Associations • Using Collocations	**Original Student Writing:** Write a paragraph of your choice. **Photo Topic:** Write about a place to visit in your town or city. **Timed Writing Topic:** Is it a good idea to require all students to wear a school uniform?

Unit	Writing	Grammar for Writing	Building Better Vocabulary	Original Student Writing
5 **p. 94** **PARAGRAPH REVIEW**	• Review • Working with the Structure of a Paragraph • Analyzing Paragraphs	• Reviewing Articles	• Word Associations • Using Collocations	**Original Student Writing:** Write a paragraph of your choice. **Photo Topic:** Write about something interesting to do. **Timed Writing Topic:** What are the best snack foods?
6 **p. 116** **DEFINITION PARAGRAPHS**	• What Is a Definition Paragraph? • Quotation Marks • Putting the Paragraph Together: Sequencing	• Using Adjective Clauses • Creating Sentences with Variety	• Word Associations • Using Collocations	**Original Student Writing:** Write a definition paragraph. **Photo Topic:** Define an emotion. **Timed Writing Topic:** What does the word courage mean to you?
7 **p. 138** **PROCESS PARAGRAPHS**	• What Is a Process Paragraph?	• Using Sequence Words and Chronological Order	• Word Associations • Using Collocations	**Original Student Writing:** Write a process paragraph. **Photo Topic:** Write about a process or how something happens. **Timed Writing Topic:** What are the steps in correcting an error on a bill?
8 **p. 154** **DESCRIPTIVE PARAGRAPHS**	• What Is a Descriptive Paragraph? • Describing with the Five Senses • Using Positive and Negative Adjectives for More Precise Meanings	• Using Adjectives in Writing • Using Prepositions of Location to Describe • Using Correct Word Order with Prepositions of Location	• Word Associations • Using Collocations	**Original Student Writing:** Write a paragraph that describes something. **Photo Topic:** Describe a national monument that is important to you. **Timed Writing Topic:** Describe your ideal teacher.
9 **p. 180** **OPINION PARAGRAPHS**	• What Is an Opinion Paragraph? • Facts and Opinions • Topic Sentences for Opinion Paragraphs • Choosing a Topic for an Opinion Paragraph	• Recognizing Word Forms and Common Suffixes	• Word Associations • Using Collocations	**Original Student Writing:** Write an opinion paragraph. **Photo Topic:** Write your opinion about the best kinds of zoos. **Timed Writing Topic:** What minimum age should be required to get a driver's license?

(Continued)

Unit	Writing	Grammar for Writing	Building Better Vocabulary	Original Student Writing
10 p. 198 **NARRATIVE PARAGRAPHS**	• What Is a Narrative Paragraph? • Working with Ideas for Narrative Paragraphs	• Maintaining Verb Tense Consistency	• Word Associations • Using Collocations	**Original Student Writing:** Write a narrative paragraph about an experience that you have had. **Photo Topic:** Write about a surprising, frightening, happy, or funny experience you have had. **Timed Writing Topic:** Write about a specific event from your childhood.
11 p. 222 **PARAGRAPHS IN AN ESSAY: PUTTING IT ALL TOGETHER**	• From Paragraphs to Essays • Getting to Know Essays • What Does an Essay Look Like? • Putting an Essay Together		• Word Associations • Using Collocations	**Original Student Writing:** Write a narrative, comparison, cause-effect, or argumentative essay. **Photo Topic:** Write about the effect of technology in rural places. **Timed Writing Topic:** What should happen to students who are caught cheating on an exam?

Overview

Framed by engaging **National Geographic** images, the new edition of the *Great Writing* series helps students write better sentences, paragraphs, and essays. The new *Foundations* level meets the needs of low-level learners through practice in basic grammar, vocabulary, and spelling, while all levels feature clear explanations, student writing models, and meaningful practice opportunities. The new edition of the *Great Writing* series develops academic writing skills for learners at all levels.

Great Writing: Foundations focuses on basic sentence construction, emphasizing grammar, vocabulary, spelling, and composition.

Great Writing 1 focuses on sentences as they appear in paragraphs.

Great Writing 2 teaches paragraph development.

Great Writing 3 transitions from paragraphs to essays.

Great Writing 4 focuses on essays.

Great Writing 5 practices more advanced essays.

The earliest ESL composition textbooks were merely extensions of ESL grammar classes. The activities in these books did not practice English composition as much as they did ESL grammar points. Later books, on the other hand, tended to focus too much on the composing process. We feel that this focus ignores the important fact that the real goal for English learners is both to produce a presentable product and to understand the composing process. From our years of ESL and other L2 teaching experience, we believe that the *Great Writing* series allows English learners to achieve this goal.

Great Writing 2: Great Paragraphs offers introductory material on paragraph writing. The book is designed for intermediate students; however, the language is controlled as much as possible so that dedicated upper beginners and weak advanced students may also benefit from the instruction. Depending on the class level and the amount of writing that is done outside of class, there is enough material for 60 to 80 classroom hours. If a more substantial amount of writing is done outside of class, the number of hours for a faster group can be as little as 40.

Organization

In *Great Writing 2*, Units 1–5 deal with the elements of a good paragraph. Units 6–11 feature five different kinds of paragraphs and an introduction to writing essays. While it is not necessary to cover these five paragraph modes in the given order, the current sequencing will allow for some recycling of grammatical and lexical items. *The Brief Writer's Handbook with Activities* and the *Appendices* contain additional practice material to support both the process and the mechanics of writing.

Contents of a Unit

Although each unit has specific writing objectives (listed at the beginning of the unit), the following features appear in every unit:

Example Paragraphs

Because we believe that writing and reading are inextricably related, the 101 example paragraphs model a rhetorical mode and/or provide editing activities. Many models are often preceded by schema-building questions and are followed by questions about organization, syntactic structures, or other composition features. New, potentially unfamiliar vocabulary words are glossed next to each paragraph. These words can provide students with a list of vocabulary to add to a separate vocabulary notebook.

Grammar for Writing

Since good writing requires good knowledge of the mechanics of English, *Great Writing* includes clear charts and detailed instruction that relates directly to the writing assignments. In addition, numerous activities give students the opportunity to practice and refine their grammar and writing knowledge and skills.

Activities

The new, fourth edition contains more than 150 activities, 55 suggestions for additional paragraph writing assignments and 31 supplemental activities in the *Brief Writer's Handbook with Activities.* These writing, grammar, and vocabulary activities gradually build the skills students need to write well-crafted sentences and paragraphs and provide learners with more input in English composition, paragraph organization, and cohesion.

Building Better Vocabulary

Each unit includes two vocabulary-building activities to build schema and collocations. In the first activity, Word Associations, the student identifies words that best relate to the target vocabulary word. This allows them to build connections to more words and thus grow their vocabulary more quickly. Words from the Academic Word List are starred (see pages 275–276 for the complete list). The second activity, Using Collocations, helps students learn specific word combinations, or collocations, which will help their original writing sound more advanced. It is helpful to encourage students to use these new words in their Original Student Writing assignment and to add them to a vocabulary notebook.

Writer's Notes

Great Writing 2: Great Paragraphs features small pieces of writing advice that help writers understand more about use and format. Content includes brainstorming techniques, peer editing guidelines, citing original sources, and plagiarism.

Building Better Sentences

Periodically in each unit, students are asked to turn to Appendix 1 and work on building better sentences. Each practice is intentionally short and includes only three problems. In each problem, there are three to five short sentences that the students must combine into a single sentence that expresses all the ideas in a logical and grammatically correct manner.

Original Writing

Each unit includes an activity that requires students to do some form of writing. *Original Student Writing* includes writing prompts and a set of directions to encourage students to follow the writing process and refer back to the lessons taught in the unit.

Additional Writing Topics give students the opportunity to continue practicing their writing skills. The first topic always links back to the opening photograph and writing prompt. It is up to the teacher to decide whether all students will write about the same topic or if each student is free to choose any of the topics listed.

Peer Editing

At the end of each unit, a peer editing activity offers students the opportunity to provide written comments to one another with the goal of improving their paragraphs. A unique peer editing sheet for each unit can be found online at NGL.Cengage.com/GW2, and each one provides the guidance and structure that is necessary for students at this level to successfully perform this task. We recommend that students spend 15 to 20 minutes reading a classmate's paragraph and writing comments using the questions on the peer editing sheet.

Timed Writing

One way to improve students' comfort level with the task of writing under a deadline, such as during a testing situation, is to provide them with numerous writing opportunities that are timed. The final activity in each unit features a timed-writing prompt that is geared toward the grammar and sentence structure presented in that unit. Students are given five minutes to read the prompt and make a quick writing plan, followed by 25 minutes of actual writing. Instructors may use this activity at any time during the lesson.

What's New in This Edition?

- Engaging images from **National Geographic** connect learning to the greater world.
- New and updated readings act as springboards and models for writing.
- Updated Grammar for Writing sections clearly present grammar and help students learn the structures for writing.
- Streamlined instruction and practice activities offer step-by-step guidelines to focus writers on both the writing process and product.
- Words from the Academic Word List are highlighted in vocabulary activities, encouraging students to expand their word knowledge.
- The expanded *Brief Writer's Handbook* now includes a Useful Vocabulary for Writing section to help writers choose appropriate language for the different rhetorical modes.
- An all-new level, *Great Writing: Foundations* introduces students to the basics of grammar, spelling, and vocabulary.
- A new Online Workbook encourages learners to further practice grammar, vocabulary, and editing skills. Students can also write paragraphs or essays, and submit them to the instructor electronically.
- An updated Presentation Tool allows instructors to use the book in an interactive whiteboard setting and demonstrate the editing process.
- An eBook provides another option to use *Great Writing* in a traditional or blended learning environment.

Ancillary Components

In addition to the *Great Writing 2: Great Paragraphs* Student Book, the following components help both the instructor and the students expand their teaching and learning.

- **Online Workbook**: Includes a wealth of vocabulary, grammar, writing, and editing practice with immediate feedback.
- **Presentation Tool CD-ROM:** Offers instructors the ability to lead whole-class presentations and demonstrate the editing process.
- **Assessment CD-ROM with ExamView®:** Allows instructors to create and customize tests.
- **Teacher Companion Site at NGL.Cengage.com/GW2:** Provides teachers with answer keys, peer editing sheets, and teacher's notes.
- **Student Companion Site at NGL.Cengage.com/GW2:** Provides students with peer editing sheets, glossary, and interactive flashcards.
- **eBook**: Offers an interactive option.

Inside a Unit *Great Writing 2: Great Paragraphs*

Framed by engaging **National Geographic** content, the new edition of the *Great Writing* series helps students write better sentences, paragraphs, and essays. The new *Foundations* level meets the needs of low-level learners through practice in basic grammar, vocabulary, and spelling, while all levels feature clear explanations, student writing models, and meaningful practice opportunities. The new edition of the *Great Writing* series develops academic writing skills for learners at all levels.

Unit
1
Paragraphs
OBJECTIVES To learn the four main features of a paragraph
To use the correct form for verbs in a paragraph
A carnival ride throws off orbs of light in
St. Paul, Minnesota.
2

Impactful ***National Geographic*** images provide engaging topics to encourage student writing.

ACTIVITY 2 **Reading Example Supporting Sentences**

Read the paragraphs on pages 73–75. Notice how the supporting sentences tell you more about the topic sentence. Compare what you wrote in Activity 1 to the information in each paragraph. How well did you predict the content?

Example Paragraph 21

A Great Tourist Destination

New York and Boston attract millions of tourists, but I think one of the best cities to visit on the east coast of the United States is Washington, D.C. It has some of the most interesting **landmarks** and tourist **spots** in the country. There are many monuments to visit, such as the Lincoln Memorial, the Jefferson Memorial, and the Washington Monument, which is the tallest building in Washington. For more excitement, the area called Georgetown in northwest Washington is famous for its shopping and restaurants. Finally, there is the White House tour. On this tour, the guide **leads** visitors as they walk through many of the rooms in the White House and **view** the home of the president of the United States. Although Washington, D.C., does not have the large number of visitors that New York or Boston does, I think this city is one of the best destinations for tourists.

a landmark: a historical building, a well-known location

a spot: a place, a location

to lead: to show the way, organize

to view: to see, look at

Over 100 Sample Writing Models focus on specific writing skills and rhetorical modes.

Vocabulary words are glossed to encourage independent mastery of new terms.

Inside a Unit *Great Writing 2: Great Paragraphs*

Grammar for Writing

Using Pronouns in Place of Key Nouns

Because a paragraph is about one topic, writers often repeat key nouns from the topic sentence in their supporting sentences. However, too much repetition of these same nouns can sound awkward. You can avoid repeating key nouns by replacing them with **pronouns** after the nouns are first introduced.

Explanation	Examples
Pronouns take the place of a person, place, or thing: Carla → She Washington → It Giraffes → They Replace nouns with pronouns to avoid repetition.	One of the best cities to visit on the east coast of the United States is **Washington, D.C. It** has some of the most interesting landmarks and tourist spots in the country. One of the people that I most admire is **my great-grandmother Carla. She** came to the United States from Italy in 1911 as a young woman on a large ship.
Remember to be consistent. If you use *they* at the beginning of a paragraph, do not switch to *it*. The underlined words are incorrect in the example.	**Giraffes** are among the most interesting of all the animals that live in Africa. **They** are easily recognized by **their** special features. **They** have long necks and long legs, but its neck is longer than its legs. It usually lives in very dry areas.

ACTIVITY 9 **Identifying Key Nouns and Pronouns**

Read the following sentences. Write the correct pronoun in each blank. Use *it, they,* or *we.* Then underline the key noun that the pronoun refers to.

1. Tennis rackets have changed tremendously in the last ten years. ___They___ used to be small and heavy, but that is no longer true.
2. Soccer is by far the most widely played sport in the world. __________ is played professionally on nearly every continent.
3. I will never forget my childhood friends Carlos and Juan and what __________ taught me.
4. Not only is text messaging fast, but __________ is also an interesting way to practice English.
5. A bad thing happened to my classmates and me at school yesterday. __________ were late coming to class, so the teacher gave us an extra homework assignment.
6. If you travel to Budapest, Hungary, you will fall in love with the Danube River. __________ separates the city into two parts—Buda and Pest.

New **Grammar for Writing** sections provide clear explanations and examples of the target grammar, giving learners easy access to the structures they will use in their writing.

Guided, structured activities help students practice writing, grammar, and editing skills.

Building Better Vocabulary activities highlight words from the Academic Word List and prompt students to apply their vocabulary and knowledge of collocations.

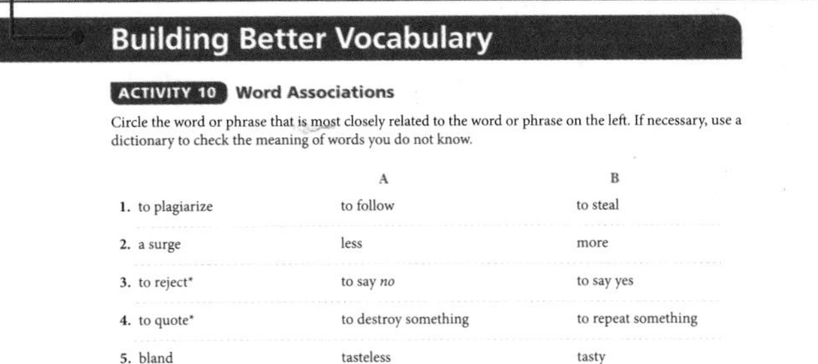

Building Better Vocabulary

ACTIVITY 10 **Word Associations**

Circle the word or phrase that is most closely related to the word or phrase on the left. If necessary, use a dictionary to check the meaning of words you do not know.

	A	B
1. to plagiarize	to follow	to steal
2. a surge	less	more
3. to reject*	to say *no*	to say yes
4. to quote*	to destroy something	to repeat something
5. bland	tasteless	tasty

Original Student Writing: Opinion Paragraph

ACTIVITY 11 **Original Writing Practice**

Develop a paragraph about a strong opinion that you have. Include facts to support your opinion. Follow these guidelines:

- Choose a topic such as the value of living abroad, connecting teachers' salaries to students' grades, or why young children need their own cell phones.
- Brainstorm your topic. If you want, use the Internet for ideas.
- Write a topic sentence with a controlling idea.
- Write supporting sentences with facts that support your opinions.
- Check for incorrect word forms.
- Use at least two of the vocabulary words or phrases presented in Activity 9 and Activity 10. Underline these words and phrases in your paragraph.

If you need ideas for words and phrases, see the Useful Vocabulary for Better Writing on pages 275–279.

Original Student Writing gives students the chance to combine the grammar, vocabulary, and writing skills together in one writing piece.

Peer Editing activities increase students' awareness of common errors.

Timed Writing

How quickly can you write in English? There are many times when you must write quickly, such as on a test. It is important to feel comfortable during those times. Timed-writing practice can make you feel better about writing quickly in English.

1. Take out a piece of paper.
2. Read the writing prompt.
3. Brainstorm ideas for five minutes.
4. Write a short paragraph (six to ten sentences).
5. You have 25 minutes to write your paragraph.

In your opinion, why do so many people want to learn English? Give a few strong examples to support your answer.

For more practice with the grammar, vocabulary, and writing found in this unit, go to NGL.Cengage.com/GW2.

Timed Writing prepares students for success on standardized and international writing exams.

Technology *Great Writing 2*

For Instructors:

The Presentation Tool CD-ROM contains time-saving, interactive activities from the student book, a set of whiteboard tools, and additional content to help the instructor guide learners through the editing process.

Teacher's Notes, Answer Keys, and Peer Editing Sheets are available online for instructors.

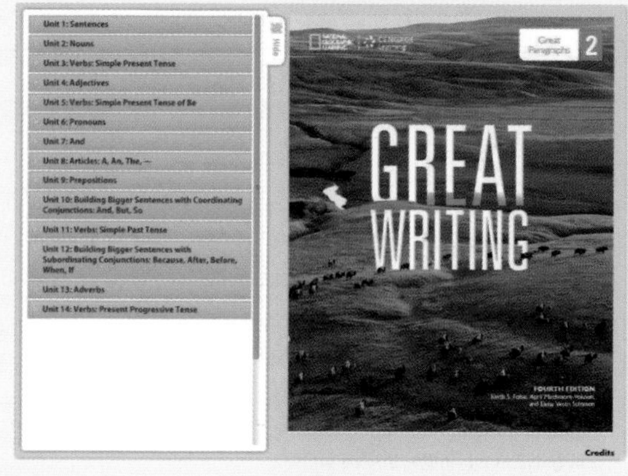

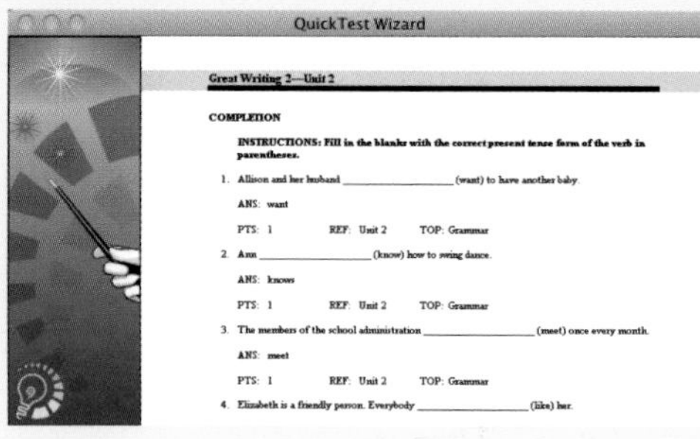

The Assessment CD-ROM with ExamView® allows instructors to create and customize tests and quizzes easily.

For Students:

The Online Workbooks: Each level features additional independent practice in vocabulary, grammar, writing, and editing.

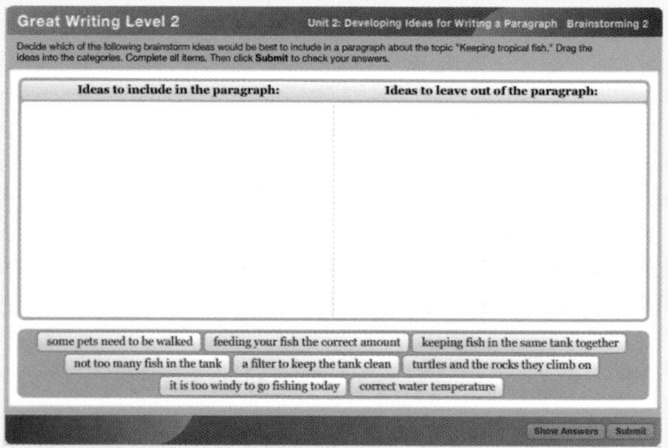

***Great Writing* eBooks** are available for all levels and are compatible with tablets, laptops, and smartphones.

Acknowledgements

We would like to thank the hundreds of ESL and English composition colleagues who have generously shared their ideas, insights, and feedback on second language writing, university English course requirements, and textbook design.

We would also like to thank Laura Le Dréan, Thomas Jefferies, Ian Martin, and Emily Stewart from National Geographic Learning for their guidance. We are extremely grateful for the support given to us by our developmental editors Katherine Carroll, Charlotte Sturdy, and Yeny Kim. We also remain forever grateful to our previous editors at Houghton Mifflin, Susan Maguire, Kathy Sands-Boehmer, and Kathleen Smith for their indispensable guidance throughout the birth and growth of this writing project.

Likewise, we are indebted to the following reviewers who offered ideas and suggestions that shaped our revisions:

Laura Taylor, Iowa State University, Iowa
Mary Barratt, Iowa State University, Iowa
Abdelhay Belfakir, University of Central Florida, Florida
Taoufik Ferjani, Zayed University, United Arab Emirates
Cheryl Alcorn, Pasadena City College, California
Paul McGarry, Santa Barbara City College, California
Fernanda Ortiz, University of Arizona, Arizona
Michelle Jeffries, University of Arkansas—Fayetteville, Arkansas
Suzanne Medina, California State University—Dominguez Hills, California
Kristi Miller, American English Institute, California
Kevin Van Houten, Glendale Community College, California
Izabella Kojic-Sabo, University of Windsor, Canada
Wayne Fong, Aston School, China
Yiwei Shu, New Oriental School, China
Raul Billini, John F. Kennedy Institute of Languages, Dominican Republic
Rosa Vasquez, John F. Kennedy Institute of Languages, Dominican Republic
Mike Sfiropoulos, Palm Beach State College, Florida
Louise Gobron, Georgia State University, Georgia
Gabriella Cambiasso, City College of Chicago—Harold Washington, Illinois
Lin Cui, Harper College, Illinois
Laura Aoki, Kurume University, Japan
Rieko Ashida, Konan University, Japan
Greg Holloway, Kyushu Institute of Technology, Japan
Collin James, Kansai Gaigo University, Japan
Lindsay Mack, Ritsumeikan Asia Pacific University, Japan
Robert Staehlin, Morioka University, Japan
Jenny Selvidge, Donnelly College, Kansas
Phan Vongphrachanh, Donnelly College, Kansas
Virginia Van Hest Bastaki, Kuwait University, Kuwait
Jennifer Jakubic, Century College, Minnesota
Trina Goslin, University of Nevada—Reno, Nevada
Margaret Layton, University of Nevada—Reno, Nevada
Amy Metcalf, University of Nevada—Reno, Nevada
Gail Fernandez, Bergen Community College, New Jersey

Lynn Meng, Union County College—Elizabeth, New Jersey
Zoe Isaacson, Queens College, New York
Sherwin Kizner, Queens College, New York
Linnea Spitzer, Portland State University, Oregon
Jennifer Stenseth, Portland State University, Oregon
Rebecca Valdovinos, Oregon State University, Oregon
Renata Ruff, Prince Mohammed University, Saudi Arabia
Ya Li Chao, National Taichung University of Science and Technology, Taiwan
Kuei-ping Hsu, National Tsing Hua University, Taiwan
Morris Huang, National Taiwan University of Science and Technology, Taiwan
Cheng-Che Lin, Tainan University of Technology, Taiwan
Rita Yeh, Chia Nan University of Pharmacy and Science, Taiwan
Nguyen Chanh Tri, Vietnam Australia International School, Vietnam
Mai Minh Tien, Vietnam Australia International School, Vietnam
Tuan Nguyen, Vietnam Australia International School, Vietnam
Nguyen Thi Thanh The, Vietnam Australia International School, Vietnam
Nguyen Vu Minh Phuong, Vietnam Australia International School, Vietnam
Colleen Comidy, Seattle Central Community College, Washington
Cindy Etter, University of Washington, Washington
Kris Hardy, Seattle Central Community College, Washington
Liese Rajesh, Seattle Central Community College, Washington

Finally, many thanks go to our students who have taught us what ESL composition ought to be. Without them, this work would have been impossible.

Keith S. Folse
April Muchmore-Vokoun
Elena Vestri Solomon

Photo Credits

Unit 1
Pages 2–3: © JUSTIN GUARIGLIA/ National Geogreaphic
Page 7: © Camera Press Ltd / Alamy
Page 10: © Peter Dazeley/Getty Images
Page 13: © Picsbyst/Shutterstock.com
Page 15: © RICHARD NOWITZ/ National Geographic Creative
Page 17: © De Agostini Picture Library / M. Seemuller /The Bridgeman Art Library
Page 18: © Mike Theiss/National Geographic Creative
Page 19: © Hulton Archive/Getty Images
Page 20: © MAHMUD HAMS/ AFP/Getty Images
Page 22: © Davis Barber / PhotoEdit
Page 24: © Andrii Gatash/E+/Getty Images

Unit 2
Page 32–33: © G. Brad Lewis/ Aurora Photos
Page 36: © Jody Watt / Pacific Stock / Aurora Photos
Page 37: © Jake Lyell / Alamy
Page 38: © Mark Skalny/ Shutterstock.com
Page 42: © Monkey Business Images/Shutterstock.com

Unit 3
Pages 46–47: © Rick Neves/Flickr/ Getty Images
Page 48: © Rainer W. Schlegelmilch/Getty Images
Page 52: © Paul Bradbury/ Caiaimage/Getty Images
Page 56: © TAYLOR S. KENNEDY/ National Geographic Creative
Page 57: © Mauricio Handler/ National Geographic Creative
Page 58: © Olga Danylenko/ Shutterstock.com
Page 59: © Mikael Damkier/ Shutterstock.com
Page 64: © BRIAN J. SKERRY/ National Geographic Creative

Unit 4
Pages 70–71: © Johan Sjolander/ Getty Images
Page 73: © JAMES P. BLAIR/ National Geographic Creative
Page 74: © Museum of the City of New York/Byron Collection/ Archive Photos/Getty Images
Page 75: © PAUL CHESLEY / National Geographic Creative.
Page 79: © David Buffington/Blend/ Aurora
Page 81: © Luciano Mortula/ Shutterstock.com
Page 83: © Poznyakov/Shutterstock.com
Page 89: © Getty Images/Handout/ Getty Images News/ Getty Images
Page 90: © CRISTINA MITTERMEIER/National Geographic Creative

Unit 5
Pages 94–95: © BARRY TESSMAN/ National Geographic Creative
Page 98: © Buddy Mays/Alamy
Page 99: © Rob Walls/Alamy
Page 101: © Tumar /Shutterstock.com
Page 102: © UDO WEITZ/EPA/ Newscom
Page 104: © Andrey Nekrasov/ Image Broker/Aurora Photos
Page 106: © TIM LAMAN/National Geographic Creative
Page 107: © VikOI/Shutterstock.com
Page 108: © ZSSD/Minden Pictures/Getty Images
Page 109: © William Silver/ Shutterstock.com
Page 112: © istockphotos/jmalov

Unit 6
Pages 116–117: © Claudio Villa/ Getty Images
Page 118: © MSPhotographic / Shutterstock.com
Page 120: © Peter & Georgina Bowater/Stock Connection/ Aurora PhotosPhotography/ Alamy
Page 122: © Irina Schmidt / Shutterstock.com
Page 128: © GETTY IMAGES INC/National Geographic Creative.
Page 133: © vicspacewalker/ Shutterstock.com

Unit 7
Pages 138–139: © MARK THIESSEN/National Geographic Creative
Page 140: © DreamPictures/Blend Images/Getty Images
Page 142: © AMNON EICHELBERG/National Geographic Creative
Page 144: © David Halbakken/ Alamy
Page 148: © Datacraft Co Ltd/Getty Images

Unit 8
Pages 154–155: © Richard Nowitz/ National Geographic Creative
Page 156: © Steve Vidler/Alamy

Page 160: © JASON EDWARDS/ National Geographic Creative
Page 161: © Todd Shoemake/ Shutterstock.com
Page 163: © Doug Menuez/ Photodisc/getty images
Page 174: © E.J. Baumeister Jr./Alamy
Page 176: © SZ Photo/Scherl/DIZ Muenchen GmbH, Sueddeutsche Zeitung Photo/Alamy

Unit 9

Pages 180–181: © AP IMAGES (SEE AP/WIDE WORLD PHOTOS INC)/National Geographic Creative
Page 183: Top: © iStockphoto.com/ Pawel Gaul
Page 185: © DESIGN PICS INC/ National Geographic Creative
Page 186: © Robert Landau/ Alamy
Page 191: © Goodluz/Shutterstock. com

Unit 10

Pages 198–199: © Joel Sartore/ National Geographic Creative.
Page 200: © Hill Street Studios/ Blend Images/Getty Images
Page 202: © Greg Balfour Evans/ Alamy
Page 204: © Datacraft Co Ltd/Getty Images
Page 206: © Purestock/Getty images
Page 209: © Alex Coppel/National Geographic My Shot/National Geographic Creative
Page 210: © AP Photo/David Tenenbaum
Page 213: © PRAKASH SINGH/ AFP/Getty Images
Page 214: © StockLite /Shutterstock.com
Page 215: © iStockphoto.com/ luisapuccini
Page 217: © Boaz Rottem/Alamy
Page 218: © Big Cheese Photo/Big Cheese Photo/Aurora Photos

Unit 11

Pages 222–223: © TAO Images Limited/Getty Images
Page 227: © Olaf Krüger/Image Broker/Aurora Photo
Page 231: © Frank Herholdt/Alamy
Page 236: © Andrew Zarivny/ Shutterstock.com

Unit 1

Paragraphs

The bungee slingshot thrills tourists in Singapore.

OBJECTIVES To learn the four main features of a paragraph
To use the correct form for verbs in a paragraph

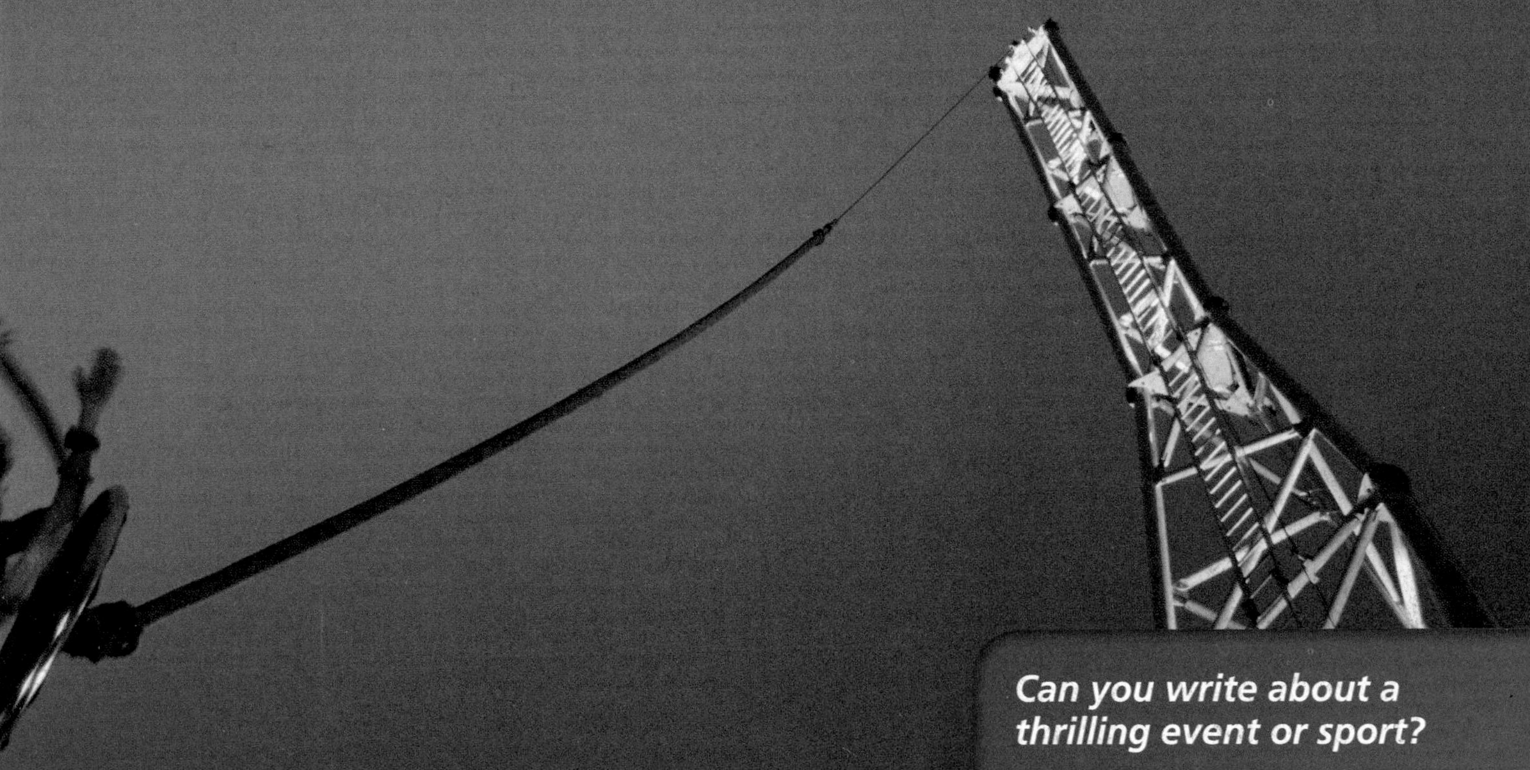

Can you write about a thrilling event or sport?

What Is a Paragraph?

A **paragraph** is a group of sentences about one topic or one idea. Learning to write a paragraph is an important academic skill. On the next few pages, you will find three example paragraphs—a comparison paragraph, a process paragraph, and a narrative paragraph. Each example shows what a good paragraph looks like.

ACTIVITY 1 Studying an Example Paragraph

This paragraph is about two countries that are near each other but have many differences. Discuss the Preview Questions with your classmates. Then read the paragraph and answer the questions that follow.

Preview Questions

1. What are some things you could compare about two cities or countries?
2. What things do you know about Brazil and Chile?

Example Paragraph 1

Chile and Brazil

Chile and Brazil are two important countries in South America. **Although** they are near each other, they are very different in **geography**, population, and language. The easiest difference to see is in geography. Brazil is much larger than Chile. In fact, Brazil is the largest nation in South America and **takes up** almost half of the **entire** South American continent. Brazil is so large that it shares a **border** with every South American country except Chile and Ecuador. In contrast, Chile is a very **narrow** country along the Pacific Coast of South America. The widest point in this long country is only 160 miles (258 kilometers). These two countries also **differ** in population. Brazil is home to almost 200 million people, but only about 17 million people live in Chile. Finally, these two countries differ in national languages. Like most countries in South America, the **majority** of people in Chile speak Spanish. In Brazil, however, the most commonly spoken language is Portuguese because the Portuguese **settled** in Brazil in 1500. These three differences make these countries extremely interesting.

although: contrast between two ideas; but

the geography: the land of a place

to take up: occupy space

entire: whole, all

a border: a line between two countries

narrow: the opposite of wide

to differ (in): be different

the majority: more than half

to settle: to come to live in a new area

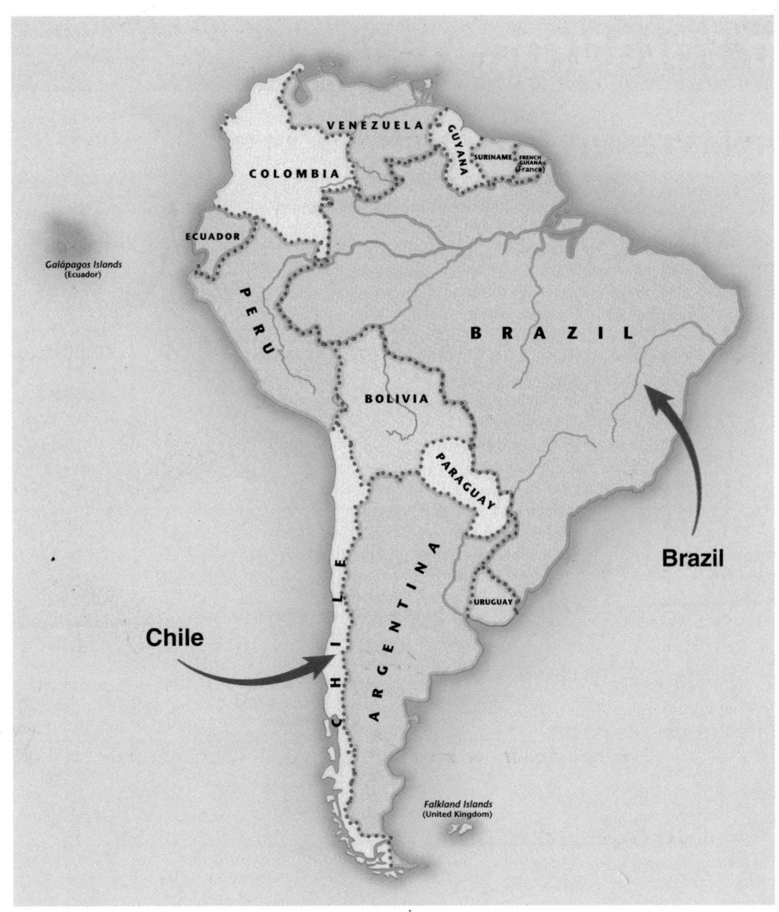

Post-Reading

1. Which three things are being compared here?

   Geography, population and language.

2. In your own words, what are the two biggest differences? Begin your sentence like this: "The two biggest differences between …"

   The two biggest differences between Brazil and Chile are their languages and populations / geography.

3. Make a list of three other things you know about each of these countries. (Interview classmates or consult the Internet if necessary.)

Group or pair work

Country 1: Brazil	Country 2: Chile
1. has the world's largest rainforest, the Amazon Rainforest. (60% of A.R.)	1. Has more active volcanoes than any country except Indonesia.
2. has the largest Japanese community outside of Japan.	2. The Andes (the longest continental mtn range in the world) covers entire length of Chile – 80% of Chile.
3. Christ Redeemer statue in Rio de Janeiro is one of the 7 Wonders of the World.	3. Easter Island has 887 monumental statues, called Moai, by the early Rapa Nui people.

4. More species of monkey in Brazil than anywhere else in the world.

4. Largest producer of copper.

has largest Japanese community outside of Japan – Largest country in S. America!

Grammar for Writing

Using the Simple Present Tense with Facts

Explanation	Examples		
Use the **simple present** to explain something that is still true today. It is a general fact.	These two countries also **differ** in population. The majority of people in Chile **speak** Spanish.		
The simple present uses the **base form** of the verb for *I, we, they,* and *you,* and the **–*s* form** for *he, she,* and *it* and other third person nouns. The subject must agree with the verb in number (singular or plural).	I / We / They / You / Brazilians He / She / It / The man	**speak** **speaks**	**Portuguese.**

Look at Example Paragraph 1 on page 4 and answer the questions.

1. Draw two lines under each verb. What tense are most of the verbs? Simple present tense
2. One verb is in the simple past. Write it here. Settled
3. Why is this verb in the simple past? It happened in the past. It's a historical fact.

Writer's Note

Repetition

Look again at the Example Paragraph 1 on page 4.

- How many sentences are there in the paragraph? 14
- How many times is the word *Brazil* the subject of a sentence? 5
- How many times is the word *Chile* the subject of a sentence? 2

The words *Brazil* and *Chile* are repeated often because this is the topic that is being explained and described. Repetition of key nouns is sometimes necessary to avoid confusion. For example, if we use the word *it* five or six times in this paragraph, we might not know if we are talking about Brazil or about Chile.

ACTIVITY 2 Writing Practice

Think of something that is unique about you. It can be about your hobby, language, or family. Write five sentences about that topic. What verb tense will you use?

1. ______________________
2. ______________________
3. ______________________
4. ______________________
5. ______________________

ACTIVITY 3 Studying an Example Paragraph

A process paragraph tells how to do something. Discuss the Preview Questions with your classmates. Then read the paragraph and answer the questions that follow.

Preview Questions

1. Can you cook? What are three things that you can cook by yourself?
2. Who taught you how to prepare them?

Example Paragraph 2

An Easy Sandwich

An egg salad sandwich is one of the easiest and most delicious foods to make for lunch. First, **boil** two eggs for five minutes. Take them out of the water and let them cool off. Next, **peel** away the **shells** and put the eggs into a bowl. Use a fork to **mash** them very well. After that, add three tablespoons of mayonnaise. Add a little salt and pepper. Mix these **ingredients** well. Put the egg salad in the refrigerator for **at least** thirty minutes. Just before you are ready to eat, **spread** the egg salad on bread. If you follow all these steps, you will certainly enjoy your creation.

to boil: to cook in water at 212°F (100°C)

to peel: to take away the outside covering

a shell: the outside covering of an egg

to mash: to push down and break into small pieces

the ingredients: the parts to make something

at least: the minimum number or amount of something that is required

to spread: to move something in many directions

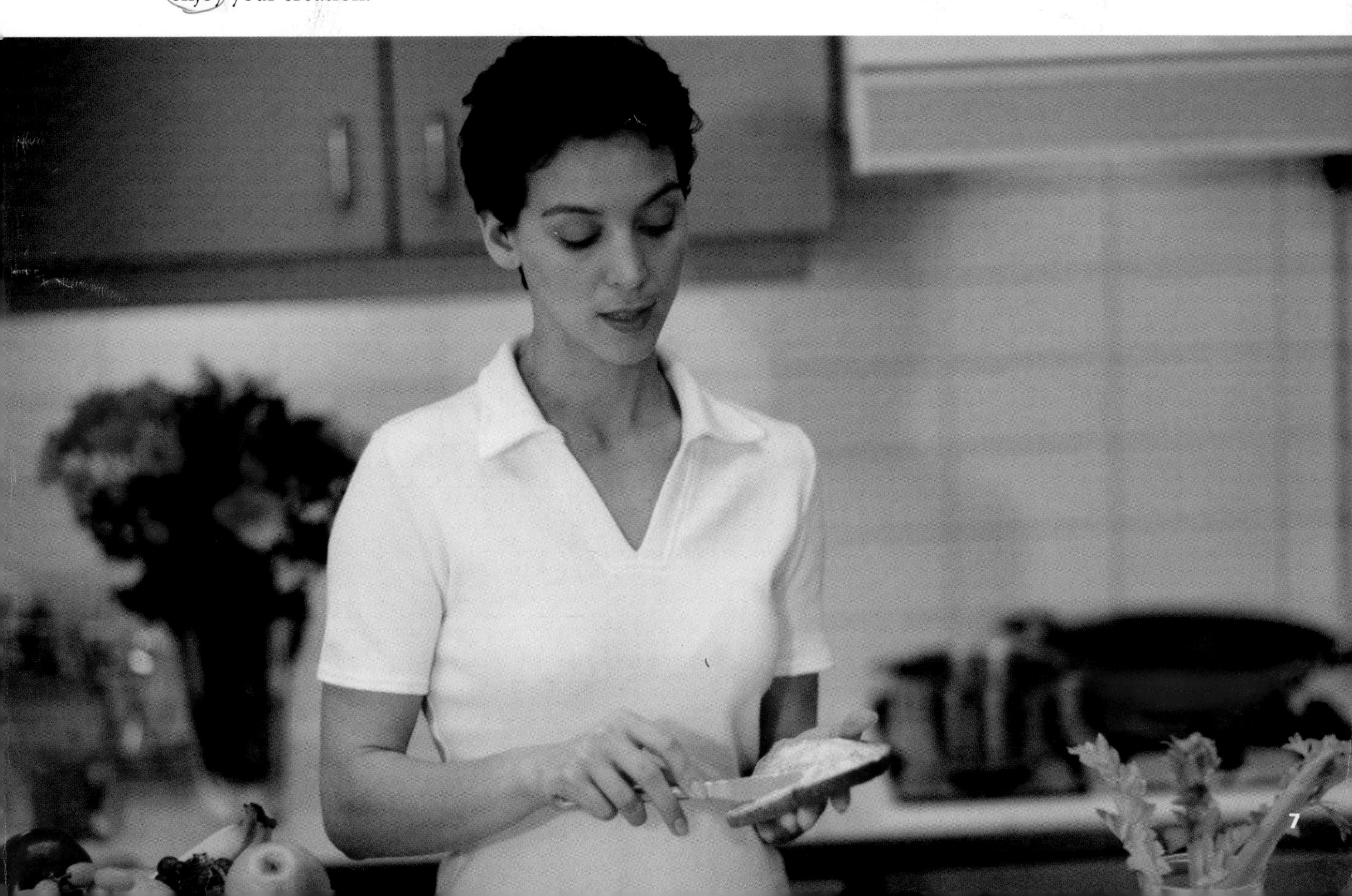

Post-Reading

1. What is the main purpose of this paragraph? (Why did the author write this paragraph?)

To explain how to make an egg salad sandwich.

2. Do you know another easy recipe? Write the main steps of the recipe. Tell it to your classmates and then listen to your classmates present their recipes.

1.

2.

3.

4.

5.

Grammar for Writing

When you teach someone how to do something!

Using the Imperative in Process Paragraphs

Imperative sentences give directions or commands.

Explanation	Examples
Use the **base form of the verb** to begin an imperative sentence.	**Mix** these ingredients well.
When you give written directions, the **sequence** or order of the steps is important. Add a **sequence word** before the imperative. Sequence words include *First, Second, Third, Next, Then,* and *Finally*. Remember to add a comma after a sequence word or phrase.	**First,** boil two eggs for five minutes. **Next,** peel away the shells.

Look at Example Paragraph 2 on page 7 and answer the questions.

1. How many sentences are there in "An Easy Sandwich?" __________
2. Circle the 15 main verbs in the sentences.
3. How many sentences begin with an imperative? __________
4. How many sentences begin with a sequence word? __________

ACTIVITY 4 Writing Practice

Think of a process that you know how to do. Write four to seven sentences that explain how to complete that process. For example, you can write about food or an everyday routine (e.g., how to bake bread or how to send a text message). Use imperative sentences and sequence words.

1. __________
2. __________
3. __________
4. __________
5. __________
6. __________
7. __________

ACTIVITY 5 Studying an Example Paragraph

Can you remember a time when you had a strong feeling about something? Perhaps you were happy or sad or angry. In the narrative paragraph on the next page, the writer tells about a day when he was afraid. This emotion was so strong that he remembers many details about the event even though it took place many years ago. Read the paragraph and answer the question that follows.

Example Paragraph 3

My First Flight

Although the first time I flew on a plane was many years ago, I can still remember how afraid I was that day. All my life, I had **wondered** what it would be like to fly in an airplane. Finally, in March of 1990, I **boarded** my first flight. I flew from New Orleans, Louisiana, to Managua, Nicaragua, on SAHSA Airlines. It was a Boeing 727 jet. There were three seats on each side of the **aisle**. It was **sort of** crowded, and this only made me more nervous. Every time we hit a little **turbulence**, my hands **turned** white. I was so nervous during the **entire** flight that I did not eat the meal they gave me. I would not even go to the bathroom. I cannot tell you how **relieved** I was when the plane finally landed at our **destination**. Since then, I have been on **over** one hundred flights, but I can still remember many small **details** of my first airplane flight.

Why didn't he eat nor go to the bathroom

to wonder: to ask yourself about something, to imagine what something is like

to board: to get on a plane (or other form of transportation)

an aisle: the row between seats on a plane (or bus or train)

sort of: somewhat, rather

the turbulence: rough air during a flight, bumpiness

to turn: to change, become

entire: complete, whole

to be relieved: the feeling when a person no longer feels pressure about something

your destination: the final place that you are traveling to

over: more than

a detail: a fact about something

Think of a happy/frightful/sad/regrettable event in your life. Use adjectives to describe how you felt before, during and after that event.

Post-Reading

Almost everyone has traveled by plane. Can you remember your first flight? Write three questions to ask a classmate about his or her first flight. Then work in small groups and take turns asking each other your questions.

1. What do you remember about your first flight?
2. How did you feel the night before your first flight?
3. " " " " When you boarded the fight?
4. " " " " during the flight?
5. " " " " when your plane landed?

Grammar for Writing

Using the Simple Past Tense in Narrative Paragraphs

Writing a story about something that has happened is called **narrative** writing. Most verbs in narrative writing are in the simple past.

Explanation	Examples
Use the simple past to tell a story or event that happened in the past.	I **boarded** my first flight.
Form the past by adding *-d* or *-ed* to the base form of the verb.	He **lived** in Chile.
Many verbs have **irregular past** forms. Be sure to check a dictionary to find the correct form.	go → went begin → began eat → ate have → had

1. Underline all the verbs in "My First Flight." How many verbs are there? 23 verbs
   flew, was, can remember, was, had wondered, would be, boarded, flew, was, were, was, made, hit, turned, was, did not eat, gave, would not go, cannot tell, was, landed, have been, can remember
2. How many of the verbs are in the simple present tense? 3 verbs
3. How many of the verbs are in the simple past tense? 16 verbs

ACTIVITY 6 **Writing Practice**

Think of something that happened to you, such as a funny event or a happy occasion. Write five to eight sentences in which you tell the story.

1. ______________________________

2. ______________________________

3. ______________________________

4. ______________________________

5. ______________________________

6. ______________________________

7. ______________________________

8. ______________________________

Building Better Sentences: For further practice with the sentences and paragraphs in this part of the unit, go to Practice 1 on page 284 in Appendix 1.

Four Features of a Paragraph

These are the four main features of a paragraph:

1. A paragraph has a topic sentence that states the main idea.

The topic sentence is usually at the beginning and is the foundation for the paragraph. The topic sentence helps the reader understand what the paragraph is about. (Topic sentences will be discussed more in Unit 3.)

2. All of the sentences in a paragraph are about one topic.

They are connected to the topic sentence. There are no unrelated or extra sentences. How do you know whether something is connected or not? Look at the main idea in the topic sentence, which is sometimes called the *controlling idea*. All of the other information in the paragraph must be connected to the controlling idea in the topic sentence. (You will learn more about this in Unit 3 on page 46.)

3. The first line of a paragraph is indented.

Indenting means moving the first line to the right about a half of an inch. On a keyboard, this is about six spaces or the first tab stop position. This gap, or open space, in the first line is called an indentation.

4. The last sentence, or concluding sentence, brings the paragraph to a logical end.

The concluding sentence usually states the main point again or summarizes the main idea of the paragraph. Often a key word or phrase from the topic sentence appears in the concluding sentence. In addition, it can offer a suggestion, an opinion, or a prediction. (Concluding sentences will be discussed more in Unit 4.)

ACTIVITY 7 Analyzing the Features of a Paragraph

Discuss the Preview Questions with your classmates. Then read the paragraph and answer the questions that follow.

Preview Questions

1. Do you have a pet?

2. Who cares for the pet? What kind of care does it need?

Example Paragraph 4

Children and Pets

At some point, most parents have to decide whether or not to **allow** their children to have pets. Some parents believe that pets teach children **a sense of** responsibility because children have to learn how to take care of their pets. In addition, many parents believe that pets can be fun for the family. Pets can also help children become more **compassionate** because children will develop a special **bond** with their pets. **On the other hand**, some parents are afraid that their children might hurt the animals or that these animals might hurt the children. Cats are good pets, but I do not like it when they shed hair **all over**. Often these parents do not allow their children to have any kind of pet. Other families do not have the extra time or money that pets **require**. In **brief**, although many children want a pet, parents are divided on this issue for **a number of** important reasons.

to allow: to permit, let

a sense of: a feeling of

compassionate: with strong feelings of caring or wanting to help

a bond: a connection, a relationship

on the other hand: an expression used for the second or opposite reason ("on one hand" versus "on the other hand")

all over: everywhere

to require: to need, must have

brief: short

a number of: several

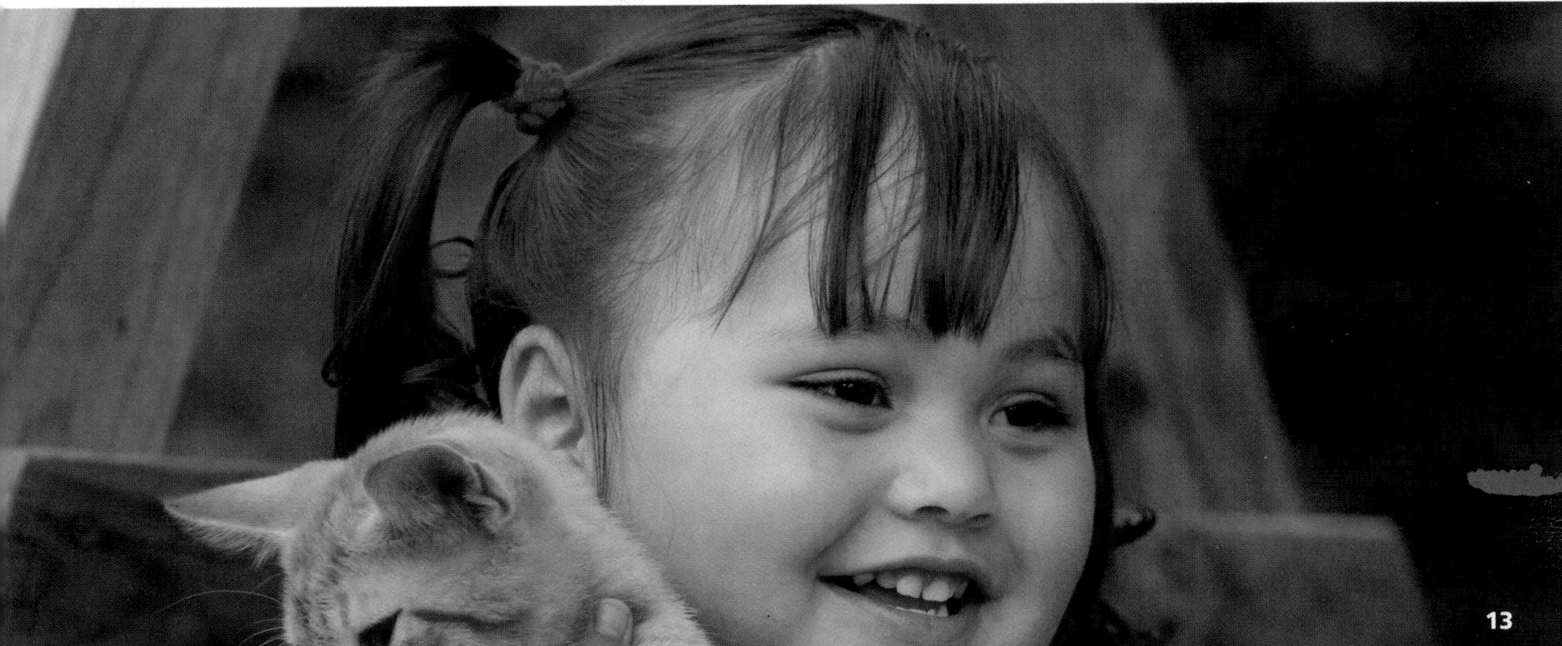

Post-Reading

1. What is the main idea of the paragraph?

Reasons why parents allow or do not allow their children to have a pet.

2. How many sentences are there in the paragraph? 9

3. How many sentences do NOT relate to the main idea? 1 Draw a line through any unrelated sentences. Cats are good pets, ... all over.

4. Draw a line under the topic sentence. (Remember that the topic sentence is the sentence that helps the reader understand the main idea.) At some point, ...

5. Is this paragraph indented? ☑ yes ❑ no

6. Draw two lines under the concluding sentence. How is the information in the concluding sentence related to the information in the topic sentence?

The info in both sentences is closely connected. The concluding sentence restates the main idea of the topic sentence.

ACTIVITY 8 Analyzing the Features of the Example Paragraphs

Look at these three example paragraphs again: "Chile and Brazil" on page 4, "An Easy Sandwich" on page 7, and "My First Flight" on page 9. Fill in the information about the features of each paragraph.

1. Write the topic sentence of each paragraph.

"Chile and Brazil" Chile and Brazil are two important countries in S.A.

"An Easy Sandwich" An egg salad sandwich is one of the easiest and most delicious foods to make for lunch.

"My First Flight" Although the first time I flew on a plane was many years ago, I can still remember how afraid I was that day.

2. What is the main idea of each paragraph?

"Chile and Brazil" The differences bet. Chile + Brazil.

"An Easy Sandwich" how to make an egg salad sandwich

"My First Flight" a depiction of the fear in the narrator's first airplane flight.

3. Is the first line of each paragraph indented?

"Chile and Brazil" ☐ yes ☐ no

"An Easy Sandwich" ☐ yes ☐ no

"My First Flight" ☐ yes ☐ no

ACTIVITY 9 Analyzing the Features of Student Paragraphs

Read the following student paragraphs and answer the questions that follow.

Example Paragraph 5

eBook Readers

eBook readers are excellent **devices** for students. Reading eBooks is just like reading a **normal** book without having to hold the book or turn the pages. These devices save students energy. Before eBook readers, students had to carry many heavy books with them each day. However, eBook readers are **extremely** lightweight and usually weigh less than a pound. eBook readers are more **efficient** and

an eBook: an electronic book

a device: a small machine or instrument

normal: usual

extremely: very

efficient: capable or productive

convenient than a regular book. They are wireless, so students can use them anywhere. They are comfortable to hold and are clear even in bright sunlight. My ~~friend has an eBook reader, and she **convinced** me to buy one~~. Finally, **purchasing** a new book for an eBook reader is simple and cheap. There are now millions of eBooks available, and many eBooks cost less than **traditional** books. It is clear that eBook readers have certainly made students' lives much easier.

to convince: persuade

to purchase: buy

traditional: normal or usual; not new

1. The general topic of the paragraph is how eBook readers help students. Does the paragraph have a topic sentence? If so, write it here. If not, create one here.

   eBook readers are excellent devices for students.

2. Are all the sentences related to the topic? If not, write the unrelated sentences here.

   My friend has an eBook reader, and she convinced me to buy one.

3. Is the first line indented? ☑ yes ☐ no

4. What is the concluding sentence?

   It is clear that eBook readers have certainly made students' lives much easier.

Example Paragraph 6

Simón Bolívar

Simón Bolívar (1783-1830) was one of South America's greatest generals and one of the most powerful people in world political history. In Spanish, Simón Bolívar is often called *El Libertador,* which means "The Liberator." ~~Spanish is the **principal** language in at least 22 countries.~~ This **nickname** is a very good one because his planning and military actions helped to gain independence from Spain for six countries: Bolivia (1809), Colombia (1819), Ecuador (1820), Panama (1821), Peru (1821), and his native country of Venezuela (1811). In fact, Bolivia is named for Bolívar, making him one of the few people to have a country named for him. These six countries together are **approximately** the same size as modern Europe, so the independence of such a large area was an amazing military and political **feat**. Although Bolívar's name is not as well-known outside Latin America, people there remember him as perhaps the most important person in their history.

the principal: main, the most important

a nickname: a short name that people use in place of a longer name

approximately: about, more or less

a feat: an accomplishment

Post-Reading

1. What is the topic of the paragraph? The importance of Simon Bolivar for many S.A. countries

   Does the paragraph have a topic sentence? If so, write it here. If not, create one here.

   Yes. Simon Bolivar (1783-1830) was one of S.A's greatest generals and one of the most powerful people in world political history.

2. Are all the sentences related to the topic? If not, write the unrelated sentences here.

   No. Spanish is the principal language in at least 22 countries.

3. Is the first line indented? ☑ yes ☐ no

4. What is the concluding sentence?

   Although Bolivar's name is not as well-known outside Latin America, people there remember him as the most important person in their history.

Class work not homework

New York City

First, many movies were made here, so people have seen the city even if they have not traveled here in person. Second, New York City has many famous tourist attractions, including the Statue of Liberty, the Empire State Building, Central Park, and Times Square. In addition, the city has some of the best shopping in the world, and many famous department stores are located here. Finally, New York City is famous for its many theaters with world-class shows. For these reasons, everyone knows about this city.

Post-Reading

1. What is the topic of the paragraph? Why New York City is famous.

   Does the paragraph have a topic sentence? If so, write it here. If not, create one here.

   No. New York City is famous in the whole world for many reasons
   New York City is well-known in the whole world.

   There are many reasons why NYC is famous.

2. Are all the sentences related to the topic? If not, write the unrelated sentences here.

   Yes.

3. Is the first line indented? ☑ yes ❑ no

4. What is the concluding sentence?

   For these reasons, everyone knows about this city.

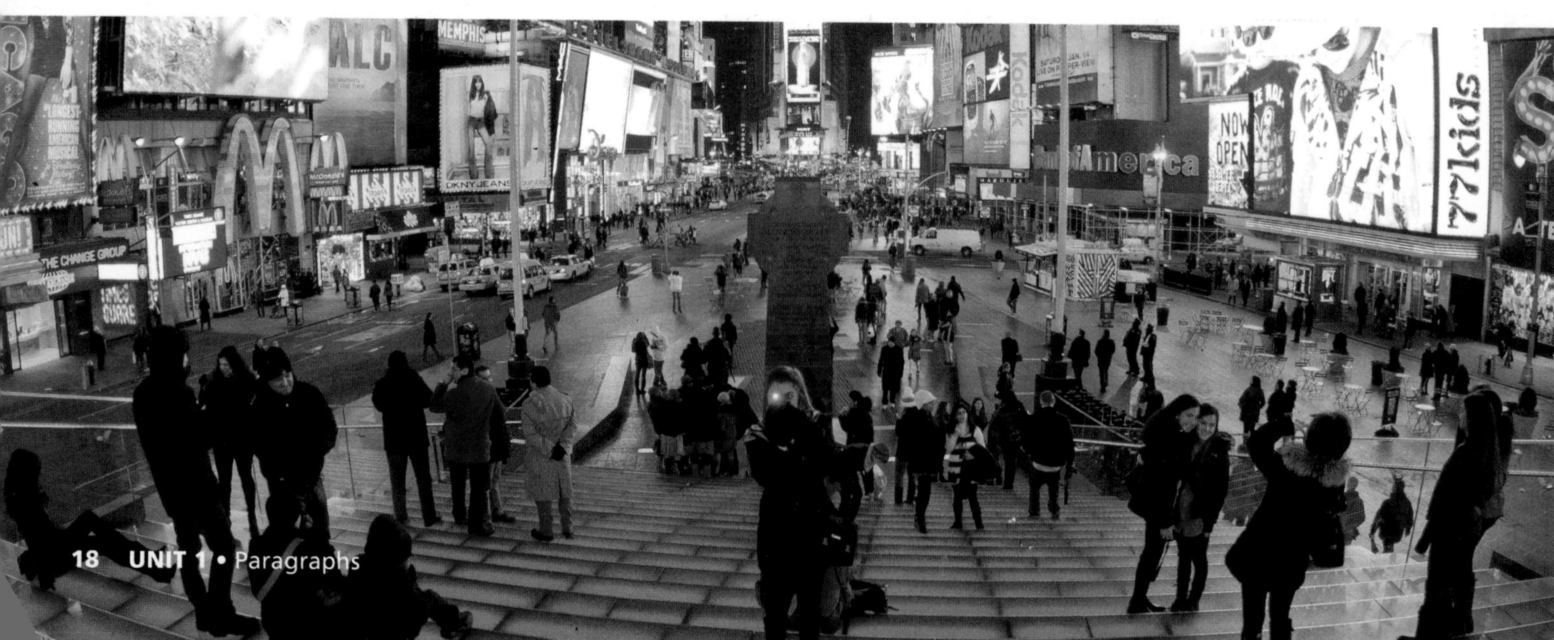

Class work not homework

Jim Thorpe's Final Victory

Jim Thorpe is a **controversial** figure in sports history. He won Olympic gold medals for running in 1912, but he was not allowed to keep them. In the 1912 Olympics, Thorpe won both the pentathlon (five events) and decathlon (ten events). However, a month later, the U.S. Olympic Committee took away his medals because Thorpe had played baseball for money. An athlete who takes money for sports is called a professional, and at that time, professional athletes were not allowed to **take part in** any Olympic Games. In 1982, the U.S. Olympic Committee **reversed** this **ruling**. Seventy years after his **achievements**, Thorpe's name was finally returned to the list of 1912 Olympic winners.

controversial: causing great disagreement or discussion

to take part in: to participate in

to reverse: to change to the opposite position

a ruling: a decision, especially one that is made by a judge or court

an achievement: something special that a person is able to accomplish or do

Post-Reading

1. What is the topic of the paragraph? Jim Thorpe, the controversial Olympic athlete.

   Does the paragraph have a topic sentence? If so, write it here. If not, create one here.

   Yes. Jim Thorpe is a controversial figure in sports history.

2. Are all the sentences related to the topic? If not, write the unrelated sentences here.

   Yes.

3. Is the first line indented? ☑ yes ☐ no

4. Underline the concluding sentence. Do you see any time words in the concluding sentence that make the sentence sound like the ending of the paragraph?

   Seventy years after his achievements, finally

Example Paragraph 9

Reasons for Not Voting

Although voting is one of the main ways that people of a country can participate in their future, some **citizens** choose not to vote. Some people decide not to vote because they think that their one vote will not matter. Other people do not vote because they are not interested in politics. Another reason that some people choose not to vote is that they do not know much about politics or **politicians** and do not have enough time to learn about them before an election. Finally, in some elections, people choose not to vote because they do not like any of the **candidates** in the election. People's reasons for not voting **vary considerably**.

a citizen: a legal member of a city, state, or country

a politician: someone who holds a government office

a candidate: a person running for political office

to vary: to be different

considerably: a great deal, by a large amount

Post-Reading

1. What is the topic of the paragraph? Reasons citizens do not vote

   Does the paragraph have a topic sentence? If so, write it here. If not, create one here.

   Yes. Although voting is one of the main ways that people of a country can participate in their future, some citizens choose not

2. Are all the sentences related to the topic? If not, write the unrelated sentences here.

   Yes.

3. Is the first line indented? ☑ yes ❑ no

4. What is the concluding sentence?

   People's reasons for not voting vary considerably.

Example Paragraph 10

My First Class as a Teacher

I can still remember a small **incident** that helped me relax on my first day of teaching many years ago. I was 23 years old at the time, and I had just graduated from college. The practice teaching that I had done for six weeks was very different from teaching my own class. When I walked into the room, I was very nervous. I carefully put my books down on the desk. Then I heard a girl say something in Spanish to another classmate. I speak Spanish, so I understood her perfectly when she told her friend to look at my hands. She said, "Look how his hands are **trembling**," and she was right. I was wearing a new watch that day, too. **Neither** of the two girls knew that I could understand Spanish. When I smiled a little, the first girl started to laugh because she realized at that moment that I understood Spanish. It seems like such a **silly** thing now, but the **humor** of the incident really helped me relax on the first day of my **career**.

an incident: a small event, usually negative

to tremble: to shake

neither: not A and not B (used with two choices)

silly: funny, crazy

the humor: funny part

a career: what a person does for a living

Post-Reading

1. What is the topic of the paragraph? ________________________________

   Does the paragraph have a topic sentence? If so, write it here. If not, create one here.

   ____

   ____

2. Are all the sentences related to the topic? If not, write the unrelated sentences here.

   ____

   ____

3. Is the first line indented? ❑ yes ❑ no

4. Underline the concluding sentence.

5. What words are repeated in both the topic sentence and the concluding sentence of this paragraph?

   ____

Building Better Sentences: For further practice with the sentences and paragraphs in this part of the unit, go to Practice 2 on page 285 in Appendix 1.

Working with Paragraphs

In this section, you will begin to learn about organizing and formatting a paragraph by copying sentences into paragraphs and then by writing a paragraph of your own. You will also look at good titles for paragraphs.

ACTIVITY 10 Reviewing Capitalization and End Punctuation

Review "Basic Capitalization Rules" on page 254 and "End Punctuation" on pages 257–258 in the *Brief Writer's Handbook with Activities.* Add correct capitalization and end punctuation to the sentences below. If you need more practice, complete the activities on pages 255–258.

1. the geography of the country of turkey is unique

   The geography of the country of Turkey is unique.

2. most countries are in one continent, but turkey lies in both asia and europe

   ____

3. the asian part is much larger than the european part

   ____

4. the eight countries that share a border with turkey are armenia, azerbaijan, bulgaria, georgia, greece, iran, iraq, and Syria

   ____

5. turkey has coasts on the mediterranean sea and the black sea

   ____

6. half of turkey's land is higher than 1,000 meters

   ____

7. in fact, two-thirds of turkey's land is higher than 800 meters

   ____

8. the unique geography of turkey is one reason that millions of tourists visit this country every year

   ____

ACTIVITY 11 Copying a Paragraph

Copy the sentences from Activity 10 in the same order. Make sure your paragraph is indented. Write a title on the top line.

Example Paragraph 11

The Title of a Paragraph

What is the title of this textbook? Look on the front cover. Write the title here.

____

What is the title of Example Paragraph 11 on page 24? Write the title here.

____

A **title** tells you what you will find in a book, a movie, a story, or a paragraph. A title is not a sentence. A title is usually very short. Sometimes the title is only one word, such as the movie titles *Spiderman, Batman,* or *Titanic.* Can you think of other movie titles in English that are only one or two words long?

A good paragraph title is catchy. It has something that catches the reader's interest, but it does not tell everything about the paragraph. As an example, imagine that you wrote a paragraph about a time when you burned some scrambled eggs. Consider these titles.

Title	Comment
I Burned the Eggs	Poor title. A title should not be a sentence.
Burning the Eggs	Poor title. The meaning is not accurate. This sounds like you will tell how to burn the eggs.
Cooking Scrambled Eggs	Poor title. The meaning is not accurate. This sounds like you will tell only how to cook scrambled eggs.
A Bad Experience with Scrambled Eggs	This is a little better, but it is not clear if this is about eating eggs or making eggs.
The Day I Tried to Make Scrambled Eggs	This is acceptable if the paragraph tells the events of that day.
A Cooking Disaster	Good title. It sums up the paragraph but does not tell exactly what happened.
A Kitchen Disaster	Good title. It sums up the paragraph but does not tell exactly what happened.

Grammar for Writing

Checking for Verbs and Fragments

Look at the **verbs** in these examples.

Explanation	Examples
Every sentence in English must have a verb. When writing, always check or proofread each sentence to make sure it has a verb!	✓ Where **is** the bank? ✓ Wheat **is grown** in Argentina. ✓ Japan **produces** many different kinds of cars. ✓ The house on the corner **does** not **have** a garage. ✓ Two amazing buildings in the United Arab Emirates **are** the Burj Al Arab and the Dubai Tower.
A sentence without a verb is called a **fragment.** The word *fragment* means a piece of something that has been broken off.	✗ Where the bank? ✗ Japan many different kinds of cars. ✗ Wheat in Argentina. ✗ The house on the corner not a garage. ✗ Two amazing buildings in the United Arab Emirates the Burj Al Arab and the Dubai Tower.

You will study more details about sentence fragments in Unit 3 on page 62.

ACTIVITY 12 Checking Subjects and Verbs

Read each sentence. The subject is in *italics*. Underline the verb that goes with each subject. If every subject in the sentence has a verb, write C for correct on the line. If a subject does not have a verb, write X on the line and add an appropriate verb in the correct place. (Many different verbs can be used. Use one that you think is appropriate.)

1. ___X___ *We* know that *languages* vary, but other important communication *methods* exist.
2. ______ For example, when two *people* are talking, the appropriate *amount* of space between them varies by culture.
3. ______ In some cultures, *people* near each other when having a conversation.
4. ______ Sometimes these *people* might touch each other during the conversation.
5. ______ *Not standing near the speaker or not touching* might be seen as "cold" or disinterested behavior.
6. ______ In other cultures, *people* stand farther apart.

7. ______ If *one* of the speakers too close, the other *person* might see this as aggressive or strange behavior.

8. ______ The *amount* of personal space from culture to culture.

9. ______ *It* also a form of communication.

10. ______ Just as there is no universal *language*, there is no universal personal *space*.

ACTIVITY 13 Copying a Paragraph

Copy the sentences with your corrections from Activity 12 in the same order. Make sure your paragraph is indented. On the top line, write an original title for your paragraph.

Example Paragraph 12

Building Better Vocabulary

ACTIVITY 14 Word Associations

Circle the word or phrase that is most closely related to the word or phrase on the left. If necessary, use a dictionary to check the meaning of words you do not know.

	A	B
1. a destination	a place	a time
2. ingredients	for a recipe	for a suitcase
3. a term	a direction	a word
4. to require*	to give	to need
5. a detail	a general idea	a specific idea
6. catchy	people like it	people hate it
7. to state	to believe	to say
8. to allow	to let	to put
9. to spread	to move	to stay
10. trembling	afraid, nervous	sleepy, tired
11. to take up	to move to a new area	to occupy space
12. majority*	less than half	more than half
13. an achievement*	something bad	something good
14. to purchase*	to buy	to persuade
15. entire	50 percent	100 percent

*Words that are part of the Academic Word List. See pages 275–276 for a complete list.

ACTIVITY 15 Using Collocations

Fill in each blank with the word on the left that most naturally completes the phrase on the right. If necessary, use a dictionary to check the meaning of words you do not know.

Look for more words on p. 19

1. in / on	___in___ brief
2. composed / spread	water is ___composed___ of
3. bright / large	a ___large___ gap
4. convince / vary	___vary___ considerably
5. hand / month	on the other ___hand___
6. banana / flower	to peel a ___banana___
7. almost / principal	the ___principal___ reason for doing something
8. flight / meeting	to board a ___flight___
9. aisle / though	even ___though___
10. of / in	differ ___in___

Original Student Writing

ACTIVITY 16 Original Writing Practice

Write a simple paragraph. Follow these guidelines:

- Choose a general topic or look at the list on the next page for some ideas.
- Think of some specific aspect of that topic. Try to be as specific as you can. For example, you might choose "sports" as your first idea. Then you might choose "tennis." Finally you might choose "how to keep score in tennis."
- Write five to twelve related sentences.
- Include a topic sentence.
- Indent the first line.
- The last sentence should be a good concluding sentence.
- Give your paragraph a title.
- Use at least two of the vocabulary words or phrases presented in Activity 14 and Activity 15. Underline these words and phrases in your paragraph.

If you need ideas for words and phrases, see the Useful Vocabulary for Better Writing on pages 277–281.

Topic Ideas

Topic	Topic Sentence
Food	The easiest food to prepare is ________.
	The best meal I ever had was ________.
Color	Each color in my country's flag represents something special.
	Colors can affect the way you feel.
Sports	________ (name a player) is an excellent ________ (name a sport) player.
	The rules for ________ (name a sport) are not (easy / difficult).
People	________ has taught me many things about life.
	If I could meet anyone in history, I would like to meet ________.

Introduction to Peer Editing

Editing Your Writing

Good writers **proofread** their work and rewrite it several times. Think of the first draft of a paragraph as a first attempt.

Before you rewrite your paragraph or paper, it is also helpful to let someone else read it, offer comments, and ask questions to clarify your meaning. Many writers do not always see their own mistakes, but a reader can help you see where you need to make improvements.

In class, **peer editing** is an easy way to get opinions about your paper. In this method, other students (your peers) read your paper and make comments using a set of questions and guidelines. (See Peer Editing Sheets on NGL.Cengage.com/GW2.) You will read someone else's paper too. Peer editing can help you strengthen any areas in your paragraph that are weak or that appear confusing to the reader.

Suggestions for Peer Editing

1. Listen Carefully

In peer editing, you will receive some comments and suggestions from other students. It is important to listen carefully to comments about your writing. You may think that what you wrote is clear and accurate, but readers can often tell you what needs improvement. Remember that the comments are about the writing, not about you!

2. Make Helpful Comments

When you read your classmates' papers, choose your words and comments carefully so that you do not hurt their feelings. For example, instead of saying "This is bad grammar," or "I can't understand any of your ideas," make helpful comments, such as "You need to make sure that every sentence has a verb," or "What do you mean in this sentence?"

3. Study an Example of "Editing Your Writing"

Study the "Editing Your Writing" section of the *Brief Writer's Handbook with Activities* (pages 251–253). There are examples of edits and comments that a teacher made on a student's first draft and an example of the student's second draft.

4. Read, Read, Read!

It is important for you to understand why a piece of writing is good or is not good, and the best way to do this is to read, read, and read some more! The more writing styles you become familiar with, the better your writing can become, too.

ACTIVITY 17 Peer Editing

Exchange papers from Activity 16 with a partner. Read your partner's paragraph. Then use Peer Editing Sheet 1 on NGL.Cengage.com/GW2 to help you comment on your partner's paragraph. There is a sample in the Appendix. Be sure to offer positive suggestions and comments that will help your partner write a better paragraph. Consider your partner's comments as you revise your own paragraph.

Additional Topics for Writing

Here are more ideas for writing. When you write, be sure to include the four features of a paragraph.

PHOTO TOPIC: Look at the photo on pages 2–3. Write about something thrilling, such as a sport or a ride at an amusement park. When was it? Who did you go with? Was it scary or exciting? What happened?

TOPIC 2: Write about something easy to cook. What things do you need to make it? What are the steps you take to make it? How does it taste?

TOPIC 3: Write about a famous living person. What does this person do? Why is he/she famous?

TOPIC 4: Which is more difficult to learn: English or your language? What parts of the language do you find hard? Can you give suggestions for someone learning the language?

TOPIC 5: Write about your favorite season. What do you do during this season? How does it make you feel?

Timed Writing

How quickly can you write in English? There are many times when you must write quickly, such as on a test. It is important to feel comfortable during those times. Timed-writing practice can make you feel better about writing quickly in English.

1. Take out a piece of paper.
2. Read the writing prompt.
3. Brainstorm ideas for five minutes.
4. Write a short paragraph (six to ten sentences).
5. You have 25 minutes to write.

Describe the daily life of a police officer. Is being a police officer a good job? Is it easy? What kinds of things does a police officer do every day?

UNIT 2

Developing Ideas for Writing a Paragraph

Lava flows out of the Pu'u O'o vent of Kilauea Volcano in Hawaii.

OBJECTIVES To learn how to brainstorm ideas for writing
To practice subject-verb agreement

Can you describe a scary event?

Brainstorming

How do writers find great topics for their paragraphs? One way to identify a really good topic for a paragraphs is **brainstorming**. Brainstorming is quickly writing down all the thoughts that come into your head. When you brainstorm, you do not think about whether an idea is good or bad or whether your writing is correct. You simply write to put your ideas on paper. This process is called brainstorming because it feels like there is a storm in your brain—a storm of ideas!

Imagine there is a fire in your hotel. What should you do? Study the ideas that one person might brainstorm.

FIRE!
Run away?
Call fire department?
Shout?
Find hose?
Get to car?
Get back to house?

Brainstorm your ideas!

ACTIVITY 1 Brainstorming Practice

Use this topic and situation to practice brainstorming. Work quickly. Do not worry about how good each idea is. For now, do not worry about correct spelling or grammar. Your immediate goal is to create a list of as many ideas as possible in just a few minutes.

Next Saturday is your grandmother's birthday. She is going to be 88 years old. What will you get for her? Make a list of five suitable birthday gifts for her.

Brainstorm as a Class – Plan your best friend's wedding – Write on the board,

1. ______________________________

2. ______________________________

3. ______________________________

4. ______________________________

5. ______________________________

Compare your list to a classmate's list. Can you combine your best ideas with your classmate's best ideas? Sometimes it is helpful to work with other writers and share ideas. Remember that in brainstorming, there are no bad ideas. The purpose of brainstorming is to produce as many ideas as possible.

How Brainstorming Works

A good writer brainstorms about a topic by completing these two important steps:

- thinking about the topic
- writing down words and ideas

It is important to remember that the first step in writing a paragraph is not writing—it is **thinking**.

Brainstorming involves associating ideas because one idea can produce another. Some writers brainstorm in **lists**. Others **cluster** or connect their ideas in some other way. Consider this example of brainstorming for Example Paragraph 2, "An Easy Sandwich," on page 7. You can see that the writer wrote many ideas and crossed out some of them. There are several ideas that were not included in the final paragraph. In addition, a few ideas in the final paragraph are not in this list.

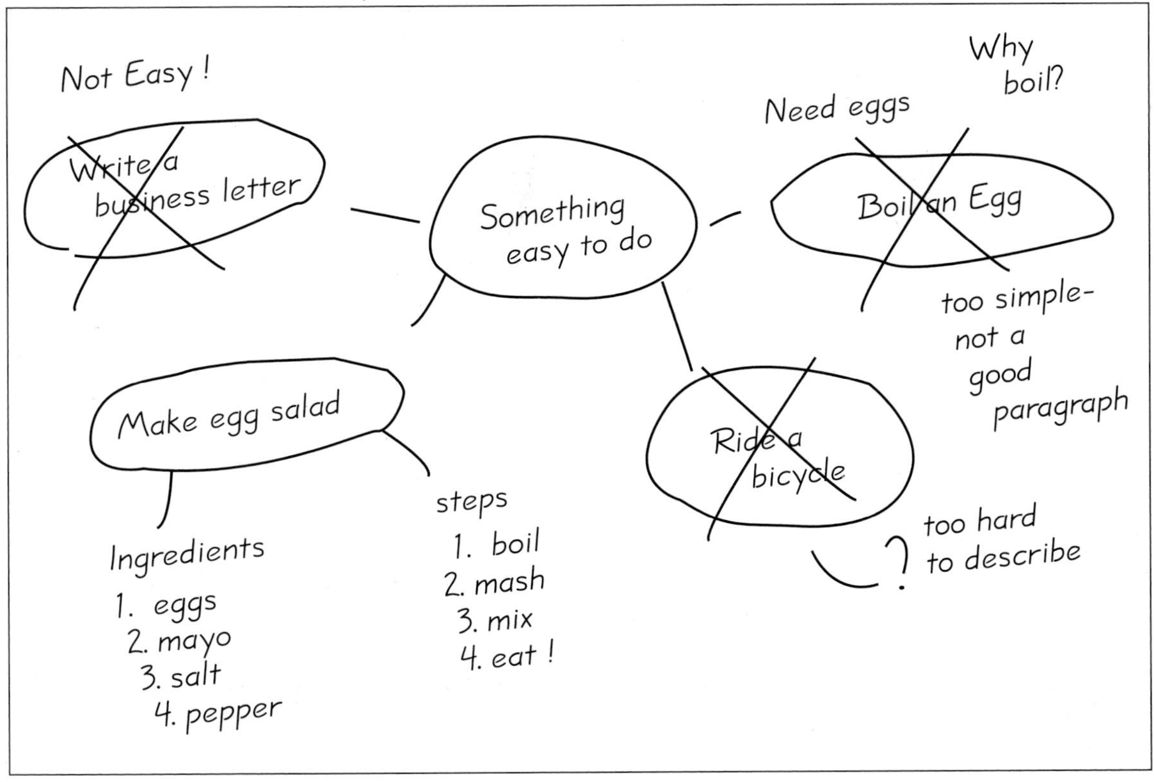

ACTIVITY 2 Brainstorming Practice

Follow these steps for each of the example topics:

1. Read the topic and brainstorm about the topic in the box. Make a list of ideas in English or use the diagram on page 35 as an example of how to connect ideas.
2. Circle the ideas that you think are the best ones to include in a paragraph.
3. Compare and discuss your ideas with a partner. When you compare your notes, be prepared to say why you want to keep some ideas and why you want to take out others. What information will be in the final paragraph?

Topic A: Terrifying Events

Brainstorm area:

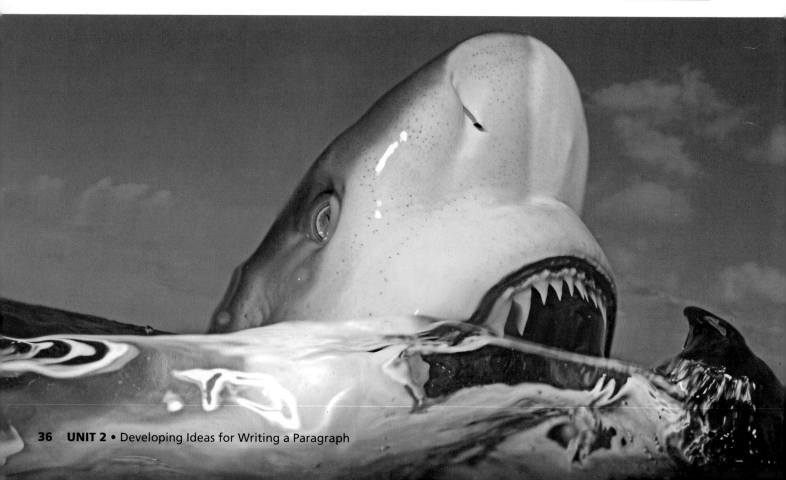

Topic B: Important Inventions

Brainstorm area:

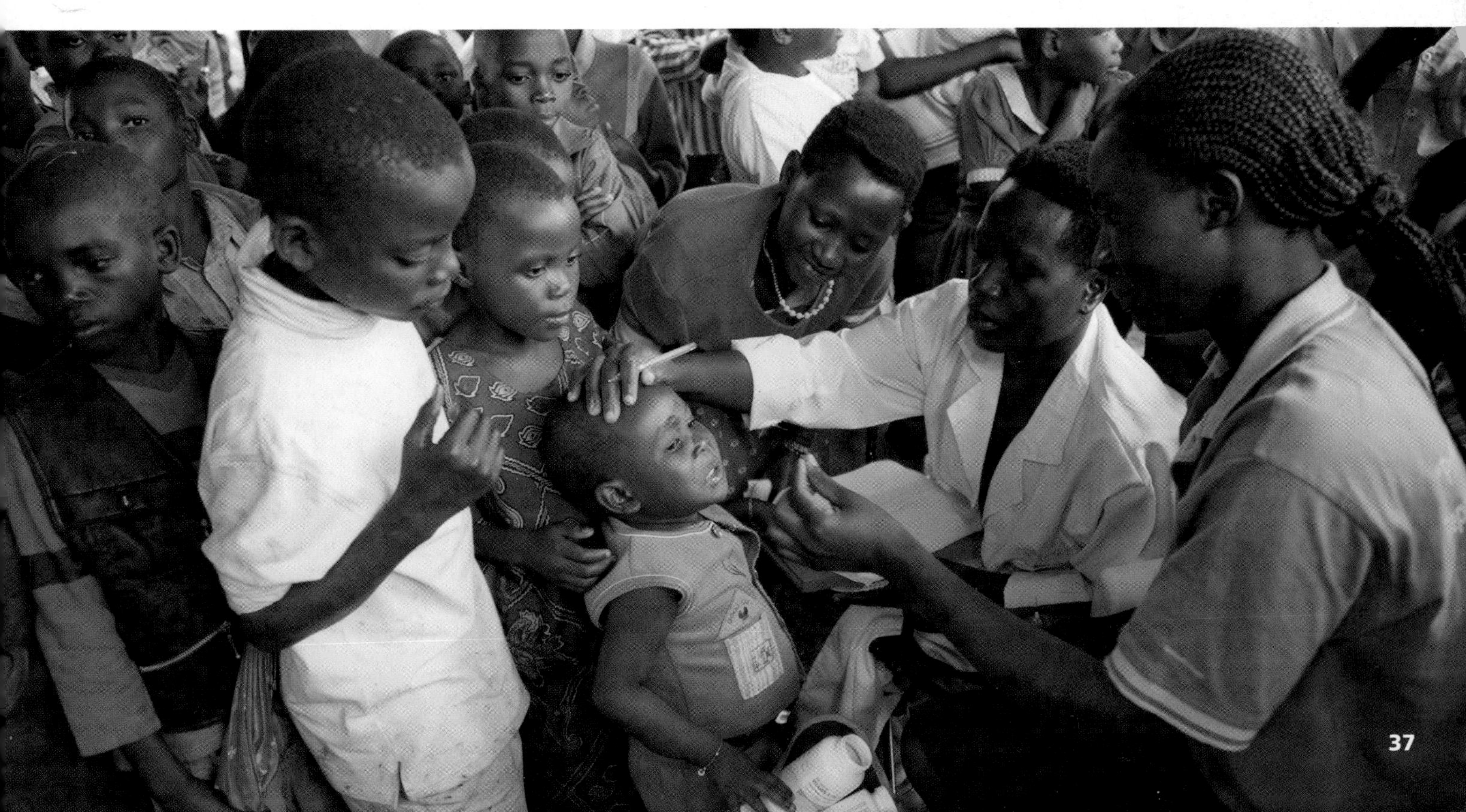

Topic C: Ideal Travel Destinations

Brainstorm area:

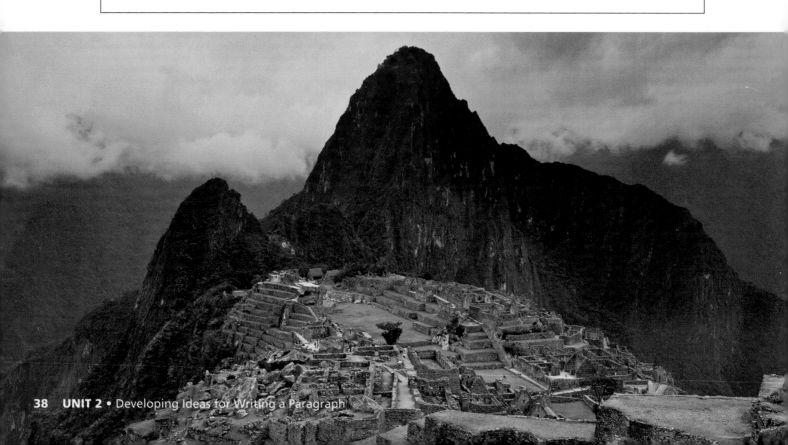

ACTIVITY 3 Brainstorming Practice from Example Paragraphs

Choose an example paragraph that you read in Unit 1: "Chile and Brazil," "An Easy Sandwich," or "My First Flight." Brainstorm ideas that are related to the topic of one of these paragraphs. For example, if you choose "My First Flight," you might brainstorm about a frightening experience you had on an airplane or another experience that was scary.

- Which paragraph did you choose? ______________________________
- Why did you choose this paragraph? ______________________________

  ____

Use the space below to brainstorm. If you prefer, work with another student who chose the same topic. Sometimes when you work with another writer, you get more ideas.

Brainstorm area:

Grammar for Writing

Subject-Verb Agreement

When writing, it is important that the verbs agree with the subjects. Notice the subject-verb agreement rules for the simple present.

Explanation	Examples
Use the base **form of the verb** for *I*, *you*, or plural words or pronouns.	I **prepare** you **prepare** we **prepare** they **prepare** my parents **prepare**
Use the **–s** form with third-person singular nouns or pronouns (*he*, *she*, *it*). The third person singular is formed by adding **–s** or **-es** to the end of the verb.	he **prepares** she **prepares** it **prepares** the cook **prepares** Bruno **cooks**
When writing, make sure the verb form matches the subject in number.	One boy **reads**. (singular) Two boy**s** **read**. (plural)
Remember to match the verb to the subject, not to other words in the sentence. Tip: Prepositional phrases start with prepositions (*at, for, by, with, without, in, of*) and include an object of the preposition (another noun). This is **not** the subject.	✗ The main **product** of Brazil and Colombia **are** coffee. ✓The main **product** of Brazil and Colombia **is** coffee. ✗ The main **products** of Brazil **is** coffee and aluminum. ✓ The main **products** of Brazil **are** coffee and aluminum.
Tip: Collective nouns in North American English are often singular. Use the third person singular.	The United States **makes** many products. The team **wins** every game. The couple **works** in the city.
Tip: The noun after ***there is*** or ***there are*** is the subject of that sentence.	There **is a dictionary** on the table. There **are** three **reasons** for my decision.
Pronouns with ***every-, some-,*** or ***any-*** are always singular. Nouns with ***each*** or ***every*** are also singular.	**Everyone has** an accent of some kind. **Every** student **needs** a book and a workbook.
Spelling notes for the third person singular: When a verb ends in a consonant **+ *y,*** change the ***-y*** to ***–i*** and add ***–es***. When a verb ends in ***–ch, -sh, -ss, -x,*** or ***–zz,*** add ***–es***.	I try ➔ he **tries** I watch ➔ she **watches** I wash ➔ he **washes** You miss ➔ it **misses** They tax ➔ the city **taxes** You buzz ➔ it **buzzes**

ACTIVITY 4 Finding Subject-Verb Errors

Read the sentences. Find the 12 mistakes and correct them. If the sentence is correct, write *C* on the line.

1. ________ Everybody lives near the coast because the interior is too dry.
2. ________ A pair of scissors are necessary for this project.
3. ________ Laura carry her guitar from class to class every Thursday.
4. ________ The main method of transportation in all of those tropical islands are the public bus system.
5. ________ The trees behind my house is dense.
6. ________ Earth revolve around the Sun.
7. ________ A pilot and a co-pilot flies the plane.
8. ________ The baby elephants at the zoo weighs just under 300 pounds.
9. ________ The coffee cups in the sink is still dirty.
10. ________ Professor Jones teachs Latin at 9 A.M. on Tuesdays and Thursdays.
11. ________ Most people in my town has a car.
12. ________ My family live near the ocean.
13. ________ There are many interesting things to do in San Francisco.
14. ________ Every term the students tries new activities.

ACTIVITY 5 Practicing Subject-Verb Agreement

Underline the correct verb form in each sentence.

1. One reason I want to visit Asia (is, are) to see Japan.
2. In my opinion, the best tourist destinations in Japan (is, are) Tokyo and Kyoto.
3. Tokyo (is, are) a very modern city with many tall buildings.
4. In fact, the skyscrapers in Tokyo (is, are) some of the tallest buildings in the world.
5. However, the city skyline with these incredibly tall buildings (do, does) not look like the scenery in Kyoto at all.
6. Life in Kyoto (move, moves) at a much slower pace.
7. Kyoto (is, are) not only smaller but also much older.
8. In fact, Kyoto (was, were) the capital of Japan a long time ago.
9. Many of the traditional buildings still (exist, exists) there, so tourists can see them all over.
10. Life in these two places (is, are) quite different, and tourists (visit, visits) each city for very different reasons.

ACTIVITY 6 Correcting Subject-Verb Agreement Errors

Read this student paragraph. It contains seven errors in subject-verb agreement. Underline each error and write the correct form above it.

Example Paragraph 13

The Hard Work of a Teacher

Some people **may** think that Mimi Robertson has an easy job, but she really do not. Mimi is a kindergarten teacher at King Elementary School. She teaches 22 very young children. Mimi's class of kindergarten students begin at 8:30 a.m., but she does a lot before then. Every day she arrive at work just after 7:30 a.m. Mimi has to organize her supplies and prepare the room for her students. If one of the parents is in class that day to help, then Mimi have to explain the lesson plan to the parent before class. After the students arrive at 8:30, the class begins. The young students in her class keeps her **extremely** busy for the rest of the day. They play games and learn new things. However, there is always a few small problems. Mimi's young students does not always listen to her, and sometimes they fight or cry. Every now and then, one child **shouts**, but Mimi tries to be very patient with all of her students. After school, she **must** attend meetings and create new lessons. Mimi says she loves her job, but it really is **a great deal** of work.

may: possibly, might

extremely: very, to a high degree

to shout: to speak in a very loud voice, yell, scream

must: to be necessary, have to

a great deal (of): a large amount, a lot (*A lot* is used more in spoken English; *a great deal* sounds more formal and is more common in written English.)

Building Better Sentences: For further practice with the sentences and paragraphs in this unit, go to Practice 3 on pages 285–286 in Appendix 1.

Building Better Vocabulary

ACTIVITY 7 Word Associations

Circle the word or phrase that is most closely related to the word or phrase on the left. If necessary, use a dictionary to check the meaning of words you do not know.

	A	B
1. frightening	afraid	happy
2. to omit	to forget	to remember
3. interior	inside	outside
4. to revolve	to become	to turn
5. however	and	but
6. to shout	loud voice	soft voice
7. to share	to buy half	to give half
8. the purpose	goal	help
9. suddenly	perhaps	surprise
10. to create*	to make	to take
11. dense	a little in a big space	a lot in a small space
12. a skyscraper	a type of building	a type of weather
13. kindergarten	adults	children
14. suitable	bad idea	good idea
15. extremely	a little	a lot
16. a destination	a bus or a train	a city or a town

*Words that are part of the Academic Word List. See pages 275–276 for a complete list.

ACTIVITY 8 Using Collocations

Fill in each blank with the word on the left that most naturally completes the phrase on the right. If necessary, use a dictionary to check the meaning of words you do not know.

1. in / on	depend ________
2. cloud / room	a messy ________
3. at / for	that book is not suitable ________ a child
4. list / storm	make a ________ of (something)
5. and / but	________ so on
6. in / out	cross ________ an error
7. in / on	talking ________ the phone
8. a page number / a long report	write down ________
9. deal / must	a great ________ of (something)
10. expensive / price	extremely ________

Original Student Writing

ACTIVITY 9 Writing a Paragraph from Brainstorming

Now it is your turn to write a simple paragraph. Follow these guidelines:

- Choose a topic from Activity 2 on pages 36–38.
- Use the ideas that you brainstormed about that topic to create sentences for your paragraph.
- Write five to twelve sentences.
- Include the four features of a good paragraph in this checklist from page 12.
    - ☐ **1.** Does the paragraph have a topic sentence that states the main idea?
    - ☐ **2.** Are all of the sentences in the paragraph about one topic?
    - ☐ **3.** Is the first line of the paragraph indented?
    - ☐ **4.** Is the last sentence a good concluding sentence?
- Give your paragraph a title.
- Be sure to proofread your paragraph for good sentences, vocabulary, and grammar.
- Be especially careful with subject-verb agreement.
- Use at least two of the vocabulary words or phrases presented in Activity 7 and Activity 8. Underline these words and phrases in your paragraph.

If you need ideas for words and phrases, see the Useful Vocabulary for Better Writing on page 277–281.

ACTIVITY 10 Peer Editing

Exchange papers from Activity 9 with a partner. Read your partner's paragraph. Then use Peer Editing Sheet 2 on NGL.Cengage.com/GW2 to help you comment on your partner's paragraph. Be sure to offer positive suggestions and comments that will help your partner improve his or her writing. Consider your partner's comments as you revise your own paragraph.

Additional Topics for Writing

Here are more ideas for writing. Start by brainstorming ideas. When you write, be sure to include the four features of a paragraph.

PHOTO TOPIC: Look at the photo on pages 32–33. Write about something very scary that you experienced. What happened? When was it? How did you feel?

TOPIC 2: You and some friends want to go to an inexpensive restaurant. Where would you go? What would you order? Write about your night out together.

TOPIC 3: Write about and compare two things, people, or places. How are they similar? How are they different?

TOPIC 4: Write about ways that students can save money.

TOPIC 5: Write about three things that will be very different two years from now. Give specific examples with details.

Timed Writing

How quickly can you write in English? There are many times when you must write quickly, such as on a test. It is important to feel comfortable during those times. Timed-writing practice can make you feel better about writing quickly in English.

1. Take out a piece of paper.
2. Read the writing prompt.
3. Brainstorm ideas for five minutes.
4. Write a short paragraph (six to ten sentences).
5. You have 25 minutes to write.

In your opinion, is English easy or difficult to learn? Why do you think so? Give two or three strong reasons to support your opinion.

Unit

3 Topic Sentences

A woman is learning to sky dive over São Paulo, Brazil.

OBJECTIVES To learn how to write a topic sentence
To use commas in sentences
To recognize and avoid sentence fragments, run-on sentences, and comma splices.

Can you write about learning something new?

The Topic Sentence

A **topic sentence** tells about the main idea of a paragraph. It is usually found at the beginning of a paragraph. In this unit, you will learn:

- the function of a topic sentence
- what a good topic sentence looks like
- how a good controlling idea guides the flow of the information in the paragraph

ACTIVITY 1 Studying a Topic Sentence in a Paragraph

Discuss the Preview Questions with your classmates. Then read the opinion paragraph and answer the questions that follow.

Preview Questions

1. How did you learn to drive a car?
2. Can you tell someone how to drive a car? Why is it difficult to explain?

Example Paragraph 14

To Shift or Not to Shift

There are many **benefits** to driving a car with a **manual transmission**. First of all, a car with a manual transmission uses less gas than a car with an automatic transmission. A **typical economy car** can get **up to** 35 miles per gallon, but an automatic car averages 28. In addition to better gas mileage, a manual transmission allows the driver to start a car that has a low battery. With a foot on the **clutch**, the driver just needs to put the car in second **gear** and have someone push the car until it gains enough speed. The driver then **releases** the clutch quickly, and the car should start. Unfortunately, starting a car this way is impossible with an automatic transmission. Finally, people with manual transmissions say that they have much more control of their cars. For example, if the **brakes** suddenly stop working on this type of car, the driver can **shift** to a lower gear to slow the car down. In contrast, people who drive automatic transmission cars have to depend on the automatic system. If something **malfunctions**, drivers have no control of their vehicles. **While** automatic cars are more convenient, manual transmission cars certainly offer many more advantages.

a benefit: a good point; an advantage

manual: by hand

a transmission: a device in a vehicle that transfers power from the engine to the car to enable it to move

typical: usual, average

an economy car: an inexpensive car with good gas mileage

up to: not more than, that amount or lower

a clutch: the left pedal in a manual transmission car that allows shifting of gears

a gear: the part of a machine that has teeth or grooves around the edge and turns another part of the same machine

to release: to let go, allow to escape

a brake: the device that stops a vehicle

to shift: to change or move the gears in a car

to malfunction: to stop working, usually suddenly

while: although

Post-Reading

1. Which one of these ideas tells the purpose of this paragraph? Put a check mark ✓ next to the correct answer.

________ **a.** to talk about the different kinds of manual transmissions

________ **b.** to explain what a manual transmission is

________ **c.** to tell why a manual transmission is better than an automatic transmission

________ **d.** to describe how a manual transmission interacts with the brakes in a vehicle

2. Underline the topic sentence in this paragraph.

3. A good paragraph has a very clear organization that you must learn. Underline the three sentences that introduce the three benefits of a manual transmission.

4. What is the purpose of the sentence that comes immediately after each of your three underlined sentences?

It gives an example

5. The following expressions are important to the organization of the paragraph. What does each one mean? What is the purpose of each expression?

   a. first of all

   the most important detail

   b. in addition to

   also, an added point is, besides, additionally

   c. finally

   the last or concluding point is

ACTIVITY 2 Recognizing Effective Topic Sentences

What do you already know about topic sentences? Read each set of sentences. Write the general topic that the sentences share. Then put a check mark ✓ on the line next to the best topic sentence. Be prepared to explain your answers.

1. General Topic: winter

   ____ Winter is a good season.

   ____ Winter weather is cold, and it snows.

   _✓_ The best season for kids is winter.

2. General Topic: Soccer

   _✓_ Soccer is popular for many reasons.

   ____ You need a leather ball to play soccer.

   ____ Soccer is a nice game.

3. General Topic: Los Angeles

   ____ There are many people in Los Angeles.

   _✓_ People from many different cultures live in Los Angeles.

   ____ Los Angeles is a big city in California.

4. General Topic: Bilingual dictionaries

_____ Monolingual dictionaries have only one language, but bilingual dictionaries have two languages.

__✓__ Many language students prefer bilingual dictionaries to monolingual dictionaries.

_____ Dictionaries that have two languages, such as French and English, are called bilingual dictionaries.

5. General Topic: Perfumes

__✓__ French perfumes are expensive for a number of reasons.

_____ My mother's perfume smells flowery.

_____ You can purchase perfumes in expensive blue crystal bottles.

6. General Topic: The book, An American Education

_____ *An American Education* has 540 pages.

_____ A woman graduates in *An American Education.*

__✓__ *An American Education* is an excellent historical novel.

How did you decide which sentences were the best topic sentences? What were you looking for? Discuss your ideas with your classmates.

Features of a Good Topic Sentence

A good topic sentence has the following features:

1. It controls or guides the whole paragraph.

When you read the topic sentence, you know what to expect in the paragraph.

2. A good topic sentence is not a fact that everyone accepts as true.

For example, a bad topic sentence would be, "Libraries have books." The information in this sentence is true, but it is a fact and is not a good choice for a topic sentence.

3. A good topic sentence is specific.

"Tea is delicious" is not a good topic sentence because the information in the sentence is too general. The reader does not know what to expect in the paragraph. If you want to write a paragraph about tea, make your topic sentence more specific, such as "Green tea has many health benefits."

4. However, a good topic sentence is not too specific.

"This dictionary contains more than 42,000 words" limits the topic too much—there is nothing else for the writer to say.

5. A good topic sentence has a controlling idea.

It includes words or phrases that help guide the flow of ideas in the paragraph. The controlling idea focuses the content of the following sentences.

·ontrolling Ideas

Here are some example topic sentences with controlling ideas. The controlling ideas have been derlined.

1. Many language students prefer bilingual dictionaries to monolingual dictionaries.

   Explanation: The reader expects the paragraph to explain *why* this statement is true.

2. The best season for kids is winter.

   Explanation: The reader expects the paragraph to give reasons and examples of *why* winter is the best season for children.

3. People from many different cultures live in Los Angeles.

   Explanation: The reader expects the paragraph to include information about various groups of people *who* make up the population of Los Angeles.

4. Soccer is popular for many reasons.

   Explanation: The reader expects the paragraph to give a variety of information about soccer and *why* it is popular around the world.

ACTIVITY 3 Recognizing Controlling Ideas in Topic Sentences

Read the following topic sentences. The main idea for each sentence has been circled. Underline the controlling idea. Then explain what information you expect to find in the paragraph.

1. The SAT Reasoning Test™ contains three distinct sections that deal with three important skills.

   Explanation:

   Controlling idea: 3 distinct sections, 3 important skills.
   Explanation: a listing of the 3 sections and the 3 skills in the SAT Reasoning Test

2. The shocking crash of a 747 jumbo jet off the coast of New York baffled investigators.

   Explanation:

   What (about the crash) baffled investigators?

3. Crossword puzzles are not only educational and fun but also addictive.

   Explanation:

   Reasons people do crossword puzzles.

4. Recent research has confirmed that eating dark green, leafy vegetables, such as broccoli and cabbage, may reduce the risk of some types of cancer.

   Explanation:

   Examples of research that suggests these vegetables reduce the risk of some types of cancer.

5. Although buying a house may seem appealing, renting an apartment has many advantages.

   Explanation:

   Why renting an apt. is better than buying a house.

Building Better Sentences: For further practice with the sentences and paragraphs in this part of the unit, go to Practice 4 on page 286 in Appendix 1.

ACTIVITY 4 More Practice Recognizing Controlling Ideas

Read the three sentences in each item and then put a check mark ✓ next to the best topic sentence. Underline the controlling idea in that sentence. Be prepared to explain your selections.

1. ________ Most of the girls in the class get higher grades in English than the boys.

   ___✓___ Research has shown that girls are better at languages than boys. What does the research say about this topic?

   ________ Many students like languages very much.

2. ________ Cats are better pets than goldfish for many reasons.

________ Cats and goldfish are both animals.

________ Cats cannot swim very well, but goldfish can.

3. ________ Yesterday I did not have lunch with my coworkers.

________ Yesterday I went to work late.

________ Yesterday was the worst day of my life.

4. ________ Some people call Paul Cézanne the father of modern art.

________ Paul Cézanne, the father of modern art, made important contributions to the history of art.

________ Paul Cézanne's art was not recognized until the end of his career, but he is often called the father of modern art.

5. ________ Many Canadians speak French, and some of them speak Chinese and Japanese.

________ The current population of Canada is a reflection of the international background of its citizens and immigrants.

________ A large number of new immigrants live in the western province of British Columbia, but not many of them speak German.

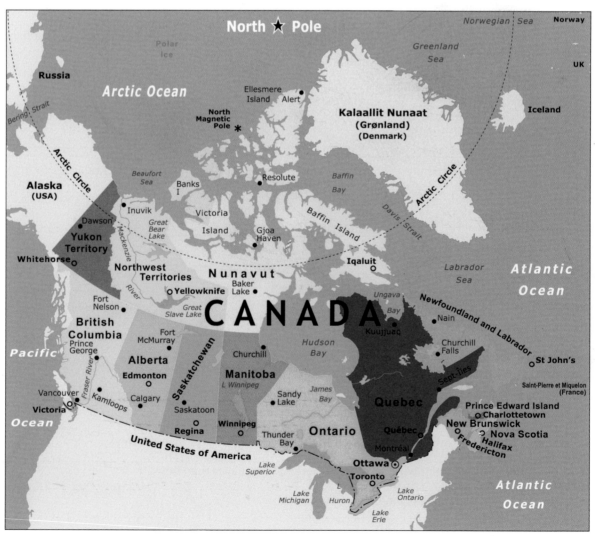

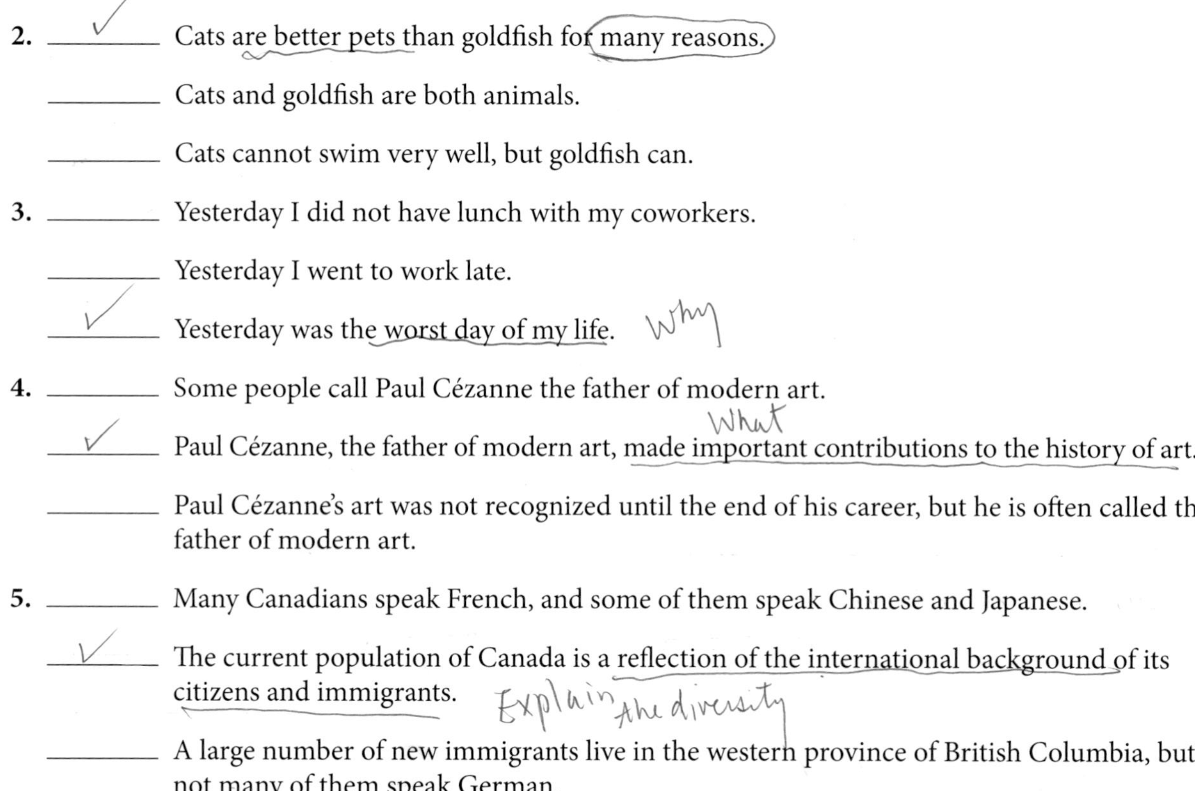

First individual then pair!

ACTIVITY 5 Adding Controlling Ideas to Create Better Topic Sentences

All of these topic sentences are too general. Rewrite each sentence and add a controlling idea. Compare your sentences with other students' sentences.

Example: Flowers are beautiful.

Flowers are the best gift to receive when you are feeling down.

OR

Only four kinds of flowers grow during the short summers in Alaska.

1. Cats are nice.

   There are many benefits to raise a cat.

2. Paris is the capital of France.

   You can visit many cultural sights in Paris.

3. The English alphabet has twenty-six letters.

   There are 3 reasons why English is popular
   ① Easy to learn, ② useful in science and computer, etc. ③ English is the official language of 53 countries

4. Reading blogs is interesting.

   There are many reasons why people read blogs.
   ① convenient info. seeking ② non-traditional news sources. ③ Variety of opinions

5. Running is an enjoyable hobby.

   Running offers us 3 benefits

ACTIVITY 6 Studying a Topic Sentence in a Paragraph

Answer these questions about how a topic sentence is related to the information in the body of the paragraph.

1. Copy the topic sentence from Paragraph 14 (page 49) here.

   There are many benefits to driving a car w/ a manual transmission.

2. Underline the controlling idea(s) in that topic sentence.

3. Give at least three examples of how the controlling idea(s) in the topic sentence are directly connected to the information in the paragraph.

   a car w/ a manual transmission uses less gas than an automatic car; it allows the driver to start a car that has a low battery; people w/ manual transmissions say that they have much more control of their vehicles.

ACTIVITY 7 Writing Topic Sentences

Read each paragraph on pages 56–60. Then write a good topic sentence that is connected to the information in the paragraph. Be sure to end each topic sentence with correct punctuation.

Example Paragraph 15

Reasons for Playing Instruments

People play instruments for different reasons.

Some people choose to learn how to play a musical instrument because they want to have fun. They want to play it with their friends or maybe in a band. Another reason people play an instrument is that it is their hobby. They learned how to play it a long time ago, and now it is a way to occupy their time. Other people learn to play an instrument because it is part of their culture. Certain instruments are popular in one culture, **such as** the guitar in Spain or the **oud** in the Middle East. In some cases, however, people learn how to play an instrument because they think it will make them smarter. **A great deal of** research suggests that studying music can improve a person's brain function and intelligence. **In sum,** there is not just one main reason that people play a musical instrument.

such as: for example

the oud: a stringed instrument

a great deal of: much, a lot of

in sum: in conclusion

Differences Between Reptiles and Dinosaurs

Dinosaurs differ from modern reptiles in three main ways.

One is size. Most modern reptiles are small. Dinosaurs were much, much larger than any reptile that we have on earth today. Second, the legs of most reptiles today are on the sides of their body. However, dinosaurs' legs were on the bottom of their body. In this way, dinosaurs could stand up on their back legs. Third, today's reptiles use the environment to control their body temperature. In contrast, dinosaurs controlled their own body temperature. They did not depend on their surroundings. While reptiles and dinosaurs may seem very similar, they are actually quite different.

Example Paragraph 17

Reasons for Exercise

Exercise can benefit people in several important ways.

First, your body will look better. Exercise is perfect for staying trim and healthy looking, and it does not have to take a long time. Second, you will actually have more energy. A person who exercises will have fewer problems walking up stairs or climbing hills. In addition, your heart will be healthier. A good, strong heart is necessary for a long, healthy life. Finally, exercise reduces stress and keeps your mind in shape. Therefore, if you want to improve your overall health, you should exercise three or four times each week to accomplish this goal.

Example Paragraph 18

Popular Popcorn

Popcorn is a simple but excellent snack food.

It is one of the easiest foods to eat. You can eat it with your fingers, and it does not have to be served piping hot like some foods do. In addition, with only 20 calories per cup and almost no fat, it is both a filling and a heart-friendly snack. Furthermore, it can be an important **source** of natural fiber, a substance that is important in limiting certain types of cancer. Based on this information, can anyone be surprised that sales of popcorn are **soaring** in many countries?

a source: a place of origin

to soar: rise quickly

Example Paragraph 19

A Method for Learning New Words

____

In this method, learners form their own sound association between the foreign language word they are trying to learn and any word in their native language. In the second stage, learners form an image link between the target word and the native language word. For example, a Japanese learner of English might look at the English word *hatchet* and connect it to the Japanese word *hachi,* which means "eight." In this case, the learner might remember that he can use a hatchet eight times to cut down a tree. For many language students, this particular method is effective in learning new vocabulary in a foreign language.

Building Better Sentences: For further practice with the sentences and paragraphs in this part of the unit, go to Practice 5 on page 287 in Appendix 1.

Grammar for Writing

Using Commas in Sentences

Commas are very important for clarity of meaning, but commas also represent the grammar of a sentence. Remember:

Explanation	Examples
A comma separates a list of three or more things.	I speak English**,** Spanish**,** and Japanese.
A comma separates two sentences when there is a combining word.	I speak three languages**, but** Adam speaks five.
A comma separates an introductory word or phrase from the rest of the sentence.	**First**, you will need to get a pencil.
A comma separates a dependent clause that comes at the beginning of a sentence.	**Because I speak three languages**, I can communicate with many people.
A comma separates an appositive from the rest of the sentence. (An appositive is a group of words that renames or explains the noun before it.)	Fiber**, a substance that is important in limiting certain types of cancer**, is found in popcorn.
A comma separates extra information that is provided in adjective clauses.	*The History of Korea***, which is on the teacher's desk**, is the book for the course.

For more information and examples, review the section on "Commas" in the *Brief Writers Handbook with Activities*, pages 258–260.

ACTIVITY 8 Comma Practice

Insert commas in these sentences where necessary. Be prepared to explain your choices. Some sentences are correct with no commas.

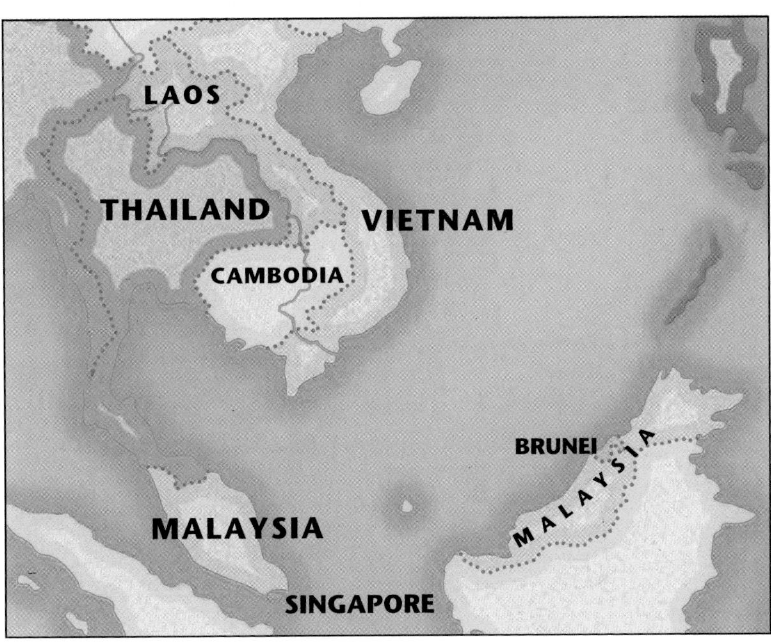

Example Paragraph 20

Malaysia and Thailand

Because Malaysia and Thailand are located next to each other we might conclude that these two nations share many similarities. To a certain extent this conclusion is true. For example both countries have temperate climates throughout the year. Thailand's economy is growing and so is Malaysia's. In addition Malaysia has many miles of beautiful beaches that attract tourists and Thailand does too. However there are also several important differences. Malaysians and Thais speak completely different languages. The population of Malaysia is about 29 million but the population of Thailand is about 69 million. Thailand has a national king but Malaysia does not. Finally Malaysia was a British colony but Thailand was never a British colony. **Thus** the fact that two countries are near each other does not always mean they are similar.

thus: therefore, for this reason

Grammar for Writing

Avoiding Three Common Sentence Errors

Three common mistakes in writing are **sentence fragments, run-on sentences, and comma splices.** These mistakes can prevent the reader from understanding the writer's message.

Explanation	Examples
A **sentence fragment** is not a complete sentence. It is usually missing either a subject or a verb, or it is a dependent clause. A dependent clause is never a complete sentence. To correct a sentence fragment: • add a subject or verb, or • combine two clauses	✗ I went to Italy last summer. Was a wonderful trip. ✓ I went to Italy last summer. **It** was a wonderful trip. *(add a subject)* ✗ Only 120 students majored in art. Because they are worried about job opportunities. ✓ Only 120 students majored in art **because** they are worried about job opportunities. *(combine two clauses)*
A **run-on sentence** is two sentences incorrectly joined without a comma or a coordinating conjunction (*and, or, but, so, yet, nor, for*). To correct a run-on sentence: • add a comma and a connecting word, or • separate the sentences into two with a period	✗ I went to Italy and saw Rome I didn't get to see Milan. ✓ I went to Italy and saw Rome**, but** I didn't get to see Milan. *(add comma and connecting word)* ✓ I went to Italy and saw Rome. I didn't get to see Milan. *(separate into two sentences)*
A **comma splice** occurs when two or more sentences or independent clauses are connected with a comma. To correct a comma splice: • add a connecting word after the comma, • create two sentences from the one, or • combine the most important words from the two sentences into one sentence and add a subordinating conjunction *(because, since, although)*	✗ I went to Italy last summer, it was a wonderful trip. ✓ I went to Italy last summer, **and** it was a wonderful trip. *(add connecting word)* ✓ I went to Italy last summer. It was a wonderful trip. *(create two sentences)* ✗ Only 120 students majored in art, because they are worried about job opportunities. ✓ Only 120 students majored in art **because** they are worried about job opportunities. ✓ **Because** they are worried about job opportunities, only 120 students majored in art. *(add a subordinating conjunction)*

ACTIVITY 9 Correcting Sentence Fragments

Read each group of words. If it is a complete sentence, write *C* on the line. If it is a sentence fragment, write *SF* on the line. Then write a correct sentence. More than one correction may be possible.

1. SF One of the most common reasons that people make a decision to become a vegetarian.

   One of the most common reasons that people make a decision to become a vegetarian is to improve their health.

2. SF Because the wind and rain were so incredibly strong between noon and 4 p.m. yesterday,

   we didn't go out. (or many people lost power.)

3. C Although the price of gasoline is extremely high, people just complain and pay the high prices.

4. SF In order to cash a check at a bank where you do not have an account and no one there knows you,

   you have to present a photo ID.

5. C Of course the main ingredient that you have to have in order to make chicken soup is chicken.

6. C For some teachers, a sentence fragment is a very serious type of mistake because it shows a lack of understanding of what a sentence is.

7. SF ~~Although~~ The economic forecast for the housing market does not contain any especially bright news for those who wish to buy a house in the near future.

8. C When the vice-president was sworn in as the new number two person in the entire country, her husband and her children as well as her grandchildren attended the ceremony.

ACTIVITY 10 Correcting Sentence Fragments, Run-On Sentences, and Comma Splices

Read each sentence or set of sentences. If it is correct, write *C* on the line. If there is an error, circle it and indicate the type of error by writing SF for a sentence fragment, *RO* for run-on sentence, or *CS* for a comma splice. Then write the correct sentence(s). More than one correction may be possible.

1. ___CS___ A whale is one of the largest animals on the planet, few people have seen one in person.

   A whale is one of the largest animals on the planet. Few people have seen one in person.

   OR

   Although the whale is one of the largest animals on the planet, few people have seen one in person.

2. ________ Yesterday's weather caused problems for many travelers. Most of the flights were canceled. Due to the torrential rains and high winds.

   ____

   ____

   ____

3. ________ Computer programs can help students learn a foreign language, many students use the language programs in the computer center.

   ____

   ____

   ____

4. ___C___ It was definitely a nervous time for many people. When we had the economic crisis, prices and unemployment soared. The government did everything possible to make sure that people did not panic.

____

____

____

5. ___CS___ *Dancing with the Stars* is an internationally known television show, the dancing is very exciting.

____

____

____

6. ___SF___ This magazine won several awards last year. For the content and the style of its stories. The last issue had two superb short stories that were written by distinguished authors.

____

____

____

7. ___R-O___ Lázaro Cárdenas was the president of Mexico from 1934 to 1940. His original goal was to become a teacher the political situation in Mexico at that time caused him to change his mind.

____

____

____

8. ___SF___ Despite all of the extremely depressing news that we recently heard from that part of the world.

The people remain optimistic.

____

____

Building Better Sentences: For further practice with the sentences and paragraphs in this part of the unit, go to Practice 6 on pages 287–288 in Appendix 1.

Building Better Vocabulary

ACTIVITY 11 Word Associations

Circle the word or phrase that is most closely related to the word or phrase on the left. If necessary, use a dictionary to check the meaning of words you do not know.

	A	B
1. a reptile	animal	disease
2. utensils	people	things
3. distinguished	known	secret
4. brakes	you use them to start a car	you use them to stop a car
5. to reduce	to become smaller	to become bigger
6. an axle	wheels	windows
7. a device*	a person	a thing
8. to purchase*	to buy	to sell
9. to baffle	to confuse	to decide
10. up to six things	four or five things	seven or eight things
11. while	after	although
12. an appealing idea	people hate it	people like it
13. a risk	a danger	a product
14. a snack	a kind of animal	a kind of food
15. the source*	where something came from	why someone did something

*Words that are part of the Academic Word List. See pages 275–276 for a complete list.

ACTIVITY 12 Using Collocations

Fill in each blank with the word on the left that most naturally completes the phrase on the right. If necessary, use a dictionary to check the meaning of words you do not know.

1. by / with	handicrafts are made ____________________ hand
2. car / fiber	an economy ____________________
3. from / with	interact ____________________

4. first / next — ____________ of all

5. bilingual / soaring — ____________ prices

6. as / for — vegetables such ____________ onions

7. than / that — one thing is easier ____________ another

8. by / of — one thing is a reflection ____________ another thing

9. in / on — depend ____________ a good friend

10. filling / trembling — a ____________ meal

Original Student Writing

ACTIVITY 13 Brainstorming Ideas for a Paragraph

Choose one of the general topics below. Brainstorm your ideas about it in the space provided. When you have finished, circle the ideas that you think are best to include in a paragraph.

Topics:

1. animal communication
2. international flights
3. pollution
4. smart phones

Brainstorming area:

ACTIVITY 14 Original Writing Practice

Use your brainstorming notes from Activity 13 on page 67 to write a paragraph.

- Make sure that your paragraph has the four features explained on page 12.
- Use at least two of the vocabulary words or phrases presented in Activity 11 and Activity 12. Underline the words and phrases in your paragraph.

If you need ideas for words and phrases, see the Useful Vocabulary for Better Writing on pages 277–281.

ACTIVITY 15 Peer Editing

Exchange papers from Activity 14 with a partner. Read your partner's paragraph. Then use Peer Editing Sheet 3 on page NGL.Cengage.com/GW2 to help you comment on your partner's paragraph. Be sure to offer positive suggestions and comments that will help your partner improve his or her writing. Consider your partner's comments as you revise your own paragraph.

Additional Topics for Writing

Here are more ideas for writing. Start by brainstorming. When you write your paragraph, be sure to include the four features of a paragraph.

PHOTO TOPIC: Look at the photo on pages 46–47. Write about learning something new. What would you learn? Would you learn about it inside or outside? What would you do with the new information or skill?

TOPIC 2: Write about your daily routine. What do you do and when? How many things do you do in a day? What is the best part of your day or week?

TOPIC 3: Write about a famous person you would like to meet. What has this person done that is interesting to you? What would you talk about? What would you hope to learn from the experience?

TOPIC 4: Write about two vacation destinations. Which is better? Compare the sights. What is similar, and what is different? What are some activities you can do while in each of these places?

TOPIC 5: Write about your favorite relative. Who is this person? What qualities make this person special? How does this person make others feel?

Timed Writing

How quickly can you write in English? There are many times when you must write quickly, such as on a test. It is important to feel comfortable during those times. Timed-writing practice can make you feel better about writing quickly in English.

1. Take out a piece of paper.
2. Read the writing prompt.
3. Brainstorm ideas for five minutes.
4. Write a short paragraph (six to ten sentences).
5. You have 25 minutes to write your paragraph.

In your opinion, why do so many people want to learn English? Give a few strong examples to support your answer.

Unit 4

Supporting and Concluding Sentences

A cable car is going toward the top of Sugerloaf Mountain in Rio de Janeiro, Brazil

OBJECTIVES To learn how to write supporting sentences
To learn how to write concluding sentences
To substitute pronouns for key nouns

Can you write about a place to visit in your city?

Supporting Sentences

Supporting sentences give information that explains and expands the topic of the paragraph. They answer questions—*who? what? where? when? why?* and *how?*—and give details. Good writers think of these questions when they write supporting sentences for the topic sentence.

ACTIVITY 1 Predicting Paragraph Content from the Controlling Idea

Read each topic sentence. Circle the main idea. Underline the controlling idea. Then predict the kind of information you will find in the paragraph.

1. New York and Boston attract millions of tourists, but I think one of the best cities to visit on the east coast of the United States is Washington, D.C.

   What kind of information do you think is in this paragraph?

   Main idea: Washington, D.C;
   Controlling idea: best cities to visit on the east coast;
   Prediction: reasons & examples showing why Wash. D.C. is such a good city to visit in comparison to New York and Boston.

2. One of the people that I most admire is my great-grandmother Carla.

   What kind of information do you think is in this paragraph?

   Main idea: my great-gran
   Controlling idea: one of the people that I most admire;
   Prediction: admirable qualities of my great-grandmother

3. The Grand Palace is one of the most popular tourist destinations in Thailand.

   What kind of information do you think is in this paragraph?

   Main idea: The Grand Palace;
   Controlling idea: One of the most popular tourist destinations in the world
   Prediction: Reasons why The Grand Palace is a top tour destination in Thailand.

As you can see, the topic sentences are all very different. As a result, the supporting sentences that you write will depend on your topic sentence.

ACTIVITY 2 Reading Example Supporting Sentences

Read the paragraphs on pages 73–75. Notice how the supporting sentences tell you more about the topic sentence. Compare what you wrote in Activity 1 to the information in each paragraph. How well did you predict the content?

Example Paragraph 21

A Great Tourist Destination

New York and Boston attract millions of tourists, but I think one of the best cities to visit on the east coast of the United States is Washington, D.C. It has some of the most interesting **landmarks** and tourist **spots** in the country. There are many monuments to visit, such as the Lincoln Memorial, the Jefferson Memorial, and the Washington Monument, which is the tallest building in Washington. For more excitement, the area called Georgetown in northwest Washington is famous for its shopping and restaurants. Finally, there is the White House tour. On this tour, the guide **leads** visitors as they walk through many of the rooms in the White House and **view** the home of the president of the United States. Although Washington, D.C., does not have the large number of visitors that New York or Boston does, I think this city is one of the best destinations for tourists.

a landmark: a historical building, a well-known location

a spot: a place, a location

to lead: to show the way, organize

to view: to see, look at

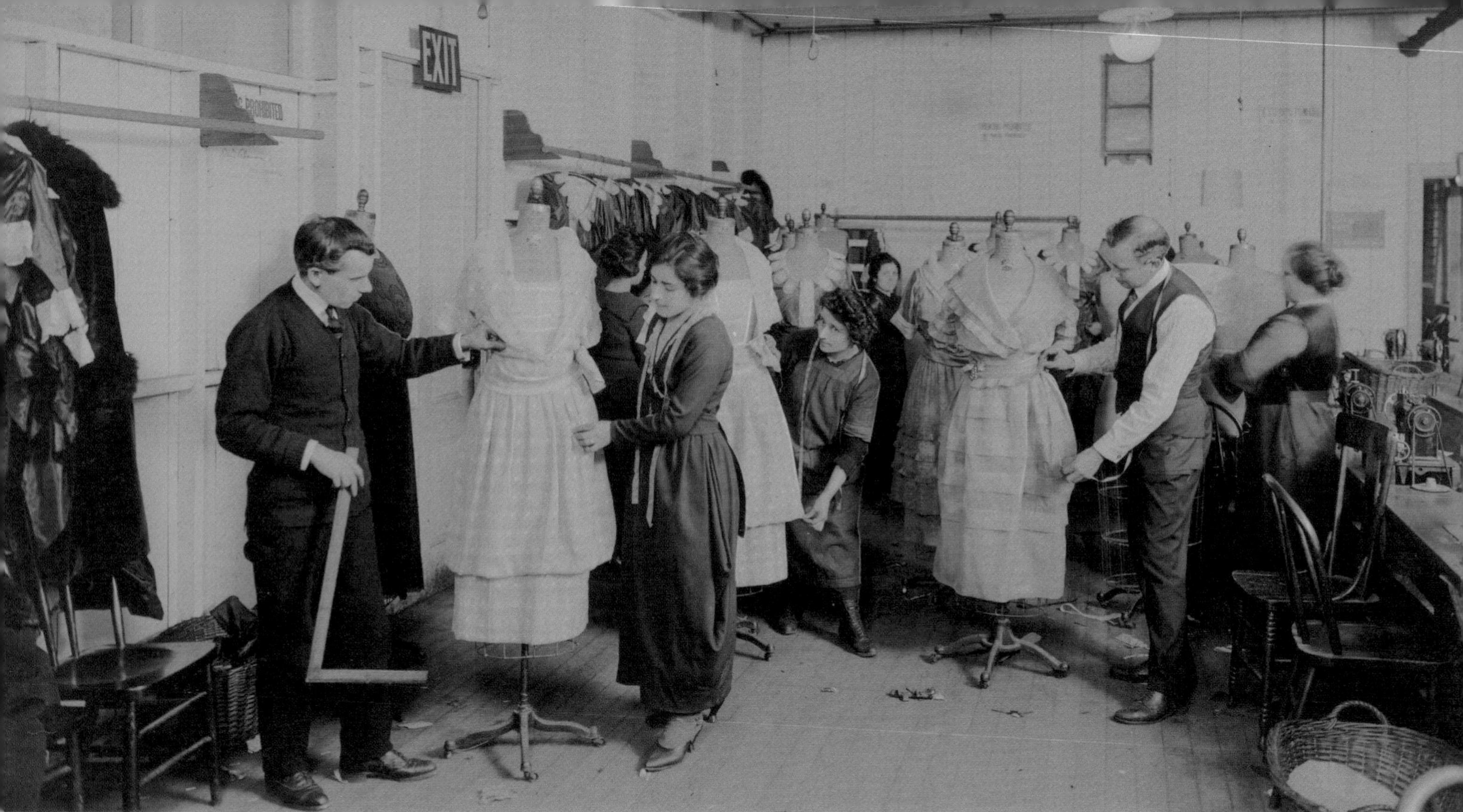

Example Paragraph 22

An Immigrant in the Family

One of the people that I admire the most is my great-grandmother Carla. She came to the United States from Italy in 1911 as a young woman on a large ship. She had little money and no **property**. Soon after landing at Ellis Island in New York, she began working as a **seamstress** in Brooklyn. She met and married my great-grandfather not long after that. They immediately began their large family. Great-grandma Carla had eight children—five boys and three girls. In addition to taking care of **such** a large family in a new country, my great-grandmother survived **discrimination** as an **immigrant**, two world wars, the Great Depression, and a long list of illnesses. However, she rarely **complained**, and she was very happy with her new life in America. Whenever I think of my great-grandma Carla, I am always filled with **admiration** for her.

the property: land or buildings that a person owns

a seamstress: a woman who sews for a living

such: to a great degree, very

the discrimination: unfair treatment, especially because of race, age, or gender

an immigrant: a person who comes to live in a new country

to complain: to express unhappiness or dissatisfaction about something

admiration: a feeling of approval or pleasure for someone

Example Paragraph 23

The Grand Palace in Bangkok

The Grand Palace is one of the most popular tourist destinations in Thailand. The **construction** of the palace began in 1782, and the royal family lived there until 1925. The palace area **consists of** over two million square feet, and the wall that surrounds the Grand Palace is more than 6,000 feet long. This huge area includes countless buildings, gardens, and special rooms. The public cannot visit all of these areas, however, because some areas are still used for official events. The palace includes some examples of European influence on the design, such as the Greek columns and the French windows. It is certainly easy to understand why so many tourists visit the Grand Palace each year.

the construction: the act of building something

to consist of: contain, include

Kinds of Supporting Sentences

Good supporting sentences have different goals. Writers vary them to:

- **explain:** The family moved from the village to the capital for economic reasons.
- **describe:** She lived in a lovely three-story castle surrounded by a forest.
- **give reasons:** Lukas finally quit his job because of the stressful working conditions.
- **give facts:** More than ten percent of the university's student population is international.
- **give examples:** Oranges and grapefruits grow in California.
- **define:** Many tourists visit Bangkok, which is the capital and largest city in Thailand.

ACTIVITY 3 Matching Supporting and Topic Sentences

Read the two topic sentences below. Then read the list of supporting sentences. Match each supporting sentence with the corresponding topic sentence by writing the correct topic sentence number on the line beside the supporting sentences. Notice that each sentence is labeled in parentheses with the kind of supporting sentence that it is.

Topic sentences

TS 1: Low-fat diets are an excellent way to stay healthy and trim.

TS 2: High-protein diets are favored by athletes and competitors.

Supporting sentences

a. ___2___ These foods help build muscles and increase energy. (fact)

b. ___1___ They are preferred by the general public because they help with weight reduction. (reason)

c. ___1___ Low-fat diets are recommended by most physicians. (fact)

d. ___2___ Many athletes eat high-protein foods, such as meat, beans, and nuts. (example)

e. ___1___ Low-fat foods include fruits, vegetables, and pasta. (example)

f. ___1___ Because they are easy to find in stores, low-fat foods are convenient. (reason)

g. ___2___ Athletes generally eat high-protein diets to give them more energy. (reason)

h. ___1___ Crispy steamed vegetables and grilled fish and chicken are all tasty parts of a low-fat, heart-friendly diet. (description)

ACTIVITY 4 Asking Questions about Topic Sentences

Read each topic sentence. What information would you expect the writer to include in the paragraph? Write a question that the supporting sentences should answer. Use a *who? what? where? when? why?* or *how?* question.

In 2008, smoking was banned in all public facilities.

Why was smoking banned?

1. Texas is home to several kinds of poisonous snakes.

What are the different kinds of poisonous snakes in Texas?

2. Classrooms without windows have negative effects on students.

What are the adverse effects of windowless classrooms?

3. Computer technology will one day eliminate the use of libraries.

How will computer technology eliminate libraries?

4. Quebec City is a wonderful place to raise children.

Why is Quebec City a wonderful place to raise children?

5. I will never forget the day I got married.

What was so memorable about the day you got married?

Building Better Sentences: For further practice with the sentences and paragraphs in this part of the unit, go to Practice 7 on pages 288–289 in Appendix 1.

Choose 2 topics

ACTIVITY 5 Brainstorming Topic Sentences

For each of the general topics in the left column, brainstorm some ideas in the space provided. Then write a topic sentence with a controlling idea in the right column. Underline the controlling ideas.

Brainstorming Topic	Topic Sentence with Controlling Idea
1. vacation • types (summer; honeymoon) • 5 common destinations (national parks, Caribbean islands). • memories (Why was it special?)	I will <u>never forget</u> my summer vacation.
2. mathematics	
3. a best friend	

4. a meal you ate at a restaurant	
5. a (specific) sport	

ACTIVITY 6 Asking for More Information

Choose two of your topic sentences from Activity 5 and write them below. Then write four questions about each topic. Remember to use *who? what? where? when? why?* or *how?* questions. If you cannot think of four questions, brainstorm some ideas with a classmate.

1. Topic Sentence: I will never forget my summer vacation.
   a. Why was this vacation so memorable?
   b. Where did you go?
   c. What did you do?
   d. How old were you at that time?
2. Topic Sentence: ______
   a. ______
   b. ______
   c. ______
   d. ______
3. Topic Sentence: ______
   a. ______
   b. ______
   c. ______
   d. ______

Unrelated Information

Sometimes writers give information that is not closely related to the topic. When this happens, the paragraph does not read smoothly, and the reader might get confused about the writer's message. It is necessary that each sentence in a paragraph be connected to the controlling idea or ideas in the topic sentence of the paragraph.

ACTIVITY 7 Identifying the Unrelated Sentence

Read the paragraphs on pages 79–81. In each paragraph, underline the one sentence that does not belong because it is not connected closely with the supporting ideas in the topic sentence.

Example Paragraph 24

My Evaluation of Dining at Fresh Market

The menu at Fresh Market, one of the newest restaurants in downtown Springfield, consists of only five main dishes that are simple but very delicious. My number one dish there is pasta with fresh vegetables. The pasta is cooked just right, and the vegetables include broccoli, onions, tomatoes, and corn. My second favorite main dish is the spicy chicken and brown rice soup. The chicken is a little hot for some people's tastes, but many people really like the fact that you get brown rice instead of the usual bland white rice. The other main dishes are fried chicken with curry potatoes, Greek salad with grilled shrimp,

and fried fish with vinegar chips. All three of these use the freshest of ingredients and taste great. This paragraph will not include any information about the beverages at this restaurant. If you eat a meal at Fresh Market, I am sure you will enjoy it tremendously.

Example Paragraph 25

Counting the Continents

The number of continents should be a simple fact, but the number you identify depends on where you live. In the United States, students learn that there are seven continents. These seven are North America, South America, Europe, Africa, Asia, Australia, and Antarctica. In Europe, however, students learn that there are six continents. They learn that North America and South America are one continent, which they call the Americas. Panama is the southern end of North America, but it used to be part of Colombia, which is in South America. In some places, Europe and Asia are combined into one continent called Eurasia. In other places, Antarctica is not considered a continent. It is very interesting that different cultures clearly disagree on the definition of a continent and therefore the number of continents on our earth.

Traveling between Rome and Paris

There are three good options for traveling between Rome and Paris. The fastest way is by plane. However, flying between these two cities can be a little expensive unless you can find a discounted airline ticket. The second way is by train, which is very popular with many tourists. In fact, Rome and Paris are visited each year by millions of students from all over. The train fare is not so expensive and the service is very good, but the overnight trip takes about 14 hours. Finally, many people take a bus. The bus is the cheapest of the three options, but it takes up to 22 hours, which means it takes the most time. If you research each of these three travel options, you will find the best way for you to travel between Rome and Paris.

ACTIVITY 8 Identifying Supporting Sentences

Read each paragraph on pages 82–84.

1. For each of the underlined, numbered sentences, write *good supporting sentence* or *unrelated sentence* on the corresponding lines below the paragraph. (One sentence in each paragraph is unrelated to the topic.)

2. Write a reason for each choice.

Remember: All the supporting sentences must be related to the topic sentence. The first paragraph has been done for you.

Example Paragraph 27

Strict Parents

Fortunately, my parents were very strict with me when I was a child. I think that they were protective because I was an only child. However, at that time, it felt like I was in prison. I had to come straight home after school and immediately do my homework. (1) After I finished my homework, I was allowed to watch only one hour of television. While my friends were playing video games or watching cartoons, I was usually doing chores around the house to help my mother. (2) This included doing some of the laundry and ironing, mowing the lawn, and helping to prepare dinner. (3) My father was an architect, and my mother was a housewife. Looking back, I am not sorry that my parents were strict with me because I think it was the best way to bring up a child.

1. good supporting sentence — It is an example of why the writer felt he or she was in prison.

2. good supporting sentence — It is a list of the chores the writer had to do around the house.

3. unrelated sentence — The writer's parents' occupations are not related to how the writer was treated. There is no relationship between being an architect and being a strict parent.

Underwater Adventure

Snorkeling can be one of the most amazing adventures you can ever take part in. 1 Floating on the water and watching the fish swim below you is a unique experience. It is normal to be nervous in the beginning, but once you are in the water, the anxiety goes away as you slowly notice the new world around you. Coral reefs are the best places to snorkel because hundreds, sometimes thousands, of fish and other sea creatures live among the coral. 2 Depending on where you snorkel, you can see tiny squids, turtles, sea cucumbers, lobsters, and many other animals. 3 I saw a shark the last time I was snorkeling, and it really scared me. It is truly a beautiful sight, one that you can hardly believe is happening. When you are underwater, the world you know is blocked out, and the silence makes the overall experience more magical. If you want to have one of the most beautiful experiences that anyone can ever have, you should try snorkeling for a day.

1. Good — It gives more detail to the introductory sentence.

2. Good — It gives examples of other sea creatures, which is mentioned in prev. sentence

3. Unrelated — this paragraph is about snorkling in general, not the writer's personal experience

Example Paragraph 29

Sweet Dreams

When people have a hard time falling asleep at night, there are three things that they can do to relax before going to sleep. 1 One of the most pleasant ways to relax is to imagine a beautiful and peaceful place. This requires a creative mind, but it is very effective. Another common method is to practice deep-breathing exercises. These rhythmic exercises are good for getting rid of the tension that causes people to stay awake. 2 A third method is to listen to relaxing music, especially soft music. 3 Soft music is also popular because it helps students study better. Some people have developed unique ways to help them fall asleep, but these three methods are extremely effective for the majority of people with sleep problems.

1. Good — First example of how to relax.

2. Good — Another example of how to relax.

3. Unrelated — The use of soft music to study better is not related to the topic of how to relax and fall asleep.

Grammar for Writing

Using Pronouns in Place of Key Nouns

Because a paragraph is about one topic, writers often repeat key nouns from the topic sentence in their supporting sentences. However, too much repetition of these same nouns can sound awkward. You can avoid repeating key nouns by replacing them with **pronouns** after the nouns are first introduced.

Explanation	Examples
Pronouns take the place of a person, place, or thing: Carla ➔ She Washington ➔ It Giraffes ➔ They Replace nouns with pronouns to avoid repetition.	One of the best cities to visit on the east coast of the United States is **Washington, D.C.** **It** has some of the most interesting landmarks and tourist spots in the country. One of the people that I most admire is **my great-grandmother Carla**. **She** came to the United States from Italy in 1911 as a young woman on a large ship.
Remember to be consistent. If you use *they* at the beginning of a paragraph, do not switch to *it*. The underlined words are incorrect in the example.	**Giraffes** are among the most interesting of all the animals that live in Africa. **They** are easily recognized by **their** special features. **They** have long necks and long legs, but its neck is longer than its legs. It usually lives in very dry areas.

ACTIVITY 9 Identifying Key Nouns and Pronouns

Read the following sentences. Write the correct pronoun in each blank. Use *it, they,* or *we*. Then underline the key noun that the pronoun refers to.

1. Tennis rackets have changed tremendously in the last ten years. ___They___ used to be small and heavy, but that is no longer true.
2. Soccer is by far the most widely played sport in the world. ___It___ is played professionally on nearly every continent.
3. I will never forget my childhood friends Carlos and Juan and what ___they___ taught me.
4. Not only is text messaging fast, but ___it___ is also an interesting way to practice English.
5. A bad thing happened to my classmates and me at school yesterday. ___We___ were late coming to class, so the teacher gave us an extra homework assignment.
6. If you travel to Budapest, Hungary, you will fall in love with the Danube River. ___It___ separates the city into two parts—Buda and Pest.

Writer's Note

Staying on Track

As you write a paragraph, always look back at your topic sentence. Do not include any information that is unrelated to the topic sentence. It is very easy to lose track of the main idea if you do not refer to the topic sentence from time to time.

Concluding Sentences

The **concluding sentence** is the last sentence of the paragraph. It concludes, or wraps up, a paragraph. It lets the reader know that you have finished talking about the idea introduced by the topic sentence.

A concluding sentence often has one of these four important purposes:

1. It restates the main idea.
2. It offers a suggestion.
3. It gives an opinion.
4. It makes a prediction.

Restates the Main Idea

Perhaps the easiest concluding sentence to write is one that simply restates the main idea or summarizes the main points of the paragraph. The following transitional words and phrases are commonly used at the beginning of a concluding sentence:

as a result	overall	for this reason
certainly	because of this	surely
in conclusion	therefore	for these reasons
clearly	thus	in brief

Examples:

Paragraph 4, page 13

Topic Sentence	At some point, most parents have to decide whether or not to allow their children to have pets.
Concluding Sentence	In brief, although many children want a pet, parents are divided on this issue for a number of important reasons.

Explanation: The information in this concluding sentence is very similar to the topic sentence. In addition, the concluding sentence includes the phrase "a number of important reasons" because the paragraph includes several reasons for allowing or not allowing children to have pets.

Paragraph 5, page 15

Topic Sentence	eBook readers are excellent devices for students.
Concluding Sentence	It is clear that eBook readers have made students' lives much easier.

Explanation: This concluding sentence also restates the idea of the topic sentence. The examples in the paragraph show how eBook readers simplify students' lives, and the concluding sentence emphasizes this fact.

Offers a Suggestion, Gives an Opinion, or Makes a Prediction

A concluding statement can offer a suggestion, give an opinion, or make a prediction. Sometimes a concluding statement does a combination of these three options.

Examples:

Paragraph 28, page 83

Topic Sentence	Snorkeling can be one of the most amazing adventures you can ever take part in.
Concluding Sentence	If you want to have one of the most beautiful experiences that anyone can ever have, you should try snorkeling for a day.

Explanation: This topic sentence introduces snorkeling as an amazing adventure, and the concluding sentence offers a **suggestion** that the reader should try snorkeling.

Paragraph 27, page 82

Topic Sentence	Fortunately, my parents were very strict with me when I was a child.
Concluding Sentence	Looking back, I am not sorry that my parents were strict with me because I think it was the best way to bring up a child.

Explanation: This topic sentence explains that the writer's parents were very strict. In the concluding sentence, the writer gives his **opinion** that being a strict parent is the best way to raise a child.

Paragraph 24, page 79

Topic Sentence	The menu at Fresh Market, one of the newest restaurants in downtown Springfield, consists of only five main dishes that are simple but very delicious.
Concluding Sentence	If you eat a meal at Fresh Market, I am sure you will enjoy it tremendously.

Explanation: This topic sentence informs us that the menu at Fresh Market has only five dishes and they are very delicious. The concluding sentence makes a **prediction** that you will enjoy this place very much if you eat there.

ACTIVITY 10 Analyzing Concluding Sentences

Go back to the Example Paragraphs listed. Write the concluding sentence from these paragraphs and then check its purpose.

1. Example Paragraph 21 (page 73)

Topic: Washington, D.C.

Although Washington, D.C., does not have the large number of visitors that New York or Boston does, I think this city is one of the best destinations for tourists

What does the concluding statement do? restates the main idea

☑ restates the main idea ☐ offers a suggestion ☐ gives an opinion ☐ makes a prediction

2. Example Paragraph 17 (page 58)

Topic: Exercise

Therefore, if you want to improve your overall health, you should exercise three or four times each week to accomplish this goal.

What does the concluding statement do? Offers a suggestion.

☐ restates the main idea ☑ offers a suggestion ☐ gives an opinion ☐ makes a prediction

3. Example Paragraph 2 (page 7)

Topic: Egg Salad

If you follow all these steps, you will certainly enjoy your creation

What does the concluding statement do?

☐ restates the main idea ☐ offers a suggestion ☐ gives an opinion ☑ makes a prediction

4. Example Paragraph 3 (page 10)

Topic: My First Flight

____

____

What does the concluding statement do?

❑ restates the main idea ❑ offers a suggestion ❑ gives an opinion ❑ makes a prediction

ACTIVITY 11 Analyzing Paragraphs

Read each paragraph on pages 88–90 and:

1. Underline the topic sentence and write TS above it.
2. Circle any sentence that is not a good supporting sentence based on the controlling idea in the topic sentence.
3. Write a concluding sentence on the lines provided.

Example Paragraph 30

College Adjustments

When I first started going to college, I was surprised at all the studying that was required. I had to **adjust** my study habits because in high school I hardly ever studied, **yet** my grades were still fairly good. At the university, it seemed that all my professors thought their class was the most important class. Each professor gave me a **tremendous** amount of homework every night. As a result, my free time became very limited. Nights out with friends and time spent watching TV were **replaced** with reading assignments, group projects, learning activities, and research. My university classes kept me so busy that I could only go out on Saturday nights. This kind of schedule was a big change from high school, where I **used to** play sports, have fun, and go out **every other** night.

____

____

____

to adjust: to change a little

yet: but, however

tremendous: great; huge

to replace: to substitute one thing for another

used to + verb: to do an action many times in the past but no longer

every other: alternating

Example Paragraph 31

Different Names for the Same Kind of Storm

When bad weather, thunder, and strong winds mix, the result is a dangerous storm, but the name for that storm differs according to where the storm occurs. When a storm forms in the Atlantic or eastern Pacific Ocean, it is called a hurricane. This type of storm can be dangerous to people living in the United States, Mexico, Central America, or the Caribbean islands. When a large storm begins in the southern Pacific Ocean, this same type of storm is called a cyclone. Cyclones are less common **due to** the colder temperature of the water there. Finally, if this same storm begins in the western Pacific Ocean, it is referred to as a typhoon. Typhoons are usually stronger than hurricanes, and they **endanger** people living in areas such as Japan, Guam, or the Philippines.

due to: because of

to endanger: put in danger

Example Paragraph 32

Four Ways to Cook an Egg

There are four easy ways to prepare a delicious egg. Some people believe that brown eggs taste better than white eggs. The first and probably the easiest way is to boil an egg. Just drop the egg into a pot of water and boil it for five minutes. Another easy way is to **scramble** an egg. All you need is a fork to beat the egg **mixture** before you put it into the hot frying pan. A third way is to fry an egg "over easy." This **involves** breaking the egg into the pan without breaking the **yolk**. After a few moments, turn the egg over to cook it on the other side. Finally, **poaching** an egg involves cooking the egg in a small dish that is sitting in boiling water. Break the egg into a small metal cup that is sitting in a pan of very hot, **shallow** water. Poaching an egg takes only four to five minutes.

____

____

____

to scramble: to mix, blend

a mixture: the ingredients after they have been mixed together

to involve: to include or contain as a necessary part of something

a yolk: the yellow part of an egg

to poach: to cook in hot water or other liquid

shallow: not deep

Building Better Sentences: For further practice with the sentences and paragraphs in this part of the unit, go to Practice 8 on page 289 in Appendix 1.

Final Test

ACTIVITY 12 Word Associations

Circle the word or phrase that is most closely related to the word or phrase on the left. If necessary, use a dictionary to check the meaning of words you do not know.

	A	B
1. to eliminate* something	something appears	something disappears
2. hardly ever	not difficult	not usual
3. huge	small	large
4. to scramble	123456789	739245816
5. to get rid of	to add	to subtract
6. used to go	went	will go
7. to view	to hear	to see
8. dust	date	dirt
9. a fare	work	travel
10. property	you own it	you borrow it
11. in brief*	a few words	a lot of words
12. likewise*	in the same way	very intelligent
13. a beverage	you drink it	you eat it
14. every other	A1B2C3D4	AA1BB2CC3DD4
15. a spot	a place	a time

*Words that are part of the Academic Word List. See pages 275–276 for a complete list.

ACTIVITY 13 Using Collocations

Fill in each blank with the word on the left that most naturally completes the phrase on the right. If necessary, use a dictionary to check the meaning of words you do not know.

1. complain / collapse	________ about something
2. consist / tremendous	________ of
3. insect / reason	a poisonous ________
4. extremely / widely	the most ________ played sport
5. shallow / spot	our favorite ________
6. athletes / effects	negative ________
7. collapsed / logical	a ________ idea
8. do / make	________ chores
9. careers / vegetables	crispy ________
10. mixture / shallow	a ________ pond

Original Student Writing

ACTIVITY 14 Original Writing Practice

Choose one of the topic sentences that you wrote in Activity 5 on page 77. Write a paragraph about the topic.

- In your supporting sentences, answer the questions that you wrote in Activity 6. Remember to write only about ideas that are introduced in the controlling idea of your topic sentence.
- Use the guidelines on page 86 to write a good concluding sentence for your paragraph.
- Use at least two of the vocabulary words or phrases presented in Activity 12 and Activity 13. Underline these words and phrases in your paragraph.

If you need ideas for words and phrases, see the Useful Vocabulary for Better Writing on pages 277–281.

ACTIVITY 15 Peer Editing

Exchange papers from Activity 14 with a partner. Read your partner's paragraph. Then use Peer Editing Sheet 4 on NGL.Cengage.com/GW2 to help you comment on your partner's paragraph. Be sure to offer positive suggestions and comments that will help your partner improve his or her writing. Consider your partner's comments as you revise your own paragraph.

Additional Topics for Writing

Here are some ideas for paragraphs. When you write your paragraph, follow the guidelines in Activity 14.

PHOTO TOPIC: Look at the photo on pages 70–71. Write about a place to visit in your town or city. What is special about the place? What is the history? What should a visitor do or try?

TOPIC 2: Write about a person you admire. What special qualities does this person have? What does this person do?

TOPIC 3: Write about a great career for today's job market. What kind of job is it? What skills would someone need? What are the benefits of doing this kind of job?

TOPIC 4: Give some advice about doing something, such as buying a car or choosing a school. What should someone know? What steps should the person follow?

TOPIC 5: Write about your perfect travel destination. Where would it be? Why is this a good place for you to be? What would you do there?

Timed Writing

How quickly can you write in English? There are many times when you must write quickly, such as on a test. It is important to feel comfortable during those times. Timed-writing practice can make you feel better about writing quickly in English.

1. Take out a piece of paper.
2. Read the writing prompt.
3. Brainstorm ideas for five minutes.
4. Write a short paragraph (six to ten sentences).
5. You have 25 minutes to write your paragraph.

In your opinion, is it a good idea to require all students to wear a school uniform? Give two or three strong reasons to support your opinion. Be sure to include a strong concluding sentence.

Unit

5 Paragraph Review

Hikers ascend Carlisle's steep volcano with a clear view of Chuginadak's Mount Cleveland, Alaska.

OBJECTIVES To review paragraph skills introduced in Units 1–4
To review the use of articles in writing

Can you write about something interesting to do?

Review

In the past four units, you have learned about the paragraph. Let's take a moment to review what you have learned.

Features of a Paragraph

These are the four main features of a paragraph:

✓ A paragraph has a topic sentence with a controlling idea.

✓ All of the sentences in the paragraph relate to the main idea.

✓ The first line of a paragraph is indented.

✓ The concluding sentence brings the paragraph to a logical ending.

Grammar for Writing Review

You have practiced these elements of grammar and punctuation:

✓ subject-verb agreement

✓ verb tenses

✓ capitalization, comma usage, and end punctuation

✓ sentences, fragments, run-on sentences, and comma splices

✓ pronouns

In this unit, you will continue to practice this information through more activities and original writing.

Working with the Structure of a Paragraph

If you understand how the parts of a paragraph are arranged, you will be able to write better paragraphs. The activities in this section review the structure of a paragraph.

ACTIVITY 1 Writing Topic Sentences

Read each paragraph on pages 97–99 and write a topic sentence for each one. The topic sentence states the topic and the controlling idea. Remember to indent and add appropriate end punctuation.

Example Paragra

Applying to a College or University

You need to know that there is a college that can work for every student, whether it is a private college, a state school, a community college, or a public university. The first step in the application process is to **compile** a list of schools you want to apply to. Take the list and **narrow down** your selections to a shorter list of five to ten schools, and find out the dates that the applications are due. The next step is to **figure out** which academic records, such as transcripts and test scores, each of these schools requires. Request your records be sent to each of these institutions. You may also be required to **submit** letters of recommendation along with your application. The third step is to fill out the application for the schools on your list, most of which can be found on the schools' websites. You will also most **likely** have to write an essay for each application. Be sure to express yourself in the essays so the reviewers are able to get a feel for who you are as an individual. The last step in the application process is to visit the schools you think you have the best chance of attending. Take a tour of the campuses to see if you can imagine yourself at each school. If you follow these steps in a timely manner, you should get into a school that is right for you.

to compile: create a list of, collect

to narrow down: reduce

to figure out: calculate, determine

to submit: send

likely: probable

Example Paragraph 34

The Amazing Capilano Bridge

The Capilano Bridge in British Columbia, Canada, is one of the world's longest suspension footbridges. The bridge is 450 feet (137 m) long and rises 230 feet (70 m) above the Capilano River. The original wood and rope bridge was built in 1889 to help loggers cross the **steep** canyon.

steep: rising with a very sharp angle

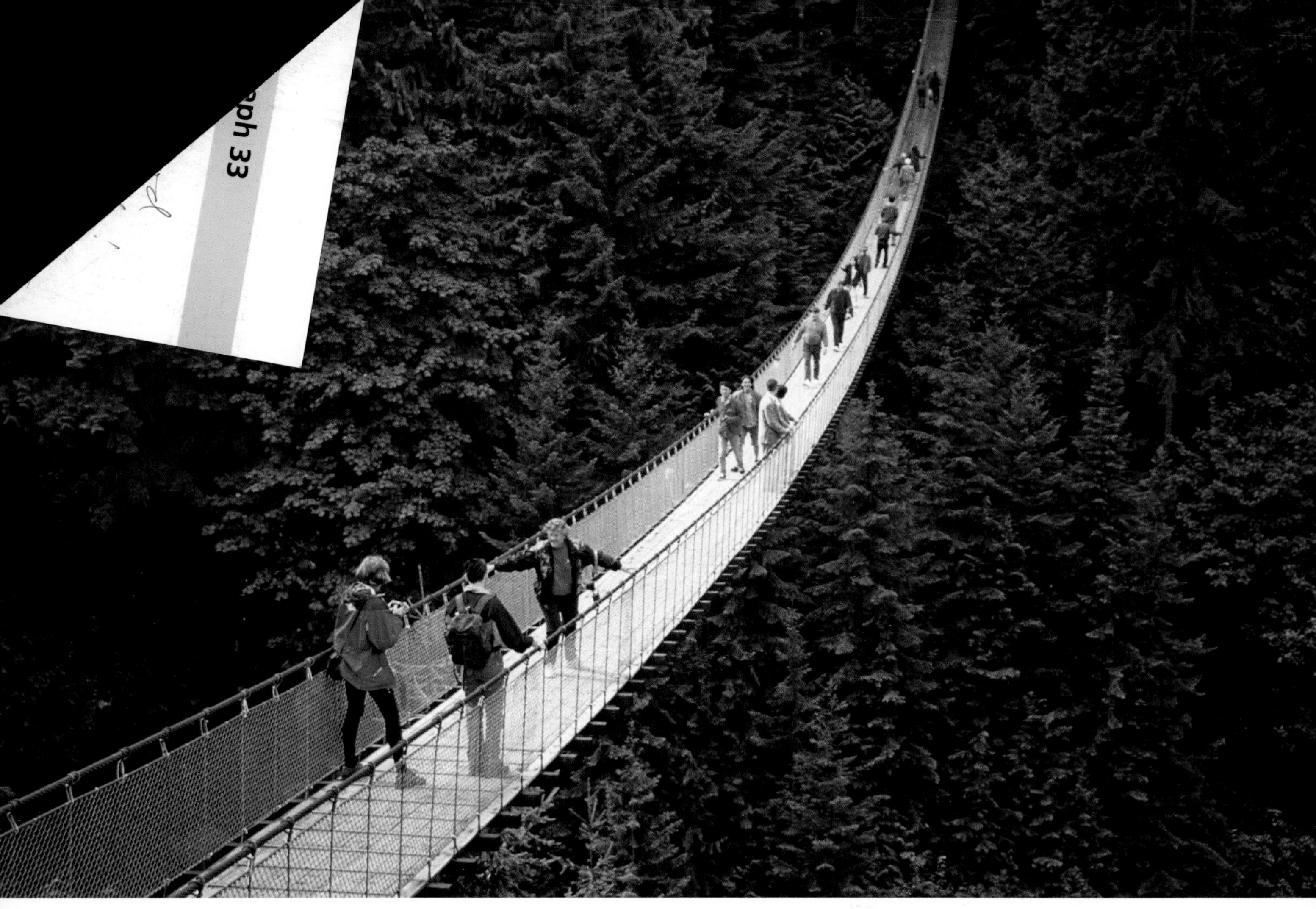

However, today only adventure-**seeking** tourists **attempt** to cross the narrow, swinging bridge. Unlike the loggers, their goal is not to take trees away from the canyon but simply to enjoy Canadian nature. This bridge is an **amazing** sight to see.

to seek: to look for; search for

to attempt: to try to do something

amazing: surprising, wonderful

Example Paragraph 35

My First Time Riding a Horse by Myself

I was excited, but my parents **warned** me about being careful. I woke up early and put on a pair of jeans and my boots, and I **grabbed** my helmet. Then I walked to the stable and greeted the horse. I groomed the horse

to warn: to tell someone about a possible problem

to grab: to take quickly

and prepared it to ride. When the horse was finally ready, I walked it outside. It was time for me to get on. I took a deep breath and stood to the left of the horse. Then I placed my left foot into the stirrup and swung over, putting my right foot into the other stirrup. I made sure to keep my heels down and my toes up. I sat up straight and held the **reins** loosely. On my signal, the horse began walking around the farm. The ride was not very smooth. I had ridden horses before, but today was my first day without my instructor, so it was hard not to feel nervous. At the end, I shouted "Whoa!" to stop the horse, and then I got off. This horseback riding experience was fun, and I **managed to** avoid any problems. I had proved for the first time that I could ride a horse all by myself.

the reins: the strings that a rider uses to control a horse's movements

to manage to + VERB: succeed in doing something

Writer's Note

Proofreading Your Work

Always proofread your work – check it for mistakes. Make sure that:

- ✓ you used correct punctuation and capitalization
- ✓ you indented the first line of the paragraph
- ✓ every sentence has a subject and a verb

It is a good idea to have someone else proofread your writing for you, too. Sometimes another reader can see mistakes that you might miss.

ACTIVITY 2 Correcting Errors in a Paragraph

The following paragraph contains ten errors in indentation, capitalization, and punctuation. Read the paragraph and correct the mistakes.

Example Paragraph 36

There is a lot to know about the sport of hockey. Hockey is popular in many countries, including Canada and the United states, the game is played on Ice, and the players wear skates to move around A hockey player can score a point if he hits a special disk called a Puck into the goal. However, this is not as easy as it seems because each goal is guarded by a special player called a Goalie The goalie's job is to keep the puck away from the goal The next time you see a hockey game on television, perhaps you will be able to follow the action better because you have this information.

ACTIVITY 3 Copying an Edited Paragraph

After you have made the corrections in Activity 2, write the paragraph on the following lines. Think of a title and write it on the line above the paragraph.

WWW.MINSKARENA.BY
Minsk2014
CCM
VAUGHN

ACTIVITY 4 Correcting Errors in a Paragraph

The following paragraph contains ten errors in indentation, capitalization, and punctuation. Read the paragraph and correct the mistakes.

Example Paragraph 37

Teh tarik is a popular **beverage** that is served in restaurants and markets in southeast asian countries such as malaysia, and singapore. Servers often perform an entertaining show as they carefully prepare it. Teh tarik is made with tea and milk, and its name translates to "pulled tea." To make teh tarik, add four tablespoons of powdered black tea to boiling water Allow the mixture, to **brew** for five minutes. Then pour the tea into a separate cup and add four tablespoons of condensed milk. **Stir** the mixture briefly. With your hands spread far apart, **pour** the mixture into an empty cup in your other hand. Then pour the mixture back into the original cup. Do this several times, taking care not to spill any As you do this, it appears that you are magically stretching or pulling the tea, and this explains the name of this delicious drink. when the mixture is thick and has white **foam** on top, pour it into a clean, clear glass and serve it. Drinking this wonderful tea is as enjoyable as watching someone prepare it.

a beverage: any kind of drink

to brew: cook over a low fire for some time

to stir: to mix the contents of a liquid

to pour: move a liquid from one container to another

the foam: liquid with a lot of tiny air bubbles in it

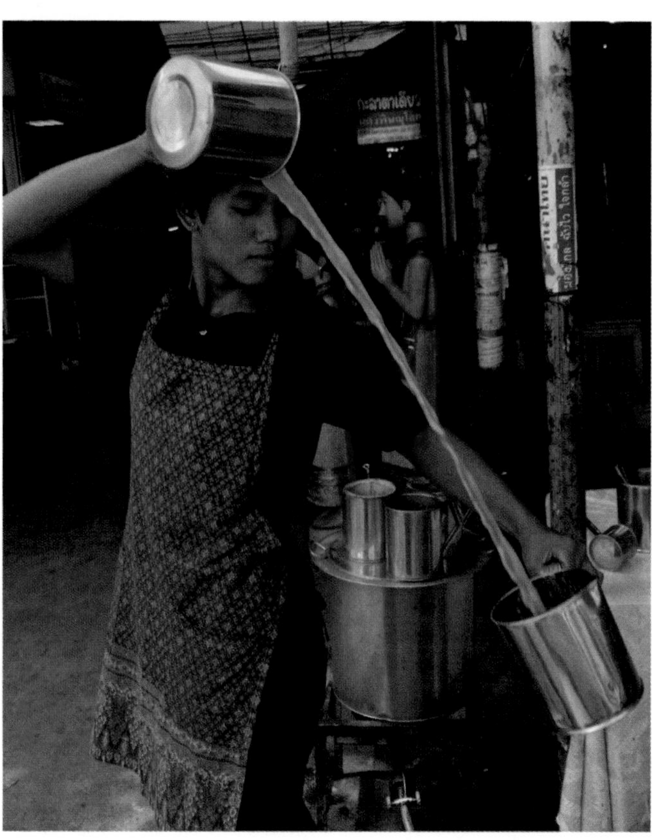

ACTIVITY 5 Copying an Edited Paragraph

After you have made the corrections in Activity 4, write the paragraph here. Think of a title and write it on the line above the paragraph.

____

____

____

____

____

____

____

____

____

____

____

____

____

____

____

____

ACTIVITY 6 Sequencing Information

These seven sentences make up a paragraph, but they are not in the best order. First, read the sentences and number them from 1 to 5 to indicate the order that they should go in. Then write the kind of sentence that each one is—*topic, supporting,* or *concluding*.

a. ________ During ancient Greek and Roman times, when a new ship was built, a small number of coins were left under the mast of the ship. The shipbuilders did this for a very special reason.

Kind of sentences: ____

b. ________ Today scientists find evidence of this long-standing tradition in a variety of locations, from the decayed remains of old Greek ships to the still active warship, the *USS Constitution*.

Kind of sentence: ____

c. ________ The art of shipbuilding has some odd traditions, and one of the most interesting of all has its roots in Greek and Roman history.

Kind of sentence: ____

d. ________ It was believed that sailors without money to cross this river would not be able to take their place in the afterlife.

Kind of sentence: ________________________________

e. ________ In case of a disaster at sea, the dead crew needed these coins to pay to get to the afterlife. According to legend, the crew members gave these coins to the ferry master Charon to take them across the river Styx to Hades, the land of the dead.

Kind of sentence: ________________________________

ACTIVITY 7 Copying a Paragraph

Create a paragraph by copying the sentences from Activity 6 in their new arrangement. On the top line, write a title for the paragraph.

Example Paragraph 38

____

____

____

____

____

____

____

____

Building Better Sentences: For further practice with the sentences and paragraphs in this part of the unit, go to Practice 9 on page 290 in Appendix 1.

Analyzing Paragraphs

It is important to be able to identify the topic, topic sentence, and writer's purpose in a paragraph. It is also important to make sure that all the supporting sentences relate to the topic sentence. Remember to refer to the controlling idea in the topic sentence to see that each supporting sentence relates to it.

ACTIVITY 8 Analyzing a Paragraph

Analyze the content and purpose of the paragraph in Activity 7. Read the paragraph again and answer the following questions.

1. What is the topic? ______________________________

2. What is the topic sentence? ______________________________

3. What is the writer's main purpose for writing this paragraph? ______________________________

4. Do you have any ideas for improving this paragraph? ______________________________

ACTIVITY 9 Identifying Poor Supporting Sentences

Read each paragraph on pages 106–107. Decide which sentence is NOT a good supporting sentence. Underline that sentence.

Example Paragraph 39

Japan's Incredible Snow Monkeys

Snow monkeys are interesting animals that live in Japan that have **adapted** in **various** ways to the cold winters in Japan. In the winter, they travel less and spend more time in hot **springs** to stay warm. Thousands of tourists come to see all of the monkeys gathered in the springs. Many snow monkeys sleep in trees to avoid being **buried** by the heavy snow that can fall during the night. In addition, their very thick **fur** can protect them from extremely cold temperatures. Snow monkeys also change their diet during the winter. During warmer months, they eat fruits, seeds, young leaves, and other foods. When these foods are not available in winter, snow monkeys dig for roots or eat fish in the hot springs. These **remarkable** changes allow snow monkeys to live farther north than any other monkeys in the world and make this animal one of the most interesting creatures on Earth.

to adapt: change

various: different, numerous

a spring: a small stream of water coming out of the earth

buried (to bury): covered

the fur: an animal's hair

remarkable: amazing, extraordinary

Example Paragraph 40

Bears of the Arctic

Polar bears have unique bodies that help them live in the **harsh** weather of the Arctic. They are large animals that weigh up to 1,800 pounds. The body fat from all this weight helps keep them warm. Their heavy white fur not only protects them from icy winds but also helps them **hide** in the large **piles** of snow. It snows a lot in the Arctic. The bears have five long sharp **claws** on each **paw**. They use these to walk safely on the ice and to catch their food. Polar bears are truly amazing **creatures**.

harsh: difficult, severe

to hide: to make invisible or difficult to see

a pile: a small hill (of books, papers, snow, etc.)

claws: fingernails or toenails of animals

a paw: a foot of an animal

a creature: an animal

ACTIVITY 10 Proofreading for Comma Errors

Below is a writing assignment that a student turned in to his teacher. Unfortunately, he did not proofread it, and it has nine comma mistakes. Correct the comma mistakes and rewrite the paragraph on the lines on page 109. (For help with comma errors, see page 60 or pages 258–259 in the *Brief Writer's Handbook with Activities.*)

Example Paragraph 41

A Great Place to Visit in California

When you go to California San Diego is a great **spot** to visit because of the many exciting things to see and do there. First you should visit the Gaslamp Quarter. In this historic area, you can easily find great food fun and culture. Next, you should visit SeaWorld to see the amazing animal shows. After you visit SeaWorld you should see a football or baseball game at Qualcomm Stadium. Finally you **ought to** see the animals at the world-famous San Diego Zoo. If you decide to go to the zoo do not forget to see the giant pandas. If you visit one two or all of these San Diego **sites**, it will certainly be a fun and interesting day!

a spot: a place, a location

ought to: should

a site: a place, a location

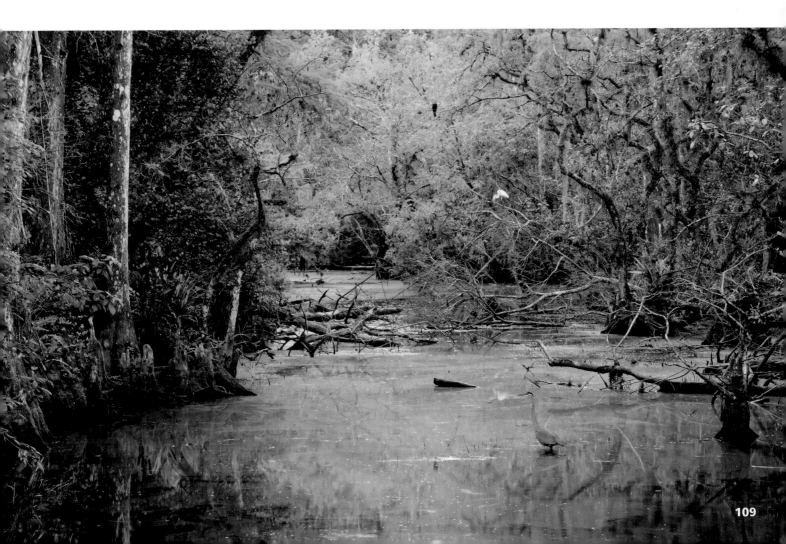

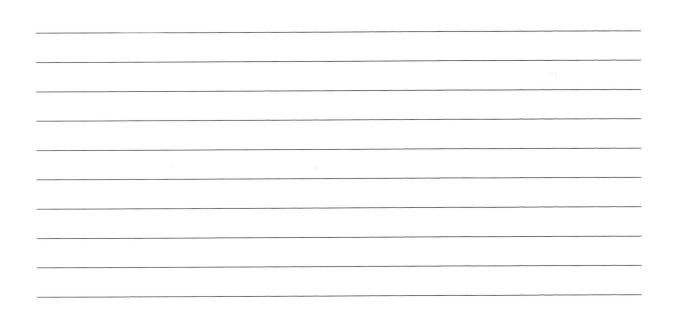

ACTIVITY 11 Guided Peer Editing

A classmate has asked you to proofread her paragraph. She wrote questions in the margin about four things that she is not sure about. Read her paragraph on page 110, answer her questions, and correct the mistakes on her draft. In addition, there are four other mistakes that she could not find. Find these mistakes, too, and correct them on this first draft.

Example Paragraph 42

The Florida Everglades

The Everglades region consists of a huge area of very wet land that can be found only in southern Florida. Water is **crucial** to this unique environment This area was formed by hundreds of years of flooding from lake Okeechobee after heavy rains. These floods always provided the land with new water to support its wide variety of plants and animals. Unfortunately people and nature are now taking too much water away from the Everglades. For example the Miami, Little and New rivers all **drain** water away from the Everglades. Even worse, man-made **dams** and canals prevents **annual** flooding, without this flooding or other source of fresh water, the everglades will **eventually** die. Only time will tell whether this unique area will be lost to future **generations** forever.

Should I capitalize "lake"?

Do I need a comma after "Unfortunately "?

Do I need to put commas in this list of river names?

Is the verb "prevents" okay with this subject?

crucial: very important, necessary

to drain: to pass or move out water or other liquid

a dam: a structure that holds back water, usually near a river

annual: happening every year

eventually: happening after a long time

a generation: all of the people born in one time period

Building Better Sentences: For further practice with the sentences and paragraphs in this part of the unit, go to Practice 10 on pages 290–291 in Appendix 1.

Grammar for Writing

Reviewing Articles

The **articles** *a, an,* and *the* are three small words, but they cause many problems for English language learners. Here are a few guidelines to help you as you write.

Explanation	Examples
Use *a* or *an* before a general singular count noun (SCN). You can answer the question *What?* Use *a* before a consonant sound. Use *an* before a vowel sound.	✗ My mother is teacher. (scn) ✓ My mother is **a** teacher. ✗ Many people believe *13* is unlucky number. (scn) ✓ Many people believe *13* is **an** unlucky number.
Use *the* when talking about something specific. You can answer the question *Which?*	✗ We're reading fifth unit. ✓ We're reading **the** fifth unit.
Use *the* for the second (or subsequent) time you talk about something.	✗ Dinner consisted of steak, potatoes, and carrots. Steak was great, but I did not like potatoes or carrots. ✓ Dinner consisted of steak, potatoes, and carrots. **The** steak was great, but I did not like **the** potatoes or **the** carrots.
Use *the* when you have a superlative form.	✗ Most interesting movie was *The Hunger Games* ✓ **The** most interesting movie was *The Hunger Games.*
Don't use an article when talking about something abstract.	✓ **Learning** is fun. ✓ People with a lot of **motivation** usually succeed.
Don't use *the* with general noncount nouns (NCN).	✗ All good chefs know that **the** salt (ncn) and **the** pepper (ncn) can make food taste better. ✓ All good chefs know that salt and pepper can make food taste better.
When you mean the thing in general, avoid using *the* + noun. It is more common to use a plural count noun (PCN) without *the.*	✗ **The** computers (scn) are found in many American homes. ✓ Computers (pcn) are found in many American homes.

Compare:

✓ My mother is **a** teacher. *(general = of any class at any school; answers What?)*

✓ My mother is **the** teacher. *(specific = of this particular class; answers Which?)*

✓ **A** teacher walked into the room *(general = some unnamed person)*

✓ **The** teacher walked into the room. *(specific = our teacher)*

✓ Teachers are friendly. *(general = teachers everywhere)*

✓ **The** teachers are friendly. *(specific = the teachers at a particular school)*

ACTIVITY 12 Correcting Articles

This paragraph has 14 errors with articles. Add four articles, delete eight articles, and change two articles where necessary. Begin with the title.

Example Paragraph 43

Best Cook in the World

Beyond any doubt, my grandmother Florence Folse is a best cook in world. Many people say that their mother or grandmother can cook a spaghetti, the fried fish, or the beans really well. However, if there were cooking **contest** right now, I am sure that my grandmother would win. My grandmother has cooked for six children, 15 grandchildren, 24 great-grandchildren, and many more **relatives**. She cooks from experience. Since my family lives in the southern Louisiana, my grandmother knows how to cook the seafood, the red beans and rice, and the gumbo, which is a kind of seafood soup. Sometimes she uses cookbook, but most of the time she cooks from memory. If you could eat the plate of her fried chicken or the meatballs, I am sure that you would agree with my conclusion about her cooking ability.

beyond any doubt: with 100 percent certainty

a contest: a competition

a relative: a family member

ACTIVITY 13 More Practice with Concluding Sentences

Choose any paragraph you have read in this book so far. Copy the concluding sentence here. Then write a new concluding sentence that works better for that paragraph. After you have completed these two steps, compare your sentence with a partner.

Paragraph Title or Topic: ____________________ Page Number: __________

Current Concluding Sentence: ____________________

____

____

Your Concluding Sentence: ____________________

____

____

Building Better Vocabulary

ACTIVITY 14 Word Associations

Circle the word or phrase that is most closely related to the word or phrase on the left. If necessary, use a dictionary to check the meaning of words you do not know.

	A	B
1. narrow	not covered	not wide
2. to bury	in the ground	in the ocean
3. to adapt*	change	destroy
4. a dam	across a highway	across a river
5. vital	you need it	you do not need it
6. decayed	very new	very old
7. to rush	fast	slow
8. a contest	a generation	a winner
9. fur	on an animal	on a bicycle
10. a flood	too much money	too much water
11. to stir	your lawn	your coffee
12. to hide something	you cannot buy it	you cannot see it

13. to pour	a liquid	a solid
14. to attempt	to do	to try to do

*Words that are part of the Academic Word List. See pages 275–276 for a complete list.

ACTIVITY 15 Using Collocations

Fill in each blank with the word on the left that most naturally completes the phrase on the right. If necessary, use a dictionary to check the meaning of words you do not know.

1. scream / steep	a ________________ canyon
2. for / to	ought ________________
3. in / on	________________ the corner of 41st and Vine Streets
4. pour / seek	to ________________ adventure
5. as / for	a large city such ________________ Paris
6. about / odd	an ________________ tradition
7. of / to	to find evidence ________________ a problem
8. glass / tree	a clean ________________
9. about / without	to know ________________ something
10. a car / a horse	to get off ________________

Original Student Writing

ACTIVITY 16 Original Writing Practice

Write a paragraph of five to ten sentences.

- Choose a general topic and brainstorm a specific idea. You may want to talk to friends or look on the Internet for ideas. Brainstorm what you could write about.
- Make sure that you have a topic sentence with a controlling idea.
- After you write your paragraph, check to see if all the supporting sentences are related to the controlling idea in the topic sentence.
- Your concluding sentence should restate the topic or make a prediction about it.
- Use at least two of the vocabulary words or phrases presented in Activity 14 and Activity 15. Underline these words and phrases in your paragraph.

If you need ideas for words and phrases, see the Useful Vocabulary for Better Writing on pages 277–281.

ACTIVITY 17 **Peer Editing**

Exchange papers from Activity 16 with a partner. Read your partner's paragraph. Then use Peer Editing Sheet 5 on NGL.Cengage.com/GW2 to help you comment on your partner's paragraph. Be sure to offer positive suggestions and comments that will help your partner improve his or her writing. Consider your partner's comments as you revise your own paragraph.

Additional Topics for Writing

Here are some ideas for paragraphs. Select one of these topics and write an original paragraph. Remember what you have learned in Units 1 through 5. If you need further help, review the writing process in the *Brief Writer's Handbook with Activities*, pages 244–250.

PHOTO TOPIC: Look at the photo on pages 94–95. Can you write about something interesting to do? What is it? What makes it interesting? What can one learn from it?

TOPIC 2: What do you think will be the highest-paying occupation 50 years from now? Give reasons to support your opinion.

TOPIC 3: What is the definition of a perfect parent? What are the characteristics of such a person?

TOPIC 4: Choose a mechanical device, such as a watch, a coffee maker, a smart phone, or an MP3 player. How does it work? Explain the process step by step.

TOPIC 5: The United Nations was formed in 1945 to promote world peace. However, some people think that the United Nations is not useful. Do you think the United Nations is doing a good job? Should the United Nations continue to exist? Why or why not?

Timed Writing

How quickly can you write in English? There are many times when you must write quickly, such as on a test. It is important to feel comfortable during those times. Timed-writing practice can make you feel better about writing quickly in English.

1. Take out a piece of paper.
2. Read the writing prompt.
3. Brainstorm ideas for five minutes.
4. Write a short paragraph (six to ten sentences).
5. You have 25 minutes to write.

What are the best snack foods? Be sure to include a topic sentence, one or two strong supporting reasons for each of your choices, and a solid concluding sentence.

Unit 6

Definition Paragraphs

World Cup soccer players display joy and disappointment after the first goal in Milan, Italy.

OBJECTIVES To learn how to write a definition paragraph
To practice using quotation marks
To study simple adjective clauses
To learn how to combine sentences for added variety

Can you define emotions?

What Is a Definition Paragraph?

A definition paragraph defines something. The word *definition* comes from the verb *to define,* which means "to state the meaning of a word or to describe the basic qualities of something." For example, a definition paragraph might define the word *gossip* and give examples. Another definition paragraph might define the term *true friendship* and give relevant examples.

In an essay, it is common to have one paragraph that defines a term or a concept before the writer gets to his or her main points. Thus, a definition paragraph can be an important part of a well-written essay.

A definition paragraph:

- explains what something is
- gives facts, details, and examples to make the writer's definition clear to the reader

ACTIVITY 1 Studying Example Definition Paragraphs

Read and study the three definition paragraphs.

Definition Paragraph 1

This paragraph is about a kind of food that is common in the state of Louisiana in the United States. Discuss the Preview Questions with your classmates. Then read the paragraph and answer the questions that follow.

Preview Questions

1. What is seafood? Give three examples.
2. What do you know about the people of Louisiana? Do you know anything about the Cajun people? You may need to consult a dictionary or the Internet.

Gumbo

The dictionary definition of *gumbo* does not make gumbo sound as delicious as it really is. The dictionary defines gumbo as a "thick soup made in south Louisiana." However, anyone who has tasted this delicious dish knows that this definition is too bland to describe gumbo. It is true that gumbo is a thick soup, but it is much more than that. Gumbo, one of the most popular of all **Cajun** dishes, is made with different kinds of seafood or meat mixed with vegetables, **such as** green peppers and onions. For example, seafood gumbo contains **shrimp** and **crab.** Other kinds of gumbo include chicken, sausage, or **turkey.** **Regardless of** the **ingredients** in gumbo, this regional dish is very delicious.

Cajun: related to people who moved from Acadia (in Canada) to Louisiana in 1755

such as: like, for example

shrimp: a kind of seafood

a crab: a kind of seafood

a turkey: a kind of bird that cannot fly long distances

regardless of: anyway, no matter

an ingredient: a food item in a dish

Post-Reading

1. What is the topic sentence of this paragraph?

____

____

2. Write one sentence in your own words that defines *gumbo.* Begin your sentence like this: "Gumbo is ..."

____

____

____

3. Notice that the writer quotes a dictionary definition of *gumbo.* Choose one of these food items and write a definition in your own words. Do not look in a dictionary.

sandwich	milk shake	dessert
hamburger	sundae	pie

4. Now look in a dictionary for the definition of the word that you chose in number 3. Is your original definition in number 3 similar to the dictionary definition? If not, how is it different?

____

____

Definition Paragraph 2

This paragraph defines something that most people think is wrong, but some people do it anyway. Discuss the Preview Questions with your classmates. Then read the paragraph and answer the questions that follow.

Preview Questions

1. What is gossip? Give an example.
2. Is gossip good or bad? Why or why not?

Example Paragraph 45

Gossip

According to *The Collins Cobuild Dictionary of American English*, *gossip* is "an informal conversation, often about other people's private affairs," but this definition makes gossip sound **harmless** when it is really not. At first, gossip might not seem so bad. One person tells a second person something about someone, and that second person tells a third, **and so on**. The information passes from person to person. However, gossip is much more than just information and rumors. As a rumor continues, it grows and changes. People do not know all the facts. They add information. As the gossip goes from one person to the next person, the **damage** continues, and the person who is the subject of the gossip cannot do anything to answer or protect himself or herself. Because the **potential** damage may **range** from hurt feelings to a lost career, gossip is much worse than simply an "informal conversation."

harmless: not causing harm; not dangerous

and so on: etc. (et cetera)

the damage: harm, negative effects, injury that reduces the value of something

potential: possible but not yet actual

to range: to extend (from X to Y)

Post-Reading

1. What is the topic sentence of "Gossip?"

____

____

____

2. What is the writer's opinion about gossip? Does the writer think it is wrong? How do you know?

____

____

3. Do all the supporting sentences relate to the topic? ❑ yes ❑ no

4. Like the writer of "Gumbo," this writer also quotes a dictionary definition. Read the following sentences. Which ones are easy to read and understand? Which ones are difficult? Rank them from 1 to 4, with 1 being the easiest to read and 4 being the most difficult.

_______ Paragraph 1: The dictionary defines *gumbo* as a "thick soup made in south Louisiana."

_______ Paragraph 1: The definition of *gumbo* is a "thick soup made in south Louisiana."

_______ Paragraph 2: According to *The Collins Cobuild Dictionary of American English*, *gossip* is "an informal conversation, often about other people's private affairs."

_______ Paragraph 2: *The Collins Cobuild Dictionary of American English* definition of *gossip* is "an informal conversation, often about other people's private affairs."

5. *Gossip* is difficult to define in your own words. Here are some other words that you may find difficult. Choose one, look it up in a dictionary, and write a definition sentence similar to the topic sentence in "Gossip." Then read your sentence to your classmates.

pride honesty friendship luck fate patience

____

____

____

____

Definition Paragraph 3

This paragraph talks about a popular snack food. Discuss the Preview Questions with your classmates. Then read the paragraph and answer the questions that follow.

1. Write a definition in your own words for *snack*. Compare your definition with your classmates' definitions.
2. Name three examples of popular snacks. Why do you think these three snacks are so popular?

Example Paragraph 46

Pretzels

The **pretzel**, which is a salted and **glazed** snack that is shaped like a **knot**, has an interesting history. The first pretzels were made in Italy in A.D. 610. These **twisted** pieces of bread were originally called *pretiola,* which means "little **reward**" in Latin. They were given as **treats** to local children. The pretzel rapidly became popular throughout Europe. Today the pretzel is an especially popular snack in Germany, Austria, and the United States.

a pretzel: a snack made of flour

glazed: having a thin, smooth, shiny coating

a knot: a part of a string that is tied in loops

twisted: turned in several directions

a reward: something given for a special service or accomplishment

a treat: something special

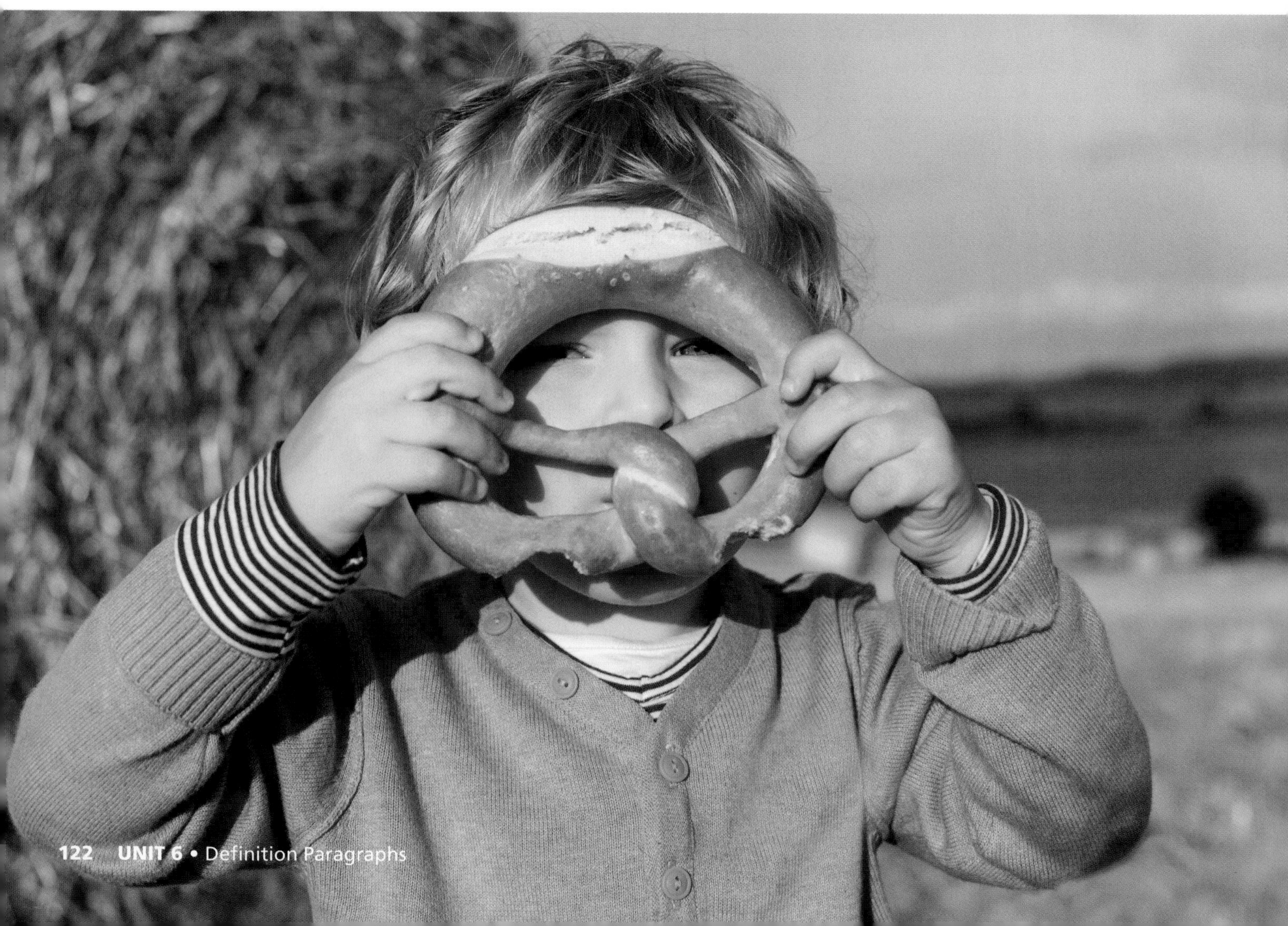

Post-Reading

1. Write the topic sentence of "Pretzels."

____

____

2. How is this sentence different from the topic sentences of "Gumbo" and "Gossip?"

____

____

____

3. When you write a definition paragraph, you can include a definition from the dictionary or use an original definition of your own. Here are four items that are difficult to define. Choose one and write your own definition.

giraffe battery flag cell phone

____

____

4. Compare your definition with your classmates' definitions. How are they the same? How are they different?

____

____

____

Building Better Sentences: For further practice with the sentences and paragraphs in this part of the unit, go to Practice 11 on pages 291–292 in Appendix 1.

Quotation Marks

When you write, the ideas and the words are usually your own. However, sometimes you might want to borrow someone else's words. When you use another person's words, you must let the reader know that these words are not yours. In English, you do this by putting the borrowed words in **quotation marks.**

For example, if you use a definition that is taken from another source, such as a dictionary, put the definition inside quotation marks.

Remember:

1. Commas, periods, and question marks are placed inside the quotation marks.

   The dictionary defines gumbo as a "thick soup made in south Louisiana."

   According to *The Collins Cobuild Dictionary of American English*, *gossip* is "an informal conversation, often about other people's private affairs," but this definition makes gossip sound harmless when it is really not.

   The professor asked, "Can anyone define this word?"

2. When quoting someone's exact words, be sure to begin the quote with a capital letter.

   The instructor said, "The university will close at 2:00 due to the weather," so the class ended early.

ACTIVITY 2 Adding Quotation Marks

The following sentences are from books and conversations. Add quotation marks where necessary. Sometimes you will have to add a comma and capitalize letters. (See pages 258–261 in the *Brief Writer's Handbook with Activities* for more information.) Items 1 and 6 have been done for you.

Words taken from a book or a similar source:

1. The dictionary defines *marriage* as "the union of a husband and a wife."

2. According to *The Collins Cobuild Dictionary of American English*, an errand is a short trip that you make in order to do a job, but my trip to the courthouse was certainly not a simple errand.

3. If we believe the dictionary definition of *drug* as a narcotic that is addictive, then surely we must say that cigarettes are used to deliver the drug nicotine.

4. The dictionary definition of *opulent,* extremely wealthy or rich, may sound good, but this word does not have a positive meaning for me.

5. Although the dictionary currently defines *a family* as parents and their children, previous definitions probably included additional family members.

Words that someone spoke:

6. Julie said, "~~we~~ W really hope the vocabulary exam is not too tough."

7. When all the students were seated, the teacher stood up and announced beginning tomorrow, no student may enter this room wearing a hat.

8. The taxi driver turned to me and asked where do you want to go?

9. The player stopped the tennis game, approached the net, and calmly asked her opponent are you sure that ball was really out?

10. I cannot wait here any longer the woman said as she walked out the door.

Writer's Note

Citing Ideas to Avoid Plagiarism

Plagiarism is using someone else's words as if they were your own words. Simply defined, plagiarism is stealing another person's words. It is a very serious academic offense, and the consequences can be severe. In many universities, for example, a student can be expelled for plagiarizing.

If you want to use another person's exact words in your paragraphs and essays, you must put those words in **quotation marks**. If you change most of the words but keep the person's idea, you do not need to use quotation marks because you are not quoting the person's exact words.

Whether you use a person's exact words or not, you must acknowledge that the idea is not yours, but rather, someone else's. You must **cite**, or show, the source of the idea. Citation methods vary according to academic professions and fields, so ask your instructor about the citation system that is required in your course work. You should list all the works, or sources, of the words and ideas you used in the final **bibliography**, or list of cited works at the end of your paper.

See the *Brief Writer's Handbook with Activities*, pages 273–274, for more information on using citations in order to avoid plagiarism.

Putting the Paragraph Together: Sequencing

Good writers order their sentences in a way that best conveys the intended meaning of their paragraph. For a definition paragraph, writers may start with a definition or clarification of a term, then continue to write about the topic using examples and descriptions.

ACTIVITY 3 Sequencing Sentences

These sentences about a learning method make up one paragraph. Read the sentences and number them from 1 to 7 to indicate the best order.

a. __5__ Similarly, an English speaker learning Malay might remember the word *pintu,* which means "door," by using the English words *pin* and *into.*

b. __4__ The learner might remember that he or she can use a hatchet eight times to cut down a tree.

c. __1__ The keyword method, which can help language learners remember new vocabulary, is gaining popularity among teachers and students.

d. __7__ Through these two simple examples, we can get an idea of how useful this method of remembering vocabulary can be.

e. __3__ For example, a Japanese learner of English might look at the English word *hatchet* and connect it to the Japanese word *hachi* ("eight") because they sound alike.

f. __2__ In this method, learners first form their own sound association between the second language word they are trying to learn and a word in their first language. In the second stage, learners form an image link between the target word and the first language word.

g. __6__ He or she can imagine putting a pin into the door to open it.

ACTIVITY 4 Copying a Sequenced Paragraph

Now copy the sentences from Activity 3 in paragraph form. The result will be a definition paragraph that describes a method for remembering vocabulary. Give the paragraph an original title.

Example Paragraph 47

____

____

____

____

____

____

____

____

____

____

____

____

____

ACTIVITY 5 Analyzing a Paragraph

The paragraph from the previous activity is a definition paragraph. You may want to read it again or refer to it as you complete the answers to these questions.

1. What is the general topic of Example Paragraph 47? ______________________________

   ____

2. What is the topic sentence? ______________________________

   ____

3. What is the writer's main purpose for writing this paragraph? ______________________________

   ____

4. How many examples are given in the supporting sentences? ____________________

Write them here. ____________________

____

____

____

5. If Example Paragraph 47 did not have any examples, how would that affect your understanding of the information?

____

____

____

6. Can you think of two more examples to further explain the keyword method?

____

____

____

Grammar for Writing

Using Adjective Clauses

Writers often use adjective clauses to define special terms. An **adjective clause** consists of a relative pronoun *(that, which,* or *who)* followed by a verb and sometimes an object. It describes the noun that comes before it.

Explanation	Examples
Use *that* or *which* for things. (*That* is more common.)	Gumbo is a thick soup (noun) [adjective clause: that (relative pronoun) contains (verb) seafood or meat (objects)].
Use *who* or *that* for people. (*Who* is preferred.)	A goalie is a player (noun) [adjective clause: who (relative pronoun) protects (verb) the team's goal (object)].

ACTIVITY 6 Recognizing Adjective Clauses

Read the next paragraph. Underline all the adjective clauses. Look for the relative pronouns *that* and *who*. Circle the noun that each clause modifies or describes.

Example Paragraph 48

Nature's Worst Storm

A hurricane is a dangerous storm that **features** high winds and heavy rains. In addition, areas along the coast may experience a major increase in the height of the water that can then flood whole towns. Hurricanes in the Atlantic Ocean occur mostly between April and November. However, the months that have the most hurricanes are August and September. Modern technology has now made it possible for people who live in a given area to know in advance if there is the possibility of a hurricane hitting their region. However, this was not always the case. For example, a hurricane that surprised the residents of Galveston, Texas, in 1900 resulted in thousands of deaths. Although we know much more about hurricanes now and can **keep track of** their movements, hurricanes continue to be one of the most dangerous weather events.

to feature: to have, to contain

to keep track (of): to have the most recent information about, follow the location of

ACTIVITY 7 Writing Sentences with Simple Adjective Clauses

Write a definition for each of the following terms. Include an adjective clause in your definition and underline the clause. Then share your sentences with a partner. Did your partner include an adjective clause in each definition?

1. turtle

   A turtle is a slow-moving, four-legged animal that goes inside its shell when there is danger.

2. co-pilot

   ____

   ____

3. skunk

   ____

   ____

4. passport

   ____

   ____

5. submarine

   ____

   ____

6. odd numbers

   ____

   ____

7. William Shakespeare

   ____

   ____

8. plumber

   ____

   ____

9. Serena Williams

____

____

10. the United Nations

____

____

Grammar for Writing

Creating Sentences with Variety

1. Combining Sentences with Connecting Words

One way to improve your writing is to write different kinds of sentences. Many beginning writers use only simple sentences that have a subject, a verb, and an object. For variety, combine two short sentences with a connecting word, such as *for, and, nor, but, or, yet,* and *so* ("FANBOYS" is an acronym to help remember them.).

Simple Sentence	Combined Sentence
I studied math for five hours last night. I failed the test.	I studied math for five hours last night, **but** I failed the test.
The scientist forgot to control the temperature. The experiment was not successful.	The scientist forgot to control the temperature, **so** the experiment was not successful.

2. Using Other Words and Phrases

In addition to connecting words, good writers use adjectives, adjective clauses, adverbs, adverb clauses, prepositional phrases, and other variations in their sentences. Study these examples. The variations are bold.

Part of Speech	Simple Sentence	Variation
Adjectives	The manager rejected the schedule.	The **current business** manager rejected **Mark's revised** schedule.
Adjective Clauses	The students liked the suggestion.	The students **who are in charge of planning the party** liked the suggestion **that Mark made**.
Adverbs	The woman picked up the chain saw.	**Next**, the woman **carefully** picked up the chain saw.
Adverb Clauses	He asked her to sit down.	**Before the doctor told the woman the news**, he asked her to sit down.
Prepositional Phrases	I did all the homework.	I did all the homework **on my computer in about three hours**.

ACTIVITY 8 Reading for Sentence Variety

Work with a partner. Read the next two examples and answer the questions that follow.

Example 1:

I was walking on Stern Street. I was in front of the bank. I heard a bang. It was loud. It was violent. The front door of the bank opened. This happened suddenly. A man left the bank. He did this hurriedly. He was tall. He was very thin. He had wavy hair. It was brown. He had a gun. It was silver. It was shiny. It was in his right hand.

Example 2:

I was walking in front of the bank on Stern Street. Suddenly I heard a loud, violent bang, and the front door of the bank opened. A tall, very thin man with wavy brown hair hurriedly left the bank. In his right hand, he had a shiny silver gun.

1. How many sentences are in Example 1? _____ Example 2? _____
2. What differences do you notice in the writing styles? Discuss your impression of each paragraph.

Did you notice that both examples include the same information? Example 1 has short, choppy sentences, which make reading uneven and difficult. In Example 2, the writer has combined phrases and ideas to make more complex sentences that sound better and read more smoothly.

ACTIVITY 9 Sentence Combining

Each paragraph is missing a sentence. Create the missing sentence from the sentences below the paragraph. You may want to circle the important information in these sentences. You do not have to use all the words, but you must keep all the ideas. Write one good supporting sentence. Write the new sentence on the blank lines in the paragraph.

Example Paragraph 49

Patience

Patience means the ability to continue doing something even if you do not see any results right away. We can see patience in a teacher who works with young children. She repeats things many times and does not get angry when a child **misbehaves**. We can see patience in a clerk who is **polite** to a customer even though the clerk has already been working with other customers for seven or eight hours. We can see patience in a person who is waiting for a bus at a street corner when it's beginning to drizzle. In our modern society people often **lack** simple patience. People nowadays expect immediate results all the time. To me, patience is one sign of a civilized society.

to misbehave: to act badly or incorrectly

polite: having good manners

to drizzle: to rain lightly

to lack: to not have

Ideas:

- We can see patience in a person.
- The person is waiting.
- The person is at a street corner.
- It is beginning to **drizzle.**

Seward's Folly

A folly is a foolish act that has a bad or an **absurd** result. The purchase of Alaska, which is now the largest oil-producing state in the United States, was once considered a foolish act. In fact, for this reason, Alaska was called "Seward's Folly." This name refers to Secretary of State William Seward, who convinced Congress in 1867 that buying Alaska from Russia was a good idea. At that time, many Americans thought that it was a waste of money to buy a cold, empty land for several million dollars. However, they were wrong. Alaska is not always cold nor is it a barren place. Most of all, it was not a waste of money.

Large amounts of gold and other minerals have been found in Alaska. Alaska is an important **source** of oil for the United States. In addition, thousands of people visit Alaska each year to see the natural beauty of the state. The purchase of Alaska in 1867 may have seemed like a bad decision at the time, but today we know that buying Alaska was certainly not a folly.

absurd: crazy

the source: the origin; where something comes from

Ideas:

- Alaska is not a cold place all the time.
- Alaska is not a barren place all the time.
- It was not a waste of money.

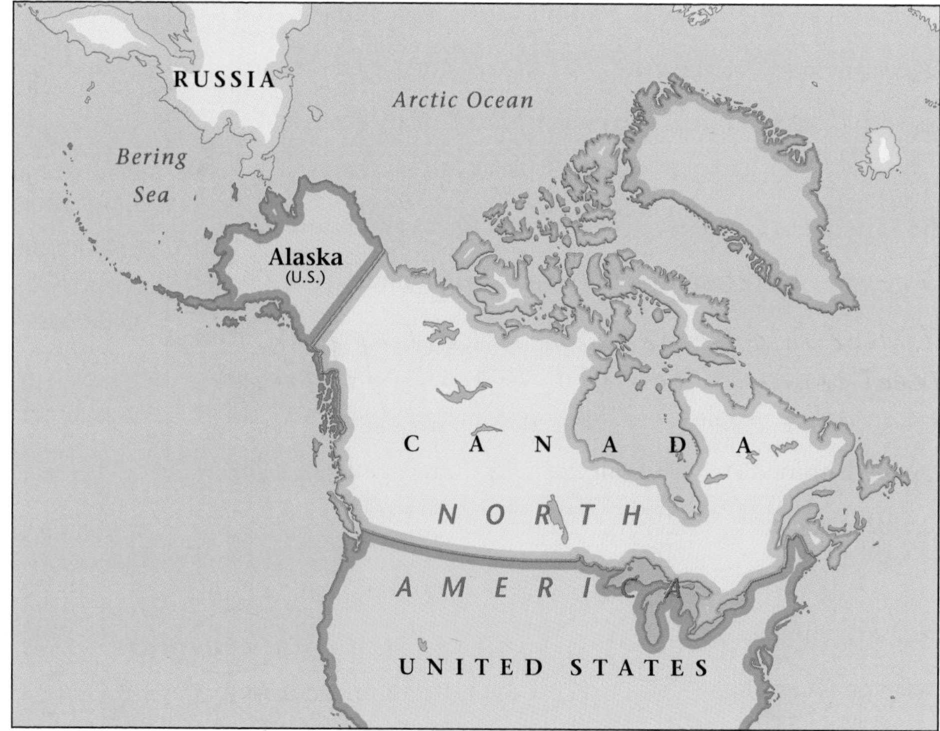

An Unusual Word Relationship

You might never guess that the word *sincere* is related to making pottery. *Sincere* comes from two Latin words: *sin* meaning "without" and *cero* meaning "wax." Thus, *sincere* means "without **wax**." In ancient times, pottery was made of clay. People used pottery for plates and bowls. It took a long time to make this pottery, and occasionally the pottery had cracks in it. Pottery with a crack in it was **worthless** and had to be destroyed. Some potters who did not want to make brand-new pottery would put wax on the crack. To the eye of the **careless** shopper, the pottery looked good. However, people soon realized which potters were good and which were not good. Thus, the most respected potters made pottery that was without wax, or "sincere," and that is how the word *sincere* began.

wax: a substance to make candles

worthless: having no value

careless: the opposite of *careful*

Ideas:

- People used pottery.
- This was in ancient times.
- The pottery was made of clay.
- The pottery was for plates.
- The pottery was for bowls.

Hint: Begin with a time phrase.

Building Better Sentences: For further practice with the sentences and paragraphs in this part of the unit, go to Practice 12 on page 292 in Appendix 1.

Building Better Vocabulary

ACTIVITY 10 Word Associations

Circle the word or phrase that is most closely related to the word or phrase on the left. If necessary, use a dictionary to check the meaning of words you do not know.

	A	B
1. to plagiarize	to follow	to steal
2. a surge	less	more
3. to reject*	to say *no*	to say *yes*
4. to quote*	to destroy something	to repeat something
5. bland	tasteless	tasty
6. gossip	ranges	rumors
7. to misbehave	a child	a paragraph
8. to measure	to find a number	to find a person
9. fate	pride	future
10. harmless	safe	dangerous
11. to purchase*	to buy	to reply
12. to strike	to hit	to tell
13. to lack money	poor	rich
14. to rank	$12 \times 8 = 96$	1st, 2nd, 3rd
15. seafood	sausage	shrimp

*Words that are part of the Academic Word List. See pages 275–276 for a complete list.

ACTIVITY 11 Using Collocations

Fill in each blank with the word on the left that most naturally completes the phrase on the right. If necessary, use a dictionary to check the meaning of words you do not know.

1. of / on regardless ________________

2. costly / quickly a ________________ action

3. area / first in a given ________________

4. from / in their ages range ________________ 18 to 24

5. give / keep to ________________ track of

6. guessed / seemed it may have ________________ difficult

7. lack / polite a very ________________ person

8. concrete / land barren ________________

9. damage / hair with wavy ________________

10. example / errand a relevant ________________

Original Student Writing: Definition Paragraph

ACTIVITY 12 Original Writing Practice

Write a definition paragraph. Follow these guidelines:

- Choose a topic. You may talk with friends or look on the Internet for ideas.
- Brainstorm some information about the topic. What do you want to include? What do your readers know about the topic? What do they want or need to know?
- Write a topic sentence with a controlling idea.
- Write a few supporting sentences that relate to the topic.
- End with a concluding sentence that restates the topic or makes a prediction about it.
- If you use words from another source, put quotation marks around them.

- Use at least two of the vocabulary words or phrases presented in Activity 10 and Activity 11. Underline these words and phrases in your paragraph.
- If you need help, study the example definition paragraphs in this unit. Be sure to refer to the seven steps in the writing process in the *Brief Writer's Handbook with Activities* on pages 244–250.

If you need ideas for words and phrases, see the Useful Vocabulary for Better Writing on pages 277–281.

ACTIVITY 13 Peer Editing

Exchange papers from Activity 12 with a partner. Read your partner's paragraph. Then use Peer Editing Sheet 6 on NGL.Cengage.com/GW2 to help you comment on your partner's paragraph. Be sure to offer positive suggestions and comments that will help your partner improve his or her writing. Consider your partner's comments as you revise your own paragraph.

Additional Topics for Writing

Here are some ideas for definition paragraphs. When you write your paragraph, follow the guidelines in Activity 12.

PHOTO TOPIC: Look at the photo on pages 116–117. Choose an emotion, such as love or jealousy. How does the dictionary define the emotion? Is it a good emotion or a bad emotion? Who usually feels this emotion and why? Give some examples.

TOPIC 2: Choose a scientific or medical term, such as *gravity, tsunami, molecule, appendix, AIDS,* or *pediatrics*. What is it? Why is it important?

TOPIC 3: Write a paragraph in which you define the word *pride*. What is it? What is its purpose? When should people feel pride? Are there any limitations on when people feel pride?

TOPIC 4: Write about a word or phrase that is borrowed from another language. Examples of borrowed words in English are *coup d'état, siesta,* and *sushi*. What is it? What language does the word or phrase come from? What does the word or phrase mean in that language? How long has the word or phrase been widely used in English?

TOPIC 5: What is freedom? Why do people want it? Should there be limitations on freedom? Can there be limitations? Explore the nature of freedom.

Timed Writing

How quickly can you write in English? There are many times when you must write quickly, such as on a test. It is important to feel comfortable during those times. Timed-writing practice can make you feel better about writing quickly in English.

1. Take out a piece of paper.
2. Read the writing prompt.
3. Brainstorm ideas for five minutes.
4. Write a short paragraph (six to ten sentences).
5. You have 25 minutes to write.

We sometimes hear or read that a certain person showed great courage in doing something. What does the word courage mean to you? Give examples to help your readers better understand your definition of courage.

Unit 7 Process Paragraphs

A Compact Muon Solenoid, a particle physics detector, looks for the Higgs boson particle.

OBJECTIVES To learn how to write a process paragraph
To use transition words and chronological order

Can you write the steps in a process for doing something?

What Is a Process Paragraph?

At times, you are required to describe how to do something or how something works. In a process paragraph, you divide a process into separate steps. You list or explain the steps in chronological order—the order of events as they happen over time. Special time words or phrases allow you to tell the reader the sequence of the steps. The process paragraph ends with a specific result—something that happens at the end of the process.

A process paragraph:

- explains a sequence or process
- presents facts and details in chronological order
- uses time words or phrases
- ends with a specified result

ACTIVITY 1 Studying Example Process Paragraphs

The three paragraphs that follow are about different topics, and each one is an example of a process paragraph. Discuss the Preview Questions with your classmates. Then read the example paragraphs and answer the questions that follow.

Process Paragraph 1

The topic of this paragraph is a popular Mexican dish. People have to be careful when they eat this food because it can be messy.

Preview Questions

1. Do you know any Mexican food dishes? Do you know the ingredients? If so, what are they?
2. Are any of these dishes messy when you eat them? If so, what makes them messy?
3. Name a food that you have eaten that was very messy. How did you eat it?

Example Paragraph 52

Eating a Messy Food

Because eating a delicious, juicy **taco** is not easy, it requires following specific directions. First, you must be sure that you are wearing clothes that you do not mind getting dirty. Eating a taco while you are wearing an expensive shirt or suit is not a smart idea. The next thing that you should do is decide if you want to eat the taco alone or in front of others. Eating a taco in front of someone you do not know well can be **embarrassing**. Finally, it is important to plan your attack! It is a good idea to pick up the taco gently and then carefully keep it in a **horizontal** position. As you raise the taco, slowly turn your head toward it and position your head at a 20-degree **angle**. The last step is to put the corner of the taco in your mouth and take a bite. By following these simple directions, eating a taco can be a less messy experience.

messy: not neat

a taco: a Mexican dish consisting of a tortilla wrapped around a mixture of meat, lettuce, tomato, cheese, and sauce

embarrassing: causing a self-conscious or uncomfortable feeling

horizontal: across, from side to side (opposite *of vertical*)

an angle: where two lines meet

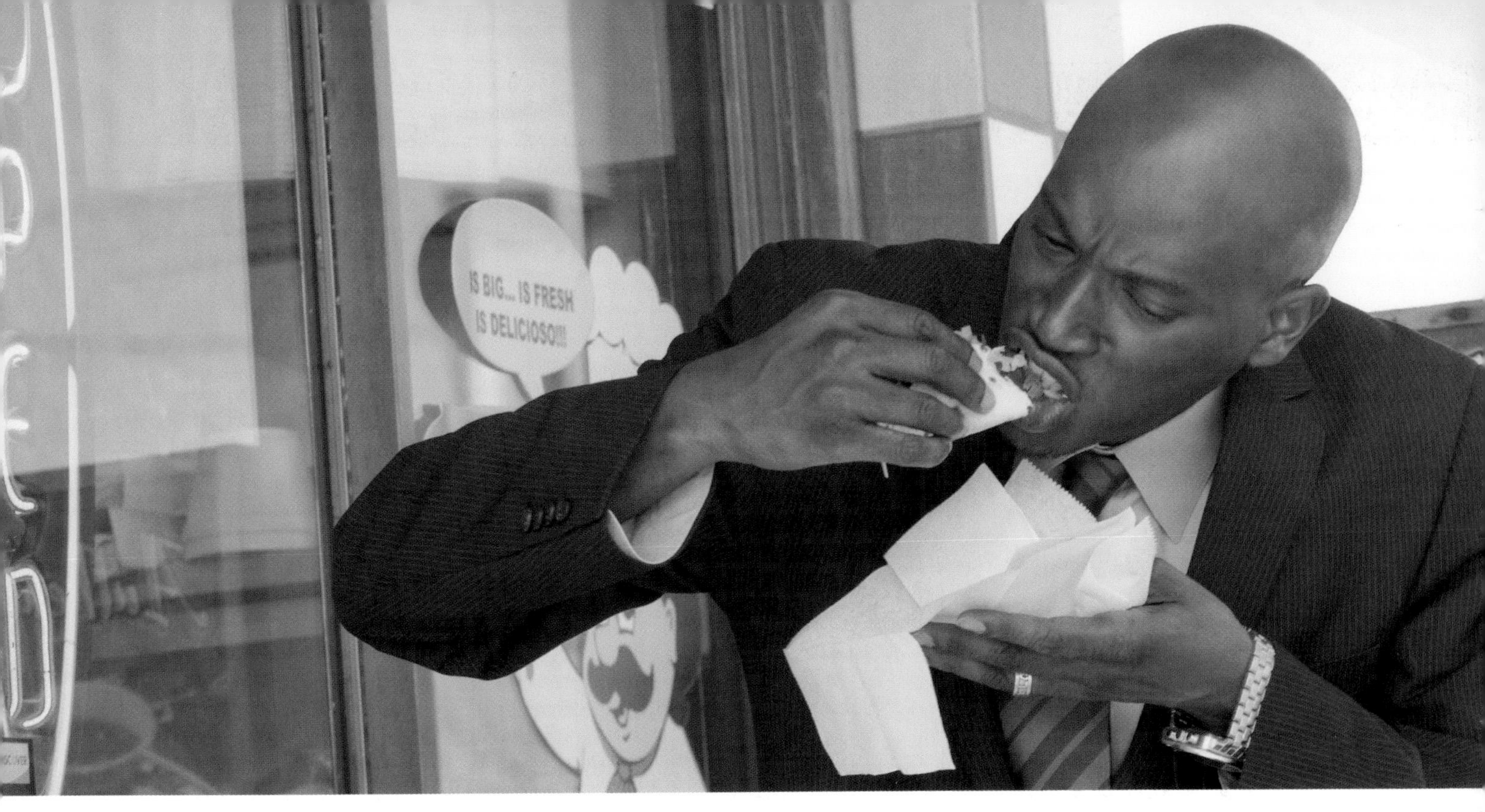

Post-Reading

1. What is the topic sentence of this paragraph?

____

____

2. This paragraph discusses three directions for eating tacos. What are they?

a. Do not wear expensive clothes because you might spill something on them.

____

b. ____

____

c. ____

____

3. Do you think that the writer's tone in this paragraph is serious, angry, or humorous?

______________ Why? ______________________________

____

4. Is there any information that you would like to add?

____

____

Process Paragraph 2

Preview Questions

1. What is your favorite strategy for increasing your English vocabulary?
2. Do you keep a vocabulary notebook or written record of new English vocabulary? Why do you do this? (OR Why don't you do this?)

Example Paragraph 53

Keeping a Vocabulary Notebook

Keeping a vocabulary notebook for learning new English words is not complicated if you follow a few easy steps. First, you must buy a notebook with at least 100 lined pages. You should select the color and size notebook that you prefer. Second, you have to write down any important words that you find when reading or listening. This step requires you to decide whether a word is important enough for you to

try to learn it by including it in your vocabulary list. Do not assume that you will remember the word later. The next step is a bit difficult because you need to decide what information about each word you will write down in your notebook. Some learners write only a translation of the word. Other people write an example phrase using the word. Some people write a synonym in English. Of course you can write all three pieces of information. When you are trying to decide what to write, you should remember that this notebook is yours, and you should include information that will help you remember the word. You can include information that matches your personality and your needs. Finally, the most important thing you can do to learn the words in your notebook is to practice these words several times. If the pages of your notebook are neat and inviting, you are more likely to review the words and their information multiple times. If you follow these important steps in keeping a good vocabulary notebook, you can improve your English greatly.

1. What is the topic sentence of the paragraph?

____

____

2. How many steps does the author give? ______________

3. Does the paragraph explain the difference between vocabulary you find in reading and the vocabulary you find in speaking? ______________ Why or why not?

____

4. What are the "three pieces of information" mentioned in the paragraph?

____

____

____

Process Paragraph 3

Preview Questions

1. Describe a magic trick that you saw someone do. Who was it? What did the person do? Do you know the secret of that trick?

2. Can you do a magic trick? If so, describe the trick.

Example Paragraph 54

Guessing Your Friend's Number

I am going to explain the steps to do a really interesting math trick that I learned yesterday that will amaze your friends. First, tell your friends that their answer will be three **no matter** what they do. Now tell your friends to think of a number **greater** than zero. Third, they should multiply their number by itself. Next, they should add their answer to their original number. Now they should divide their new total by their original number. In the sixth step, your friends should add 17 and then subtract their original answer from this last total. Finally, they should divide their answer by six. The final result is always three. Your friends will think you have the ability to know what they are thinking, but you know this is a simple math trick where the answer is always three.

no matter: it does not make any difference

greater: larger, bigger

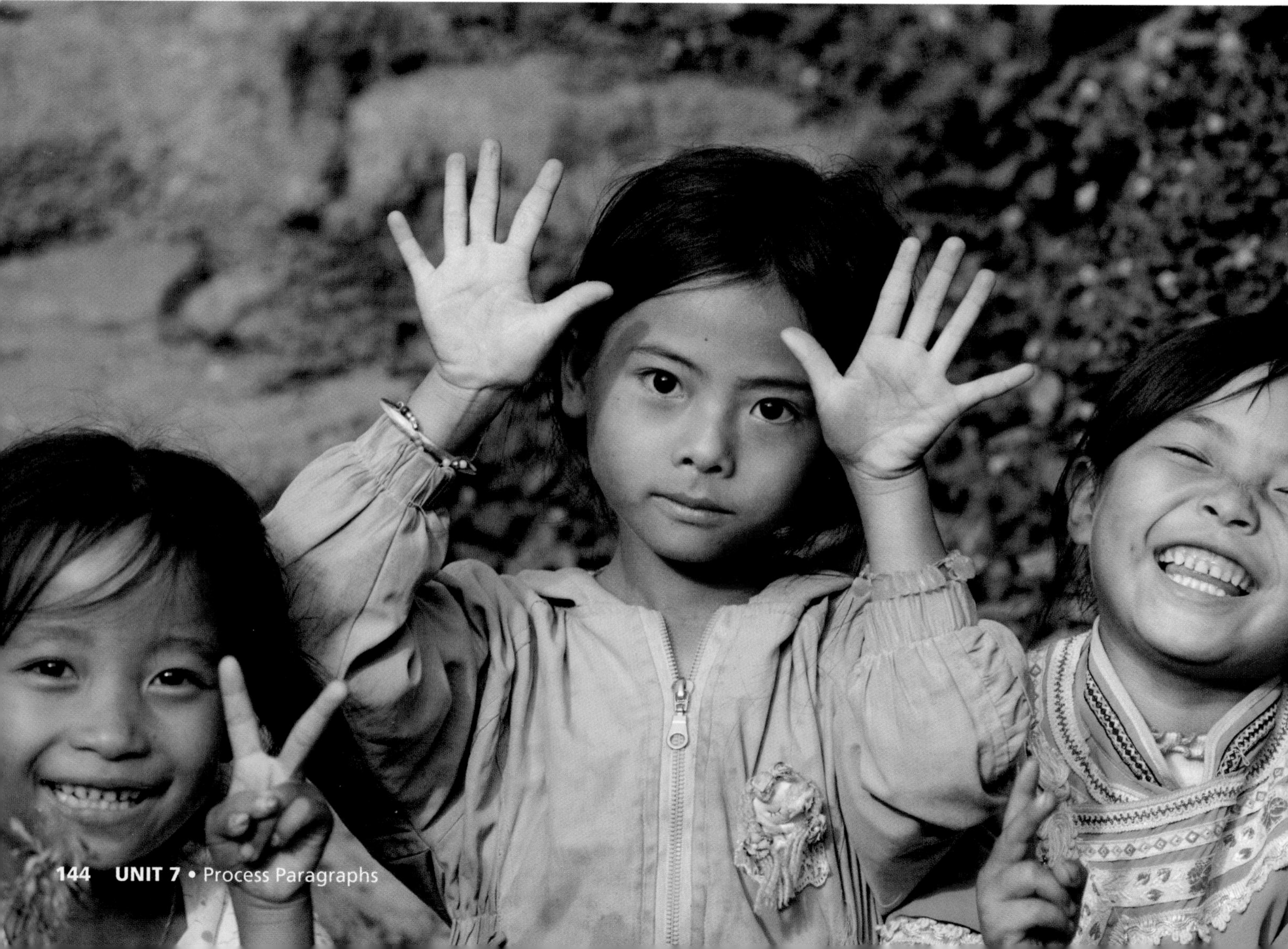

1. List the first three steps in this math trick.

____

____

____

2. This process has many small steps. Good writers do not always write one sentence for each small step. Instead, they combine some steps in longer sentences. Write a sentence from this paragraph that has more than one step in it.

____

____

3. For additional practice, choose two steps and combine them in one sentence. Compare your sentence with a classmate.

____

____

Building Better Sentences: For further practice with the sentences and paragraphs in this part of the unit, go to Practice 13 on page 293 in Appendix 1.

Grammar for Writing

Using Sequence Words and Chronological Order

The three paragraphs in Activity 1 each describe how to do or make something. The writers use chronological order to show the reader when the steps in the process occur.

To show time order in a process, writers use **time phrases, time clauses,** and **time words** such as *first, second, then, next, the next step, the last thing..., in addition, before,* and *after.* These items are also called **sequence words** or **transition words** because they mark the transition from one step to the next.

Sequence Words	Examples from Activity 1
First, (Second, Third, etc.)	**First,** you must buy a notebook with at least 100 pages.
The next thing / step Next,	**The next thing** that you should do is decide if you want to eat the taco alone or in front of others. **Next,** they should add their answer to their original number.
The last step Finally,	**The last step** is to put the corner of the taco in your mouth and take a bite. **Finally,** they should divide their answer by six.

Writer's Note

Using Notecards to Help You Organize

It is important that all the steps in your process paragraph be in the correct order. A simple way for you to organize the steps is to write each one on a small card. This organization method will allow you to arrange and rearrange the steps. It will also help point out any steps that may be missing.

ACTIVITY 2 Sequencing Sentences

The following sentences about tennis make up a paragraph. Number them from 1 to 8 to indicate the best order. Then underline all the words or phrases that show time order or sequence. (If you are not familiar with tennis, ask a person who plays tennis to explain how to serve or watch a video clip of a tennis player serving.)

________ **a.** Hit the ball into the small box on the opposite side of the net.

________ **b.** After you hit the ball, continue swinging your racket down and across the front of your body.

________ **c.** Just before the ball reaches its peak, begin to swing your racket forward as high as you can reach.

________ **d.** First, toss the ball with your left hand about three feet in the air. The best position for the ball is just to the right of your head.

________ **e.** At the same time, move your racket behind your shoulder with your right hand so that your elbow is pointed toward the sky.

________ **f.** After you have completed the serve, your racket should be near your left knee.

________ **g.** Many people think serving in tennis is difficult, but the following steps show that it is quite easy.

________ **h.** If you are left-handed, you should substitute the words *left* and *right* in the preceding directions.

ACTIVITY 3 Sequencing Information in Paragraph Form

Copy the sentences from Activity 2 in paragraph form. The result will be a process paragraph. Give the paragraph an original title.

Example Paragraph 55

____

____

____

____

____

____

____

____

____

____

____

____

____

____

ACTIVITY 4 Analyzing and Understanding a Paragraph

Read Example Paragraph 55 in Activity 3 again or refer to it as you complete the answers to these questions.

1. What is the general topic of the paragraph?

____

2. What is the topic sentence?

____

____

3. The main purpose of this paragraph is to explain how to serve a tennis ball. However, the author also expresses an opinion in the topic sentence. Read the topic sentence again. What is that opinion?

____

____

4. Look at this sentence from the paragraph: "The best position for the ball is just to the right of your head." Unlike the other sentences, this is not a step. What is the purpose of this sentence?

____

____

____

____

ACTIVITY 5 Using Commas and Sequence Expressions

Transitional words, phrases, and clauses can show chronological order. Most transitional words and clauses are followed by a comma. The following sentences make up a paragraph. Number them from 1 to 10 to indicate the best order. Then, add commas where necessary. Hint: Five sentences need commas.

_______ **a.** First put the water and the plants in the jar.

_______ **b.** One week later check the fish.

_______ **c.** The fact that the fish is still alive shows that oxygen was added. If you look carefully at a plant stem when it is in sunlight, you can see the tiny bubbles of oxygen escaping from the plant.

_______ **d.** When you do this be sure to leave about an inch of empty space.

_______ **e.** Keep the jar in a cool place indoors, but be sure that it receives some direct sunlight for a few hours each day.

_______ **f.** When you are sure that the water in the jar is at room temperature add the fish.

_______ **g.** Here is a simple science experiment that proves that plants produce oxygen.

_______ **h.** For this experiment, you will need a clean quart jar with a tight lid, some tape, a goldfish, some water, and a few green plants.

_______ **i.** Put the lid on as tightly as you can.

_______ **j.** After that wrap the lid with several layers of tape so that you are sure that no air can pass through it.

ACTIVITY 6 Writing a Paragraph with Sequence Expressions

The sentences in Activity 5 explain the steps of a simple science experiment. After you have added commas and arranged the sentences in the correct order, write the completed process paragraph on the lines below. Create a title for the paragraph.

Example Paragraph 56

____

____

____

____

____

____

____

____

____

____

____

____

____

____

____

Building Better Sentences: For further practice with the sentences and paragraphs in this part of the unit, go to Practice 14 on pages 293–294 in Appendix 1.

Building Better Vocabulary

ACTIVITY 7 Word Associations

Circle the word or phrase that is most closely related to the word or phrase on the left. If necessary, use a dictionary to check the meaning of words you do not know.

	A	B
1. the peak	the lowest point	the highest point
2. a phrase	right here	We are right here.
3. preceding*	before	after
4. a synonym	different	similar
5. to prove	to show	to try
6. horizontal	left ⇔ right	up ⇕ down
7. messy	not neat	not original
8. quite	silent	very
9. a jar	made of glass	made of paper
10. your knee	arm	leg
11. amaze	believe	surprise
12. to remind	to release	to remember
13. your shoulder	body	mind
14. a stem	an animal	a plant

*Words that are part of the Academic Word List. See pages 275–276 for a complete list.

ACTIVITY 8 Using Collocations

Fill in each blank with the word on the left that most naturally completes the phrase on the right. If necessary, use a dictionary to check the meaning of words you do not know.

1. get / put	to ______________ ready
2. make / take	______________ a bite
3. down / up	pick ______________
4. the Internet / a problem	to point out ______________
5. elbow / remind	my left ______________
6. from / than	greater ______________
7. for / of	he reminded me ______________ my father
8. comma / side	the opposite ______________
9. tape / tiny	______________ bubbles
10. from / than	greater ______________ zero
11. lid / plant	a tight ______________
12. direct / empty	an inch of ______________ space

Original Student Writing: Process Paragraph

ACTIVITY 9 Original Writing Practice

Write a process paragraph. Follow these guidelines:

- Choose a topic about something you know how to do or you know how it is done, or look at the opening photograph for an idea.
- Write some notes about the steps in the process.
- Write a topic sentence with one or more controlling ideas.

- Write supporting sentences that give the steps in chronological order. Use transition words to show that the steps are in the correct order.
- Use at least two of the vocabulary words or phrases presented in Activity 7 and Activity 8. Underline these words and phrases in your paragraph.
- If you need help, study the example process paragraphs in this unit. Be sure to refer to the seven steps in the writing process in the *Brief Writer's Handbook with Activities*, pages 244–250.

If you need ideas for words and phrases, see the Useful Vocabulary for Better Writing on pages 277–281.

ACTIVITY 10 Peer Editing

Exchange papers from Activity 9 with a partner. Read your partner's paragraph. Then use Peer Editing Sheet 7 on NGL.Cengage.com/GW2 to help you comment on your partner's paragraph. Be sure to offer positive suggestions and comments that will help your partner improve his or her writing. Consider your partner's comments as you revise your own paragraph.

Additional Topics for Writing

Here are some ideas for process paragraphs. When you write your paragraph, follow the guidelines in Activity 9.

PHOTO TOPIC: Write about a process or how something happens, for example a scientific experiment or a weather phenomenon, such as lightning, fog, a tornado, or a hurricane.

TOPIC 2: Write about the steps in writing a good paragraph. How do you start? What information do you include?

TOPIC 3: Write about the steps a successful job applicant should follow. Where do you start? What resources do you use?

TOPIC 4: Write about what you need to do to get a driver's license.

TOPIC 5: Describe how to use the Internet to find the very best price for something.

Timed Writing

How quickly can you write in English? There are many times when you must write quickly, such as on a test. It is important to feel comfortable during those times. Timed-writing practice can make you feel better about writing quickly in English.

1. Take out a piece of paper.
2. Read the writing prompt.
3. Brainstorm ideas for five minutes.
4. Write a short paragraph (six to ten sentences).
5. You have 25 minutes to write.

From time to time, a bank or other business sends a bill or statement that has a mistake. (For example, a credit card bill may have charged you twice for a certain item.) What are the steps in correcting an error on a bill?

Or

What should you do if the server at a restaurant has given you your bill with an error on it? How can you rectify this situation?

Unit 8

Descriptive Paragraphs

The illuminated Jefferson Memorial is located is Washington, D.C.

OBJECTIVES To learn how to write a descriptive paragraph
To practice describing with the five senses
To learn about adjectives; positive and negative adjectives; prepositions of location

Can you describe an important monument you know well?

What Is a Descriptive Paragraph?

A descriptive paragraph describes how something or someone looks or feels. It gives an impression of something. If, for example, you only wanted to write specific information about a certain river, you could write a paragraph filled with facts about the river. However, if you wanted to tell about the feelings you had when you sailed on a boat on the same river, you would write a descriptive paragraph.

A descriptive paragraph:

- describes
- gives impressions, not definitions
- "shows" the reader
- creates a sensory* image in the reader's mind

*related to the five senses: hearing, taste, touch, sight, and smell

ACTIVITY 1 Studying a Descriptive Paragraph

Discuss the Preview Questions with your classmates. Then read the example paragraph and answer the questions that follow.

Preview Questions

1. What are the top five adjectives that come to mind when you try to describe a very busy place?
2. How are the busiest street and river you have ever seen in person similar?

The Sights and Sounds of the Chao Phraya River

On our trip to Bangkok last year, my friends and I took a boat trip on the Chao Phraya River, which is the **principal** river of Thailand. This busy river is **crowded** with river buses, water taxis, fishing boats, and tourist boats. Every day local people use these boats because they are faster than the thousands of cars that overfill Bangkok's busy streets. Our river boat was so crowded that we could hardly move, yet we seemed to fly down the river, enjoying the cool breeze. The scenery along the shore surprised me. My mind had a hard time accepting the sight of **massive**, brand-new **skyscrapers** and tall modern hotels so near the beautiful golden palaces and temples that are more than 200 years old. While the city of Bangkok is loud from the noise of so many cars, the river is actually peaceful **in spite of** all the boat activity. I will never forget the beautiful red sun setting as we arrived at our final **destination**. Because of all the things I experienced that day on our trip, I highly recommend that you take a boat trip along the Chao Phraya River.

principal: main, most important

crowded: with many people

massive: huge

a skyscraper: very tall building that seems to touch the sky

in spite of: although; regardless of

the destination: the place you are traveling to

Post-Reading

1. What words did the writer use to describe the river?

principal, busy, crowded, peaceful,

2. How did the author feel during the ride?

The author was surprised by the surrounding skyscrapers and tall modern hotels. He also felt at ease because there wasn't the noise of the cars.

3. What other information would you like to know about this trip?

How much did it cost? How long was the ride?

Describing with the Five Senses

Good writers use words that appeal to some or all of the five senses—sight, taste, touch, hearing, and smell—to help describe a topic. Here is a list of the senses and examples of what they can describe. Add examples of your own.

Sense	Example 1	Example 2
sight	a sunset	a tree
taste	a chocolate cake	a steamed BBQ bun
touch	silk	a book
hearing	a baby's cry	a firetruck
smell	a perfume	Coffee

ACTIVITY 2 Using Adjectives to Describe Sensory Information

In the left column, write your five examples from your list above. In the right column, write three adjectives that describe each object. Try to use different senses.

	Example	Description
	sunset	purple, streaked, majestic
1.	a tree	oak, tall, full of leaves
2.	a steamed BBQ bun	hot, sweet, filling
3.	a book	Hard cover, fun, informative
4.	a firetruck	alarm, red, loud
5.	Coffee	hot, aromatic, bitter

ACTIVITY 3 Writing Sentences Using Sensory Adjectives

Use the five examples from Activity 2 to write five descriptive sentences. Use each example item as the topic of one of the sentences and include one or more of the adjectives you wrote. Share your sentences with a classmate.

1. The majestic sunset warmed the sky with orange and purple streaks.

   The oak tree

2.

3. ______________________________

____

4. ______________________________

____

5. ______________________________

____

ACTIVITY 4 Studying Example Descriptive Paragraphs

Discuss the Preview Questions with your classmates. Then read the example paragraphs and answer the questions that follow.

Descriptive Paragraph 1

This first paragraph describes the sights, smells, and sounds of a subway station.

Preview Questions

1. What is a subway? Where do you usually find a subway?
2. What kinds of people use the subway?
3. Have you ever been on a subway? How did you feel when you rode on it? Can you recall what you saw, smelled, and heard?

Example Paragraph 58

Underground Events

The subway is an attack on your senses. You walk down the steep, **smelly** staircase onto the subway **platform**. On the far right wall, a broken clock shows that the time is four-thirty. You wonder how long it has been broken. A mother and her crying child are standing to your left. She is trying to clean dried chocolate **syrup** off the child's messy face. **Farther** to the left, two old men are **arguing** about the most recent tax increase. You hear a little noise and see some paper trash roll by like a soccer ball. The most interesting thing you see while you are waiting for your subway train is a poster. It reads, "Come to Jamaica." Deep blue skies, a lone palm tree, and **sapphire** waters call you to this exotic place, which is so far from where you actually are.

smelly: smelling bad or unpleasant

a platform: a raised area

a syrup: a thick liquid

farther: comparative form of the word *far*

to argue: to fight verbally

sapphire: dark blue color like the color of a sapphire gemstone

Post-Reading

1. From the information in this paragraph, how do you think the writer feels about the subway?

2. Which of the five senses does the writer use to describe this place? Give examples from the paragraph to support your answer.

3. What verb tense is used in this paragraph? Why do you think the writer uses that tense?

Descriptive Paragraph 2

The paragraph on the next page describes a memory about a dangerous storm.

Preview Questions

1. What are some dangerous kinds of weather?
2. Have you ever experienced these kinds of weather? How did you feel?
3. When you think of these kinds of weather, what sensory adjectives come to mind?

Danger from the Sky

The long, **slender tornado** began to **descend** from the **spinning** clouds and started its horrible destruction. When the deadly storm finally touched the ground, many things were already flying in the air. The tornado **ripped** the roof from an old house and threw the contents of the home across the neighborhood. The tornado used its power to grab huge trees and toss cars around as if they were toys. Power lines and traffic lights were also victims of its deadly power. All the while, the tornado's extreme winds **roared** like a wild animal. It was hard to believe that something that looked so **delicate** could cause so much destruction.

slender: thin, narrow (positive adjective)

a tornado: a rotating column of air that moves at very high speeds

to descend: to move downwards

spinning: moving in a circle

to rip: to tear violently and quickly

to roar: to make a loud and deep sound

delicate: fragile

Post-Reading

1. What does this paragraph describe?

   The destruction caused by a tornado.

2. What verb tense does the writer use in this paragraph? Simple past (and Past Progressive)

   Choose five verbs and change them to the simple present tense.

   begins, starts, touches, are hurled, rips, throws, uses, are, are, roar, is, looks, can

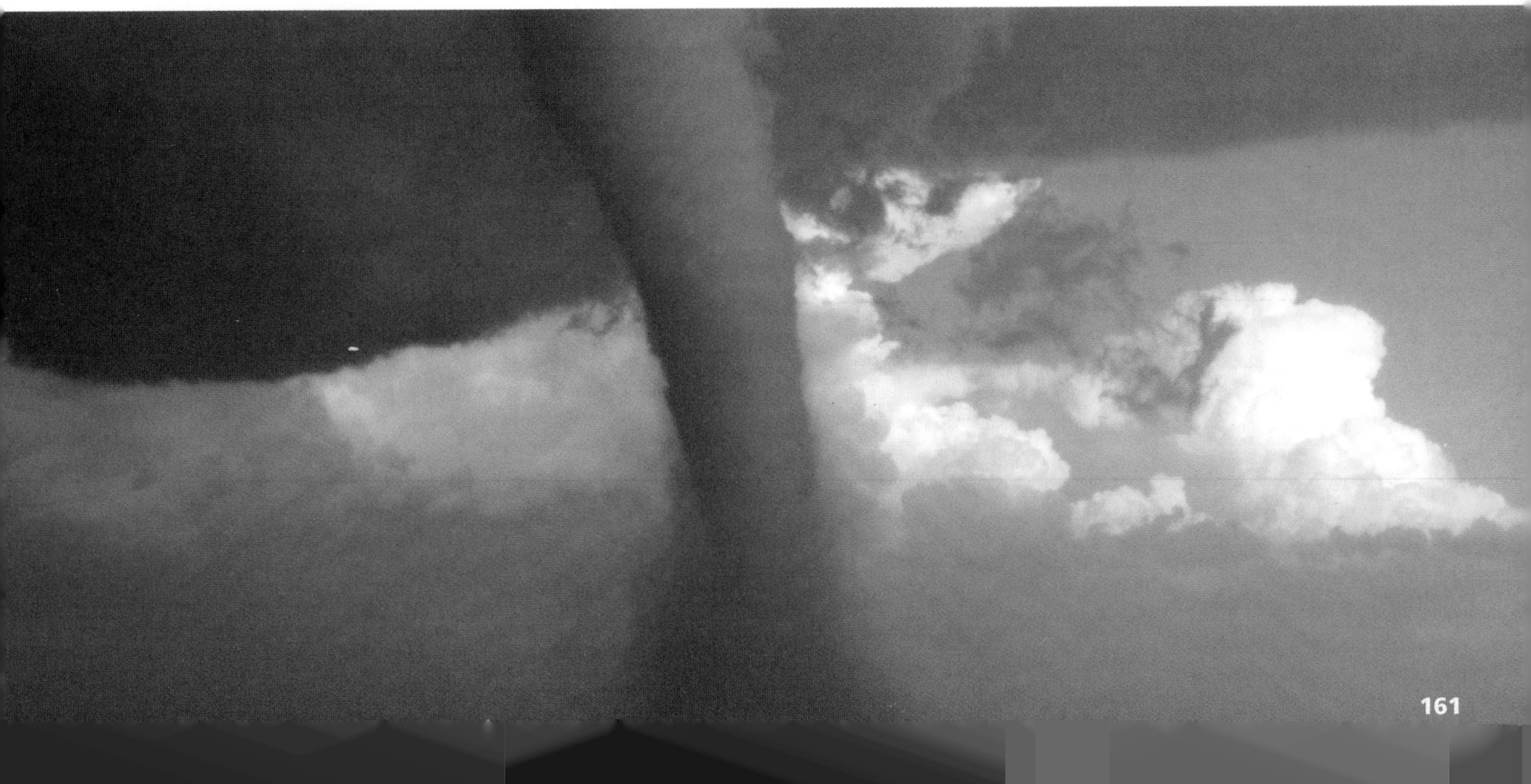

3. Which of the five senses does the writer use to describe this kind of weather? Give examples to support your answer.

Sight: long, slender tornado descends; swirling clouds; funnel, debris, huge trees, cars flying through the air, ripped the roof from an old house, looked so delicate

Hearing: Winds roared like a wild beast.

4. A good descriptive paragraph uses adjectives that help the reader feel what it is like to be in the situation. List any five adjectives in "Danger from the Sky." Then write the feelings they describe.

Adjective	Feelings
a. horrible	horrifying, scary
b. deadly	hopeless, horrifying, doomed
c. huge	very big
d. extreme	Very, very big
e. delicate	Very fragile

long, slender, swirling, horrible, deadly, old, huge, ferocious, wild, delicate

Descriptive Paragraph 3

The next paragraph describes what the writer's mother did while she worked in her garden. Notice how often the writer appeals to the readers' senses of sight and touch.

Preview Questions

1. What flowers can you name?

2. What is a rose? What does the rose symbolize to you?

3. When you think of a garden, especially a flower garden, what sensory adjectives immediately come to mind?

Example Paragraph 60

My Mother's Special Garden

My father **constantly teased** my mother about the amount of time she spent in her beautiful rose garden. He told her that she treated the garden as if it were a human being, perhaps even her best friend. However, Mom **ignored** his teasing and got up early every morning to take care of her special plants. She would walk among the thick green bushes that were covered with huge flowers of every color. While she was walking, she would **remove** any **weeds** that **threatened** her delicate beauties. She also **trimmed** the old flowers to make room

constantly: always, without stopping

to tease: to make fun of someone or something in a playful or joking manner

to ignore: to not pay attention to someone or something

to remove: to take out quickly

a weed: a useless, unwanted plant

to threaten: to put in danger, promise to harm

to trim: to cut to make something look neat

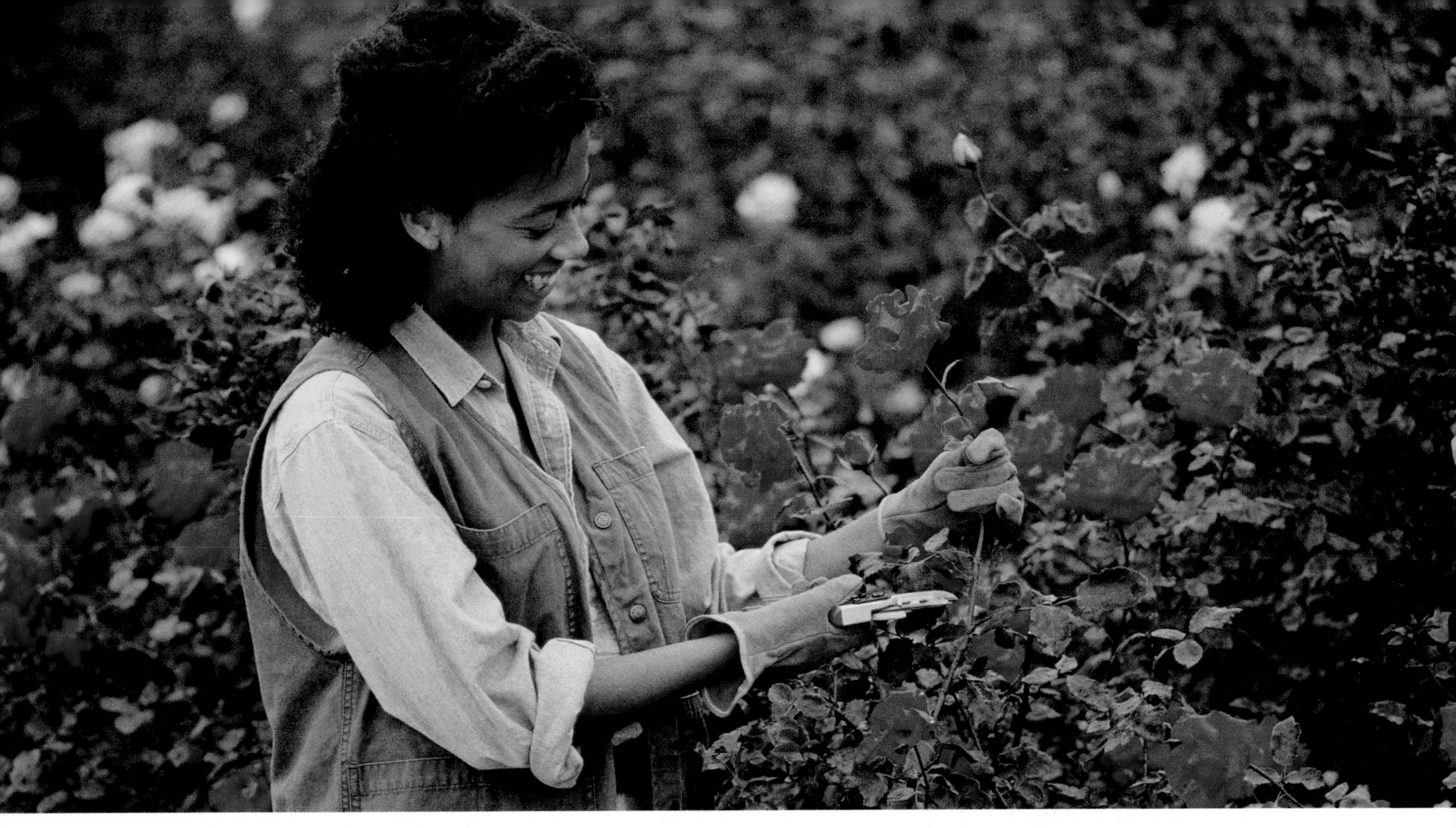

for their bright replacements. Any unwanted **pests** were quickly killed. When she was finished, she always returned from the garden with a wonderful smile and an armful of **fragrant** flowers for us all to enjoy.

a pest: an unwanted insect

fragrant: pleasant smelling

Post-Reading

1. What does this paragraph describe?

   This paragraph describes how the writer's mother cared for her rose garden.

2. Can any sentences be deleted without changing the paragraph's meaning? If yes, which ones, and why? If no, why not?

   ____

   ____

3. The writer's mother treated the roses as if they were human beings. Find two example sentences from the paragraph that show how she protected her roses.

   a. ____

   ____

   b. ____

   ____

Grammar for Writing

Using Adjectives in Writing

Adjectives are important in a descriptive paragraph. They help the reader see the person or thing the writer is describing.

The **tall**, **graceful** bride in her **white** dress walked down the **long** aisle to meet her **proud** groom.

Explanation	Examples
An **adjective** describes a noun and usually answers one or more of the following questions: *Which one?* this, that, these, those *What kind?* big, old, yellow, delicate *How many?* some, few, many, two *How much?* enough, some, less, more	her **white** dress the **long** aisle her **proud** groom
Adjectives come **before** the nouns they describe.	The **angry** (adj) customers (noun) complained about the **poor** (adj) service (noun) in the **new** (adj) restaurant (noun).
When a sentence has a linking verb, the adjective modifies the subject and comes immediately **after** the verb. Linking verbs: be become seem feel taste sound appear remain keep look	The teacher is **intelligent** and **kind**. The soup tastes **good**. Mr. Currier feels **ill**. The decorations in the café looked **horrible**.
If writers use multiple adjectives to describe a noun, the order is often: Number Observation / opinion Size Shape Age Color Origin Material	the **beautiful old stone** building a **red Italian sports** car a **round green plastic** dish

Good!

N O S S A C O M

ACTIVITY 5 Correcting the Location of Descriptive Adjectives

Read each sentence. Circle all the descriptive adjectives. Are the adjectives placed correctly? If the sentence is correct, write C on the line. If you find an adjective error, draw an arrow from the adjective to its correct location in the sentence. Add commas if needed.

1. ______ John's puppy chewed on his shoes new.
2. ______ A yellow piece of paper is on the floor.
3. ______ The teacher wrote our assignment on the blackboard old.
4. ______ My best friend wrote a letter long.
5. ______ The five black dogs chased the police car.
6. ______ Colorado is a place great to go skiing when it is cold.
7. ______ My neighbor found a large wallet stuffed with new one-dollar bills.
8. ______ The gourmet chef created a slightly spicy but delicious meal.
9. ______ The clock on the rough cement wall of the busy railway station was antique.
10. ______ Egyptian pyramids are an example excellent of ancient architecture.
11. ______ My brother bought two cotton new sheets on sale yesterday.
12. ______ To make this spaghetti sauce, you need six red juicy tomatoes.

ACTIVITY 6 Adding Adjectives

Read each sentence. Write descriptive adjectives in the blanks. You may write more than one adjective in each blank. Then compare answers with your classmates.

1. The ____tired____ teacher walked into the ____noisy____ room.
2. The ______ couple watched a(n) ______ sunset.
3. My ______ coworker is a (n) ______ athlete.
4. The ______ computer sat on a(n) ______ table.
5. That ______ spider scared my ______ sister.
6. The ______ car raced down the ______ road.
7. My ______ feet ached from walking on the ______ sidewalk.

8. Brittany wore a fancy dress to the formal / important party last night.

9. The hungry cow ate green grass in the vast field.

10. A tiny boy sat on the dirty ground and played with some new toys.

ACTIVITY 7 Writing Descriptive Sentences Using Adjectives

Read each set of nouns. Using the nouns, write an original sentence with at least two adjectives. Circle the adjectives.

1. vacation / California

   People who want the perfect vacation should visit sunny California.

2. students / computers

   The excited university students received their brand-new computers.

3. dictionaries / libraries

   There are many bilingual dictionaries in the large libraries

4. trees / forest

   Are there any rare trees in this vast forest?

5. skyscraper / city

   The gigantic skyscrapers dominated the modern city

Building Better Sentences: For further practice with the sentences and paragraphs in this part of the unit, go to Practice 15 on pages 294–295 in Appendix 1.

Using Positive and Negative Adjectives for More Precise Meanings

When you write, it is important to use words that have the precise meaning that you want. Many times English has two or more adjectives that have the same basic meaning, but one is positive and the other is negative. Knowing multiple adjectives is important to make your writing more precise.

The **thrifty** old man saved all his money for his retirement. (positive meaning)

The **stingy** old man saved all his money for his retirement. (negative meaning)

Look up *thrifty* and *stingy* in your dictionary. The basic meanings for these words are similar—they both describe someone who is careful with money. However, there is a big difference in the feeling these words give to the reader or listener. The ***thrifty*** person is wise and economical with money, but the ***stingy*** person is greedy and does not want to spend or share money.

ACTIVITY 8 Recognizing Adjectives in Paragraphs

The next two descriptive paragraphs are about the same topic. Read the paragraphs and underline the adjectives. There are 13 descriptive adjectives in Example Paragraph 61 and 11 descriptive adjectives in Example Paragraph 62. The first adjective in each paragraph has been underlined for you.

Example Paragraph 61

The Blue River is an important part of the forest, and the quality of the river shapes the environment around it. The fresh, clear water is home to a wide variety of fish and plants. Colorful trout compete with other fish for the abundant supply of insects near the beautiful river. The tall trees near the river are green and healthy. Wild deer come to drink the sweet water and rest in the shadows cast on the grassy banks of the river.

Example Paragraph 62

The Blue River is an important part of the forest, and the quality of the river shapes the environment around it. The slow brown water does not contain fish or plants. Small trout struggle with other fish to catch the limited number of insects that live near the dirty river. The old trees near the river are almost leafless. They do not provide adequate protection for the wild animals that come to drink from the polluted river.

1. Briefly, what is being described in each paragraph?

   Example Paragraph 61 ______________________________

   Example Paragraph 62 ______________________________

2. What is your impression of the topic in Example Paragraph 61? What words helped you form this opinion?

   ____

   ____

   ____

   ____

3. What is your impression of the topic in Example Paragraph 62? What words helped you form this opinion?

   ____

   ____

   ____

   ____

4. Can you find an adjective in one paragraph that has the opposite meaning of an adjective in the other paragraph? For example, we can say that *clear* in Example Paragraph 61 is opposite in meaning to *brown* in Example Paragraph 62. Can you find other examples?

   ____

   ____

   ____

   ____

Writer's Note

Using Bilingual and English Learner Dictionaries

Bilingual Dictionaries

A bilingual dictionary is very helpful when you are first learning English. However, be careful when you use this kind of dictionary. It is easy to choose the wrong word listed in the entry. In fact, the most common error is to choose the first word that you find. You should always read all of the possible translations to find the best word that accurately fits in your sentence.

English Learner's Dictionaries

An English Learner's Dictionary is helpful for developing your growing writing skills. This kind of dictionary often includes simple definitions, clear sample sentences, and synonyms. It can help you expand your vocabulary and find the correct usage for common, academic, and idiomatic words and expressions. In addition, the definitions are written using high frequency vocabulary, so it is a great opportunity to practice useful English.

ACTIVITY 9 Writing Positive and Negative Adjectives

Think of adjectives that can describe the nouns listed below. In the first blank, write one or more **positive** adjectives. In the second blank, write **negative** adjectives.

Remember: The purpose of this activity is to increase your vocabulary, so do not use simple or general words, such as *nice* or *bad*. Use your dictionary to find the precise vocabulary to express your ideas. This will help you increase your writing vocabulary.

Noun	Positive	Negative
1. cheese	creamy, buttery, light	rancid, smelly, stinky
2. rock		
3. painting		
4. laughter		
5. flavor		
6. smell		
7. music		
8. texture		

ACTIVITY 10 Changing Meaning with Descriptive Adjectives

The paragraph below describes a man walking into a room. Many of the adjectives have been deleted. Fill in each blank with an adjective and create your own paragraph.

The ______________ man entered the ______________ room. He had hair. He wore a(n) ______________ suit with ______________ shoes. The man was very ______________. Everyone in the room was ______________ when they saw him. He was such a(n) ______________ man! They could not believe that he was in the room with them.

Next, rewrite your paragraph in the space below. Be sure to indent and add an original title. Then switch books with a partner and compare paragraphs. What impression do you have of the man in your partner's paragraph? Is it positive or negative?

____

____

____

____

____

____

____

____

____

____

Grammar for Writing

Using Prepositions of Location to Describe

To be precise in description, writers often need to indicate where something or someone is, especially in relation to something or someone else. For example, if you are describing a room, you can describe what is on the right side, what is on the left side, what is on the ceiling, and what is on the floor.

When you tell the location of something, it is important to use the correct **preposition of location**, followed by a noun. This noun after a preposition is called the **object of the preposition**. This preposition and noun combination is called a **prepositional phrase** (e.g., *in the kitchen*).

Study these examples (the prepositional phrases are bold).

The new bank is **on Wilson Road near the park.**

On the left, there is an old sofa. **On the right**, there are two wooden chairs.

Next to the river, there is a grassy field that goes **from Wilson Road to the corner of Maple Street and Lee Road**.

Common Prepositions of Location			
above	before	far from	on top of
across	behind	from	opposite
after	below	in	outside
against	beneath	in back of	over
ahead of	beside	in front of	past
along	between	inside	throughout
among	beyond	near	under
around	by	next to	
at	close to	on	

ACTIVITY 11 Using Prepositions of Location to Describe a Place

Write five true sentences about the location of things or people in your classroom. Circle the prepositions and underline the objects of the preposition. The first one has been done for you.

1. The teacher's desk is in front of the whiteboard.

2. ______________________________

3. ______________________________

4. ______________________________

5. ______________________________

6. ______________________________

ACTIVITY 12 Studying Example Paragraphs with Prepositions of Location

Discuss the Preview Questions with your classmates. Then read the example paragraphs and answer the questions that follow.

Paragraph with Prepositions of Location 1

The following paragraph describes a room in a house. Notice how often the writer appeals to the reader's sense of sight by describing the location of the things in the room.

Preview Questions

1. What are three things that most people expect to find in a living room?
2. Is your living room always neat? Usually neat? Almost never neat?
3. What is in the middle of your living room? On the left side? On the right side?

Example Paragraph 63

A Great Living Room

My living room may be small, but it is **tidy** and well organized. On the right, there is a wooden bookcase with four shelves. On top of the bookcase is a small lamp with a dark base and a blue lampshade. The first and third shelves are filled with some of my favorite books, including an English-French dictionary. On the second shelf, there is an old clock with **faded** numbers on it that my grandfather gave me when I was young. The bottom shelf has a few picture frames. On the opposite side of the room is a television set with a DVD player and my small movie collection on top of it. Between the television and the bookcase is a large sofa. My cat Lucky is sleeping comfortably on the right side of the sofa. Lying near the other end of the sofa is one of his toys. Directly in front of the sofa, there is a long coffee table with short legs. On the right side of this table are two magazines. Perhaps the most **striking** thing in the room is the beautiful beach painting above the sofa. This beautiful painting shows a peaceful beach scene with a sailboat on the right, far from the beach. Although it is a small room, everything in my living room is in its place.

tidy: neat, clean, arranged, organized

faded: difficult to see

striking: exceptional, very noticeable

Post-Reading

1. Why did the writer write this paragraph?

   ________ **a.** to define a living room

   ________ **b.** to describe a living room

   ________ **c.** to explain the process of creating a good living room

2. What is the sequence of describing the room?

   ________ **a.** from right to left to middle

   ________ **b.** from left to right to middle

   ________ **c.** from right to middle to left

   ________ **d.** from left to middle to right

3. Underline the prepositional phrases. How many are there? Count carefully! ________________

4. In the topic sentence, the writer says that the room is tidy. Can you find words or phrases that paint this image for the reader?

   ____

   ____

   ____

5. Can you think of some description to add to one part of the room? Use your imagination to write a sentence for that area of the room. Use prepositions of location.

   ____

   ____

   ____

·ragraph with Prepositions of Location 2

This paragraph describes a famous monument in New York Harbor. Notice how often the writer ·als to the reader's sense of sight by describing different parts of the monument.

Preview Questions

1. If you have visited the Statue of Liberty, what was the experience like? What, if anything, was different from what you expected?
2. How high do you think the Statue of Liberty is? What does the Statue of Liberty symbolize?
3. When you think of the Statue of Liberty, what adjectives come to mind?

Example Paragraph 64

The Statue of Liberty

The Statue of Liberty, an internationally-known **symbol** of freedom that was completed in 1886, is certainly an impressive structure. The statue is of a woman who is wearing long, **flowing** robes. On her head, she has a **crown** of seven **spikes** that represent the seven oceans and the seven continents. The statue weighs 450,000 pounds and is 152 feet high. The statue appears much larger, however, because it stands on a **pedestal** that is about 150 feet high. In her raised right hand, the woman holds a **torch**. In her left hand, she carries a tablet with the date "July 4, 1776" written on the cover. At her feet lie broken chains, which symbolize an escape to freedom. The Statue of Liberty is an amazing monument.

a symbol: a figure, a representation

flowing: moving easily

a crown: a decoration for the head to show high position, often worn by kings and queens

a spike: a point

a pedestal: a base

a torch: an instrument for carrying fire as light

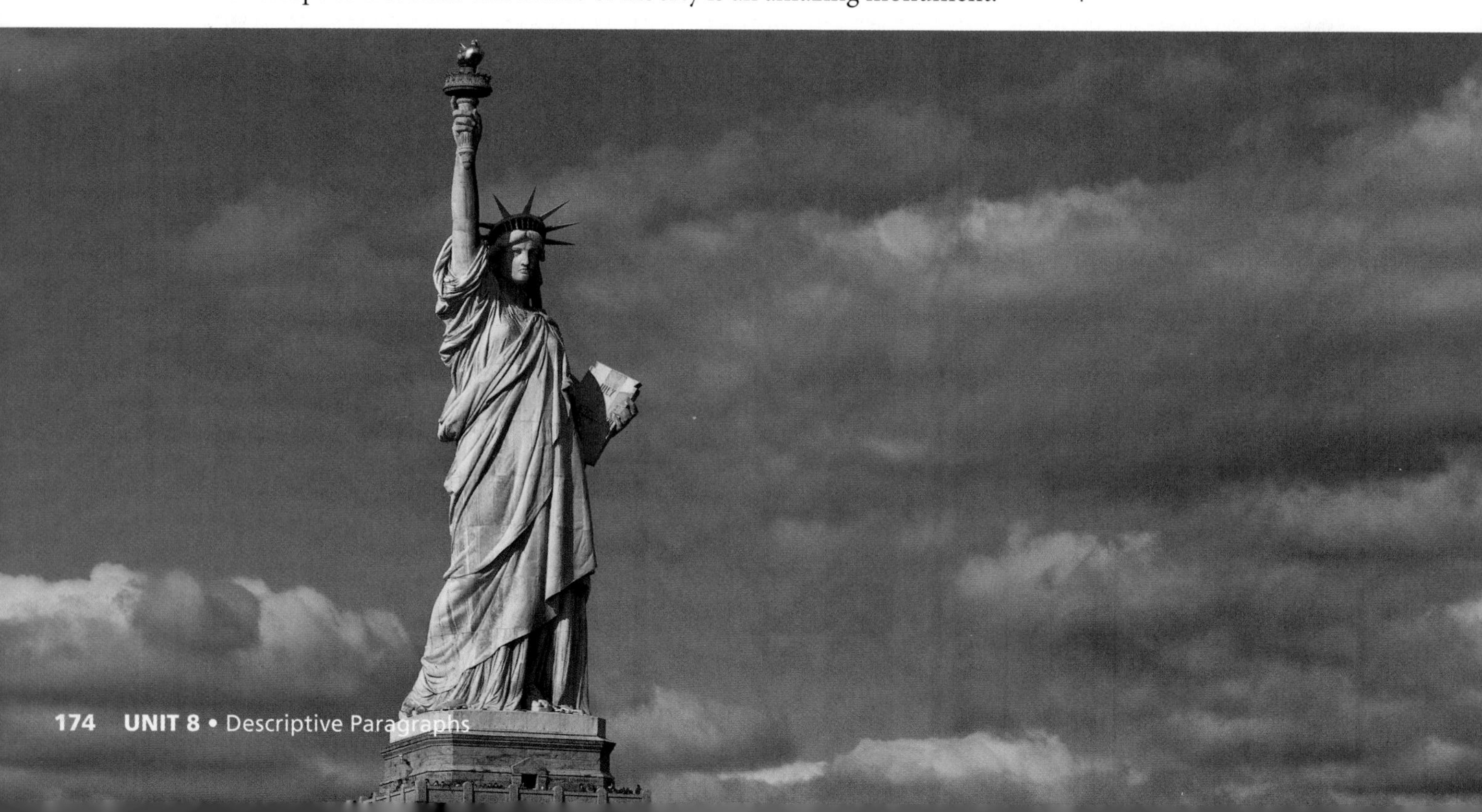

Post-Reading

1. What is the writer's purpose for writing this paragraph?

_______ **a.** to inform the reader of the history of the Statue of Liberty

_______ **b.** to explain why the Statue of Liberty was built

_______ **c.** to tell the steps in the construction of the Statue of Liberty

___✓___ **d.** to describe the Statue of Liberty

2. What is the sequence of describing the Statue?

___✓___ **a.** body — head — base — right hand — left hand — feet

_______ **b.** body — head — base — left hand — right hand — feet

_______ **c.** body — right hand — left hand — head — base — feet

_______ **d.** body — left hand — right hand — head — base — feet

3. The writer organizes the description of parts of the statue by location. To help you understand this organization better, answer these three questions:

a. Where is the tablet? In her left hand

b. Is the statue on the ground? If not, what is it on? It stands on a 150-foot-tall pedestal

c. Where is the torch? In her raised right hand

Grammar for Writing

Using Correct Word Order with Prepositions of Location

Explanation	Examples
Prepositional phrases of location can occur at the end of a sentence.	A fat, fluffy cat was sleeping **on top of the bookcase**.
Prepositional phrases of location can also occur at the beginning of a sentence. Use a comma between the prepositional phrase and the rest of the sentence.	**On top of the bookcase,** a fat, fluffy cat was sleeping.
If you want to move a prepositional phrase of location to the beginning of a sentence with the verb *be*, you must **invert the subject and the verb and drop the comma** after the prepositional phrase. This word order is more common in writing than in speaking.	✓ An empty pizza box (subject) was (verb) **under the sofa**. ✓ **Under the sofa** was (verb) an empty pizza box (subject). (No comma) ✗ **Under the sofa**, an empty pizza box was.

ACTIVITY 13 Identifying Objects of Prepositions

Read the paragraph. Circle the 20 prepositions. Underline the object of each preposition (the noun after each preposition). Then correct the two comma errors.

Example Paragraph 65

Gandhi

Although I have read about hundreds of famous people, one of the most interesting people in this group is Mahatma Gandhi of India. Gandhi was a great man who helped India win independence from Great Britain. He is most known for his peaceful methods during this important struggle, and his actions began other movements for equal rights all over the world. Gandhi was born, in 1869. This great hero's real name was Mohandas Karamchand Gandhi, but many people know him simply as Mahatma Gandhi. The title "Mahatma" means "Great Soul" and was given to him, in 1914 because he did so many good things for so many people. Unfortunately, Gandhi's life ended in 1948 when he was killed by a shooter. When I read about this great person, I realize how little I actually know about his life, and I am very eager for more information about him.

Building Better Sentences: For further practice with the sentences and paragraphs in this part of the unit, go to Practice 16 on page 295 in Appendix 1.

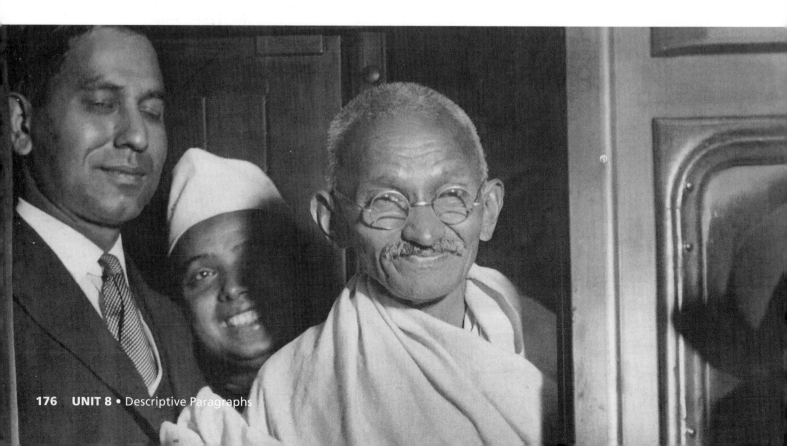

Building Better Vocabulary

ACTIVITY 14 Word Associations

Circle the word or phrase that is most closely related to the word or phrase on the left. If necessary, use a dictionary to check the meaning of words you do not know.

	A	B
1. eager for X to happen	you don't want X to happen	you want X to happen
2. delicate	can break easily	will never break
3. to recall	to remember	to understand
4. a skyscraper	high	low
5. an assault	an attack	an origin
6. to descend	10, 11, 12, 13	13, 12, 11, 10
7. to rip	to send	to tear
8. a pedestal	a statue	a person
9. constantly*	always	never
10. a syrup	a liquid	a solid
11. to argue with a person	discuss something great	discuss something bad
12. to tease	to make fun of	to try to understand
13. precise*	approximate	exact
14. a crown	your feet	your head
15. to roar	loud	soft

*Words that are part of the Academic Word List. See pages 275–276 for a complete list.

ACTIVITY 15 Using Collocations

Fill in each blank with the word on the left that most naturally completes the phrase on the right. If necessary, use a dictionary to check the meaning of words you do not know.

1. storm / worker — a skilled Worker

2. of / to — a symbol Of freedom

3. life / world — all over the World

4. bank / body — a slender body ________

5. come / go — to come ________ to mind

6. fish / photo — a faded ________

7. peaceful / principal — the principal ________ reason

8. dress / office — a tidy office ________

9. flowers / human beings — fragrant ________

10. of / with — stuffed ________ feathers

11. broken / written — ________ chains

12. common / popular — a very ________ error

Original Student Writing: Descriptive Paragraph

ACTIVITY 16 Original Writing Practice

Write a paragraph that describes something. Your goal is to give the reader an impression of what you are describing. Follow these guidelines:

- Choose a topic such as a favorite childhood memory or a famous monument.
- Brainstorm some sensory adjectives (sight, hearing, smell, taste, and touch).
- Write a topic sentence with a controlling idea.
- Write supporting sentences that relate to the topic.
- Make sure the adjectives mean precisely what you want them to mean—check both the positive and negative meanings.
- Use prepositional phrases of location in your paragraph. Put some at the beginning of sentences and some at the end of sentences because sentence variety is important to good writing.
- Make sure your concluding sentence restates the topic.
- Use at least two of the vocabulary words or phrases presented in Activity 14 and Activity 15. Underline these words and phrases in your paragraph.

If you need ideas for words and phrases, see the Useful Vocabulary for Better Writing on pages 277–281.

ACTIVITY 17 Peer Editing

Exchange papers from Activity 16 with a partner. Read your partner's paragraph. Then use Peer Editing Sheet 8 on NGL.Cengage.com/GW2 to help you comment on your partner's paragraph. Be sure to offer positive suggestions and comments that will help your partner improve his or her writing. Consider your partner's comments as you revise your own paragraph.

Additional Topics for Writing

Here are some ideas for descriptive paragraphs. When you write, follow the guidelines in Activity 16.

PHOTO TOPIC: Look at the photo on pages 154–155. Describe a national monument that is important to you. What does it look like? What feelings does the monument inspire in you?

TOPIC 2: Describe a family tradition. When do you follow the tradition? Why is the tradition important to you and your family?

TOPIC 3: Describe your favorite or least favorite meal. Be sure to tell how the food tastes, smells, and looks.

TOPIC 4: Describe something that makes you happy, sad, nervous, or afraid.

TOPIC 5: Describe a person you know. What is this person like? What are some of his or her characteristics? Make sure that the description would allow your reader to identify the person in a crowd.

Timed Writing

How quickly can you write in English? There are many times when you must write quickly, such as on a test. It is important to feel comfortable during those times. Timed-writing practice can make you feel better about writing quickly in English.

1. Take out a piece of paper.
2. Read the writing prompt.
3. Brainstorm ideas for five minutes.
4. Write a short paragraph (six to ten sentences).
5. You have 25 minutes to write.

In your opinion, what is the ideal teacher? Describe your ideal teacher. Which characteristics make this kind of teacher ideal to you? (Do not use names of current teachers, but you should use their characteristics that you consider ideal.)

Giant panda Wei Wei walks around a birthday cake made of fruits and bamboo in Wuhan Zoo.

To recognize word forms and common suffixes

Can you write your opinion about the best kinds of zoos?

What Is an Opinion Paragraph?

An **opinion** paragraph expresses the writer's thoughts and attitiude toward something. The writer attempts to persuade the reader about a certain point of view. In other words, the writer presents an argument for or against something. This kind of writing is also referred to as persuasive or argumentative writing.

Good writers will include not only opinions but also facts to support their opinions. For example, if a writer says "Smoking should not be allowed anywhere," he or she must give reasons for this opinion. One reason could be a fact, such as, "Over 160,000 people died in the United States last year because of lung cancer as a known result of smoking." This fact clearly and strongly supports the writer's opinion.

A good opinion paragraph:

- is often about a controversial issue
- gives the writer's opinion or opinions about a topic
- explains facts to support the writer's opinions
- presents a strong case that makes the reader think about an issue seriously, perhaps even causing the reader to reconsider his or her own opinion about the issue
- considers both sides of an argument (although it gives much more attention to the writer's side of the issue)

ACTIVITY 1 Studying Example Opinion Paragraphs

Discuss the Preview Questions with your classmates. Then read the paragraphs on pages 182–186 and answer the questions that follow.

Opinion Paragraph 1

This paragraph is about cell phone use while driving, which has been a topic of much interest and debate in many countries for some time.

Preview Questions

1. Do you think that using a cell phone while driving is acceptable? Why or why not?
2. Should there be laws banning the use of cell phones while driving? Why or why not?

Example Paragraph 66

Driving and Cell Phones

Because cell phones and driving are a **deadly** mix, I am in favor of a ban on all cell phone use by drivers. The most **obvious** reason for this ban is to save lives. Each year thousands of drivers are killed or seriously injured because they are talking on cell phones or texting instead of watching the road while they are driving. This first reason should be

deadly: dangerous, able to cause death

obvious: evident, clear

enough to support a ban on cell phones when driving, but I have two other reasons. My second reason is that these drivers cause accidents that kill other people. Sometimes these drivers kill other drivers; sometimes they kill passengers or even pedestrians. These drivers certainly do not have the right to **endanger** others' lives! Finally, even in cases where there are no **injuries** or deaths, **damage** to cars from these accidents costs us millions of dollars as well as countless hours of lost work. To me, banning cell phones while driving is **common sense**. In fact, a **wide range of** countries has already put this ban into effect, including Australia, Brazil, Japan, Russia, and Turkey. Driving a car is a privilege, not a right. We must all be careful drivers, and talking or texting on a cell phone when driving is not safe. For the important reasons I have mentioned here, I support a complete ban on all cell phone use by drivers.

to endanger: to cause to be in a dangerous situation

an injury: harm or hurt done to a body (for example, a foot)

the damage: harm or hurt done to thing (for example, a building)

common sense: so obvious that everyone knows it

a (wide) range of: a (great) number of

Post-Reading

1. What is the topic sentence of the paragraph? ______________________________

____

2. What is the author's opinion on cell phone usage by drivers? ______________________________

____

3. List three reasons that the writer favors a ban on cell phones while driving.

   a. ______________________________

   b. ______________________________

   c. ______________________________

4. What is your reaction to this paragraph? Do you agree or disagree with the author's opinion? Why or why not?

   ____

   ____

   ____

Opinion Paragraph 2

This paragraph is about a less serious topic than the topic that Example Paragraph 66 deals with. The subject of this paragraph is the question "Which is better, calling or texting?"

Preview Questions

1. How many phone calls do you make each day?
2. How many text messages do you send each day?
3. Do you prefer to call or text someone when you need to tell that person something? Why?

Example Paragraph 67

The Best Way to Communicate

No matter how much my friends try to convince me that I should text them more often, I prefer calling to texting. Yes, some people might say that using a telephone to make a call is **old-fashioned**, but I do not care. Texting is certainly very common now because it is convenient and fast. However, I really like to call my friends because I want to hear my friends' voices and interact with them. **Without a doubt**, calling is my preferred **mode of** communication.

no matter: it does not matter or make a difference

old-fashioned: old style, not modern

without a doubt: 100 percent, certainly

a mode: a method, manner

Post-Reading

1. What is the topic sentence of this paragraph? ______________________________

____

2. What phrases from the paragraph show the reader that the writer is giving an opinion and not a fact?

____

____

3. Do you agree with the supporting statements that the writer makes about texting and calling? Why or why not?

____

____

____

4. Can you think of at least one other reason the writer could give for preferring calling to texting?

____

____

Opinion Paragraph 3

The paragraph on the next page deals with school uniforms, a current controversial issue.

Preview Questions

1. Have you ever worn a school uniform?
2. Do you think requiring students to wear a uniform is a good idea or a bad idea?

Example Paragraph 68

An A+ for School Uniforms

School uniforms should be **mandatory** for all students for a number of important reasons. First of all, uniforms make everyone equal. In this way, kids with a lot of nice things can be on the same level as those with fewer things. In addition, getting ready for school every morning can be much faster and easier. Many kids waste time choosing what to wear to school, and they and their parents are often unhappy with their final choice. Most important, some **studies** show that school uniforms make students **perform** better in school. Some people might say that uniforms take away personal freedom, but students still have many other ways to express themselves and their individuality. For all these reasons, I believe the benefits of mandatory school uniforms are so strong that we should require them immediately.

mandatory: obligatory, something that must be done

a study: a research report

to perform: to produce work; to do

Post-Reading

1. What is the author's opinion about school uniforms?

____

____

2. The author gives three reasons to support the opinion. Write them here.

____

____

____

3. The paragraph states that some people do not think that school uniforms should be required. What is their main reason?

____

____

Writer's Note

Advanced Opinion Writing

The most important way to persuade someone to agree with what you are writing is to include strong supporting facts. Your writing will always sound better when you support what you have just written with evidence or good examples.

A second way to persuade someone to agree with the ideas in your writing is to include at least one sentence with an opposing opinion (an opinion that disagrees with your point of view). At first, this might not seem like a good idea, but it is common to state one point of view that disagrees with your own point of view. This is called a **counterargument.** This counterargument is then followed by a statement that refutes, or reduces the counterargument. This is called a **refutation** because you refute the counterargument.

When you acknowledge this other opinion, you should downplay, or minimize, it. One way to do this is to use weak words, such as *some, may,* and *might,* as we can see in the following example:

> Some people **might** say that uniforms take away personal freedom, but students still have many other ways to express themselves and their individuality.

In a good opinion paragraph, the writer:

- states an opinion about a topic
- provides supporting sentences with factual information
- briefly mentions one opposing point of view (the counterargument)
- refutes the counterargument in one or two sentences (the refutation)
- finishes the paragraph with a concluding sentence that restates the topic sentence and/or offers a solution. Study this example:

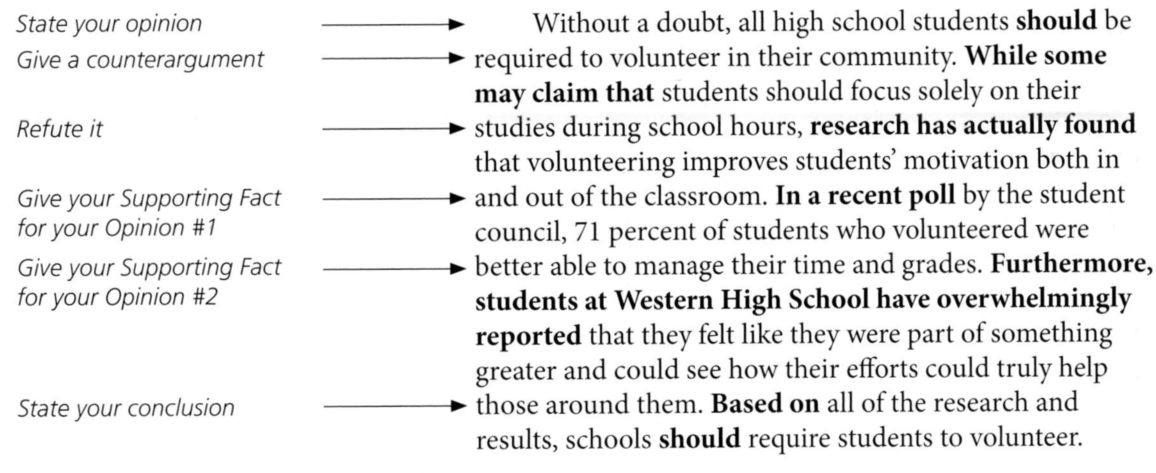

Without a doubt, all high school students **should** be required to volunteer in their community. **While some may claim that** students should focus solely on their studies during school hours, **research has actually found** that volunteering improves students' motivation both in and out of the classroom. **In a recent poll** by the student council, 71 percent of students who volunteered were better able to manage their time and grades. **Furthermore, students at Western High School have overwhelmingly reported** that they felt like they were part of something greater and could see how their efforts could truly help those around them. **Based on** all of the research and results, schools **should** require students to volunteer.

Facts and Opinions

A **fact** is information that can be verified or proved. A fact is always true. In contrast, an **opinion** is what someone thinks or believes to be true. An opinion may be true or false.

Facts	Opinions
Orlando is located in central Florida.	Orlando is a great city for people of all ages.
Orlando is home to several large theme parks.	There are many fun places to visit in Orlando.
The University of Central Florida is located in Orlando.	The University of Central Florida is an excellent university.
The average annual temperature is 73° F.	I like the weather in Orlando very much.

When you write an opinion paragraph, it is very important to include facts. If you choose helpful supporting facts with examples that the reader can clearly relate to, your opinion paragraph will be stronger and you may even convince readers to agree with you. Readers will remember good, related supporting examples, so you should try to write the most convincing examples.

ACTIVITY 2 Identifying Facts and Opinions

Read the following statements and decide if they are facts or opinions. Write F for fact and O for opinion.

__O__ **1.** Soccer is a much more interesting game to play and watch than golf.

__F__ **2.** The Nile River splits into the White Nile and Blue Nile in Sudan.

_____ **3.** The most beautiful city in the world is Paris.

_____ **4.** Citrus fruits include oranges, lemons, and grapefruit.

_____ **5.** Hawaii is the best place for a vacation.

_____ **6.** The capital of Thailand is Bangkok.

_____ **7.** Security alarms are the most effective way to protect homes from burglaries.

_____ **8.** School uniforms should be mandatory for all students.

_____ **9.** A glass of milk has more calcium in it than a glass of apple juice.

_____ **10.** Apple juice tastes better than milk.

ACTIVITY 3 Identifying Facts and Opinions in a Paragraph

Reread Example Paragraph 66 about cell phone use while driving. It contains some information that is factual and some that is the writer's opinion. Find two examples of facts and two examples of opinions in the paragraph and write them on the lines below.

Fact

1. ______________________________

____

2. ______________________________

____

Opinion

1. ______________________________

____

2. ______________________________

____

Building Better Sentences: For further practice with the sentences and paragraphs in this part of the unit, go to Practice 17 on page 296 in Appendix 1.

Topic Sentences for Opinion Paragraphs

A good topic sentence for an opinion paragraph must express an opinion that can be supported in some way. Therefore, this type of topic sentence cannot be a fact because a fact is not an opinion. A fact does not need to be proved or discussed. It is a fact. If you cannot think of at least two good reasons to support the idea in the topic sentence, then it is probably not a good topic sentence for an opinion paragraph.

Bad Topic Sentence: Paris is a large city in France.

Problem: This is a fact. Does anyone disagree that Paris is a large city and it is in France?

Bad Topic Sentence: There are several types of camels.

Problem: This is a fact. This topic sentence is going to produce a paragraph explaining the different kinds of camels, but it is not a good topic sentence for an opinion paragraph about camels.

ACTIVITY 4 Recognizing Good Topic Sentences for Opinion Paragraphs

Read the following sentences. Which ones are good topic sentences for opinion paragraphs? Put a check (✓) next to those sentences.

___✓___ 1. A hospital volunteer usually has many duties.

___✓___ 2. Soccer is a much more interesting game to play and watch than golf.

________ 3. The largest and best-known city in all of France is Paris.

___✓___ 4. Eating a vegetarian diet is the best way to stay healthy.

___✓___ 5. Hawaii is the best place for a vacation.

________ 6. The U.S. government uses a system of checks and balances.

________ 7. Although Ontario is the fourth largest of the thirteen provinces in Canada, it has about one-third of Canada's population and is therefore the most populated province in the entire country.

___✓___ 8. Security alarms are the most effective way to protect homes from burglaries.

ACTIVITY 5 Sequencing Sentences in a Paragraph

The following sentences make up a paragraph. Read the sentences and number them from 1 to 6 to indicate the correct order. Then write O or F on the line after each sentence to indicate whether the sentence contains an opinion or a fact.

___5___ a. The damage of these rays may not be seen immediately in children, but adults who spent a lot of time in the sun when they were children have a much higher chance of developing skin cancer than adults who did not spend time in the sun. ________

___1___ b. Too much time in the sun can cause severe skin damage, especially in young children. ________

___3___ c. This disease, which can be deadly if it is not treated quickly, is a direct result of the sun's harmful ultraviolet rays. ________

___6___ d. In conclusion, the information in this paragraph is enough evidence to persuade parents not to let their children play outside in the sun without sunscreen. ________

___4___ e. Although many people enjoy playing in the sun, parents should make sure that their children put on sunscreen before going outside. ________

___2___ f. The most serious example of this is skin cancer. ________

ACTIVITY 6 Copying a Paragraph

Now copy the sentences from Activity 5 in the best order to create a good opinion paragraph. Add a title of your choice.

Example Paragraph 69

Grammar for Writing

Recognizing Word Forms and Common Suffixes

Many English words have different forms for different parts of speech—**noun, verb, adjective,** or **adverb.** Some words have **suffixes** or endings that indicate the part of speech. Notice the suffixes in these parts of speech:

Part of Speech	Purpose	Common Suffixes		Examples
Noun	Names a person or thing	**-ion**	**vacation**	In this photo, you can see the **beauty** of a sunset.
		-ment	**entertainment**	
		-er	**teacher**	
		-ness	**sadness**	
		-ity	**activity**	
		-ence	**difference**	
Verb	Shows action or being	**-ify**	**classify**	The city will **beautify** several neighborhoods.
		-ize	**realize**	
		-en	**blacken**	
		-ate	**generate**	
Adjective	Describes or modifies a noun	**-ful**	**beautiful**	That is the most **beautiful** baby I've ever seen.
		-ent	**different**	
		-able	**comfortable**	
		-ish	**English**	
		-ial	**financial**	
		-y	**windy**	
Adverb	Modifies a verb, adjective, or another adverb	**-ly**	**quickly**	Susan sings **beautifully.**
			extensively	

Sometimes a word can function as different parts of speech without any change in ending. For example, the word *paint* can be a noun *(Where is the paint?)* or a verb *(Let's paint the kitchen.)*. The word *hard* can be an adjective *(The candy is hard.)* or an adverb *(She studied hard.)*. Always check your writing for the correct word forms.

ACTIVITY 7 Identifying Word Forms

Each item below contains a group of related words. Identify the word form of the words in each group. Write N (noun), V (verb), ADJ (adjective), or ADV (adverb) on the line. (Some items will not have all four forms.) Use a dictionary if necessary.

1. increasingly ADV
   increase N
   increasing ADJ
   increase V
2. believe ________
   belief ________
   believable ________
3. legality ________
   legal ________
   legally ________
   legalize ________
4. logically ________
   logic ________
   logical ________
5. finance ________
   financially ________
   finance ________
   financial ________
6. sweetly ________
   sweetness ________
   sweet ________
   sweeten ________
7. simplicity ________
   simply ________
   simple ________
   simplify ________
8. equality ________
   equal ________
   equalize ________
   equally ________
9. benefit ________
   beneficial ________
   beneficially ________
   benefit ________
10. freedom ________
    freely ________
    free ________
    free ________

ACTIVITY 8 Correcting Word Forms

Some of these sentences contain word form errors. Read each sentence. If the sentence is correct, write C on the line. If it contains an error, write X on the line and correct the word form error.

1. ________ Many people did not belief the world was round before Christopher Columbus's voyages.
2. ________ She parked her car illegally and got a $30 ticket.
3. ________ Taking multivitamins can be benefit to your health.
4. ________ Students in this class are allowed to speak freedom.
5. ________ During civil rights demonstrations, protesters fought for equality.
6. ________ Babies often speak using simply words and phrases.
7. ________ My sister is a very sweetly girl.
8. ________ Mathematicians must use their logical to solve difficult problems.
9. ________ Taxpayers do not want the government to increase taxes.
10. ________ The company's financial situation has improved dramatically this year.

Choosing a Topic for an Opinion Paragraph

In Unit 2, you learned about developing ideas for writing paragraphs. This work includes talking about topics and brainstorming. One good source for topics for opinion paragraphs is the newspaper or news websites. Top stories and editorial articles may give you some ideas.

Two methods of brainstorming work well for opinion paragraphs. One method is to brainstorm using the clusters that you did in Unit 2. A second method of brainstorming is to make two **columns** about your topic. On one side, list the negative ideas about the topic; on the other side, list the positive ideas.

Here is an example of how to set up a negative-positive brainstorm design.

TOPIC:	
Negative Points	Positive Points

When you write an opinion paragraph later in the unit, try to make a list of all of the positive and negative points of a topic. It will help you decide which points will make the strongest opinion or argument.

Building Better Sentences: For further practice with the sentences and paragraphs in this part of the unit, go to Practice 18 on pages 296–297 in Appendix 1.

Building Better Vocabulary

ACTIVITY 9 Word Associations

Circle the word or phrase that is most closely related to the word or phrase on the left. If necessary, use a dictionary to check the meaning of words you do not know.

	A	B
1. obvious*	serious	evident
2. mandatory	possible	required
3. a report	to study	to do again

4. to set up	to design, plan	to change, alter
5. a point of view	an opinion	permission
6. to split	to combine	to divide
7. to ban	to prohibit	to transport
8. severe	negative	positive
9. without a doubt	it is certain	it is possible
10. an injury	an advantage	a problem
11. to downplay	to maximize	to minimize
12. duties	fun	work
13. entirely	annually	completely
14. a voyage	a trip	a subject
15. to convince*	to persuade	to restate

*Words that are part of the Academic Word List. See pages 275–276 for a complete list.

ACTIVITY 10 Using Collocations

Fill in each blank with the word or phrase on the left that most naturally completes the phrase on the right. If necessary, use a dictionary to check the meaning of words you do not know.

1. but also / for example	not only X, ________________ Y
2. for / from	to protect your home ________________ burglaries
3. all / no	first of ________________
4. agree / offer	to ________________ a solution
5. in / on	to spend money ________________ food
6. may / than	rather ________________
7. communication / effort	a method of ________________
8. damage / evidence	to cause ________________
9. fact / issue	a controversial ________________
10. doing / to do	to waste time ________________ something

Original Student Writing: Opinion Paragraph

ACTIVITY 11 Original Writing Practice

Develop a paragraph about a strong opinion that you have. Include facts to support your opinion. Follow these guidelines:

- Choose a topic such as the value of living abroad, connecting teachers' salaries to students' grades, or why young children need their own cell phones.
- Brainstorm your topic. If you want, use the Internet for ideas.
- Write a topic sentence with a controlling idea.
- Write supporting sentences with facts that support your opinions.
- Check for incorrect word forms.
- Use at least two of the vocabulary words or phrases presented in Activity 9 and Activity 10. Underline these words and phrases in your paragraph.

If you need ideas for words and phrases, see the Useful Vocabulary for Better Writing on pages 277–281.

ACTIVITY 12 Peer Editing

Exchange papers from Activity 11 with a partner. Read your partner's paragraph. Then use Peer Editing Sheet 9 on NGL.Cengage.com/GW2 to help you comment on your partner's paragraph. Be sure to offer positive suggestions and comments that will help your partner improve his or her writing. Consider your partner's comments as you revise your own paragraph.

Additional Topics for Writing

Here are some ideas for opinion paragraphs. When you write, follow the guidelines in Activity 11.

PHOTO TOPIC: Look at the photo on pages 180–181. In your opinion, what are the best kinds of zoos?

TOPIC 2: Do you think professional athletes receive too much money? Why or why not?

TOPIC 3: Should students have to take an entrance exam to enter a college or university? Why or why not?

TOPIC 4: Should schools last all year?

TOPIC 5: Who is the person that you admire the most? Give reasons for your choice.

Timed Writing

How quickly can you write in English? There are many times when you must write quickly such as on a test. It is important to feel comfortable during those times. Timed-writing practice can make you feel better about writing quickly in English.

1. Take out a piece of paper.
2. Read the writing prompt.
3. Brainstorm ideas for five minutes.
4. Write a short paragraph (six to ten sentences).
5. You have 25 minutes to write.

In many places, the minimum age necessary to obtain a driver's license is 16 or 17. Many people say this minimum age should be increased to 21. In your opinion, what minimum age should be required to get a driver's license?

Unit

10 Narrative Paragraphs

A photographer lets two trained grizzly bears nuzzle him.

OBJECTIVES To learn how to write a narrative paragraph
To practice verb tense consistency

Can you write a story about something that happened in the past?

What Is a Narrative Paragraph?

A **narrative paragraph** tells a story or relates an event. Narratives have a beginning, a middle, and an end. Any time you go to a movie or read a fiction book, you are enjoying a narrative. A narrative paragraph can be fun to write because you often describe an event from your life.

A narrative paragraph:

- tells a story
- gives background information in the opening sentence or sentences
- has a clear beginning, a middle, and an end
- entertains and informs
- uses descriptive words to paint a picture so realistic that the reader can almost feel the experience of witnessing the event live

Beginning, Middle, and End

Every narrative paragraph has a beginning, a middle, and an end. Read this example paragraph from a student whose fear of public speaking causes her great grief in her speech class. Then read the explanation of the parts of the narrative paragraph that follows.

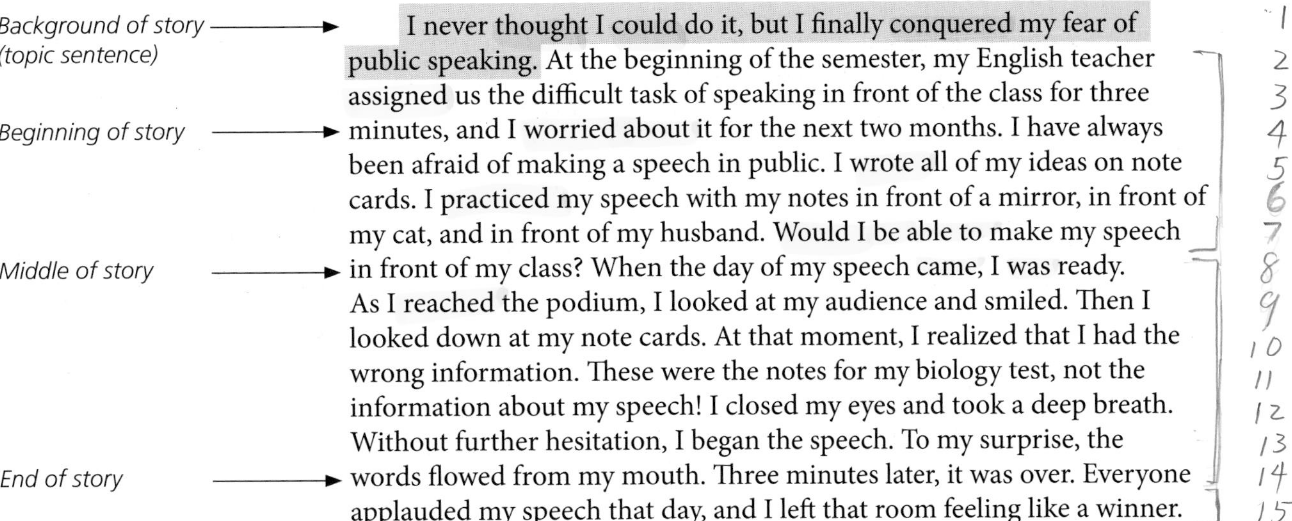

I never thought I could do it, but I finally conquered my fear of public speaking. At the beginning of the semester, my English teacher assigned us the difficult task of speaking in front of the class for three minutes, and I worried about it for the next two months. I have always been afraid of making a speech in public. I wrote all of my ideas on note cards. I practiced my speech with my notes in front of a mirror, in front of my cat, and in front of my husband. Would I be able to make my speech in front of my class? When the day of my speech came, I was ready. As I reached the podium, I looked at my audience and smiled. Then I looked down at my note cards. At that moment, I realized that I had the wrong information. These were the notes for my biology test, not the information about my speech! I closed my eyes and took a deep breath. Without further hesitation, I began the speech. To my surprise, the words flowed from my mouth. Three minutes later, it was over. Everyone applauded my speech that day, and I left that room feeling like a winner.

The Topic Sentence

The first sentence in the paragraph—the topic sentence—gives background information about the story. The writer introduces the main character—the writer herself—and prepares her readers for the action that will come. The reader can guess from this first sentence that the story will probably be about what the writer did or what happened that made her less afraid of public speaking.

The Beginning of the Story

The topic sentence is the beginning of the paragraph, but it is not usually the beginning of the story. The main action begins after the topic sentence. Not all narratives contain action. They may be about a problem or a conflict. In this paragraph, the writer has a problem—she has to make a speech in front of the class, but she is afraid of public speaking.

The Middle of the Story

After the beginning part, you will find the middle part of the story. The middle part is where the main action or problem occurs. In this paragraph, that action or problem is the speech. When the writer stood in front of the class, she discovered that she had biology notes instead of speech notes.

The End of the Story

The end of the story gives the final action or result. If there is a problem or conflict in the story, the solution is presented here. In this paragraph, the story has a happy ending. Because the writer had practiced the speech so many times, she was able to remember it without her notes. The writer learned that she had the ability to make a speech in front of a group.

ACTIVITY 1 Analyzing Example Narrative Paragraphs

Discuss the Preview Questions with your classmates. Then read the example paragraphs on pages 202–206 and answer the questions that follow.

Narrative Paragraph 1

The following paragraph is a personal story about a time when the writer was scared.

Preview Questions

1. Have you ever felt really scared? Describe the situation.
2. What was going on around you during the scary event? Give some adjectives that describe the surroundings.
3. How did the situation end?

Example Paragraph 71

My Department Store Nightmare

I will never forget the first time I got lost in New York City. I was traveling with my parents during winter vacation. We were in an incredibly large department store, and I was so excited to see such a huge place. Suddenly I turned around to ask my mom something, but she was gone! I began crying and screaming **at the top of my lungs**. A salesclerk came up to me and asked if I was OK. She got on the public address system and **notified** the customers that a little boy with blue jeans and a red cap was lost. Two minutes later, my mom and dad came running toward me. We all cried and hugged each other. This story took place over 20 years ago, but every time that I see a department store, I am reminded of that terrified little boy.

at the top of my lungs: very loudly

to notify: to give information

Writer's Note

Including Background Information

The topic sentence of a narrative paragraph, usually the first sentence, gives background information about the action that is going to happen in the story. The background sentence is not usually the beginning of the story—it sets up the story. Try to think of what information you need to give your reader so that the story flows smoothly.

Post-Reading

1. What is the topic sentence of this paragraph? I will never forget the first time I got lost in N.Y.C.
2. Where does the story take place? In an incredibly large department store
3. What is the beginning of the story? *(Circle one.)*

   a. He was in a large New York department store. (circled)
   b. A salesclerk spoke to him.
4. What is the middle of the story? *(Circle one.)*

   a. He bought some jeans and a cap.
   b. He got separated from his parents. (circled)
5. What is the end of the story? *(Circle one.)*

   a. His parents found him. (circled)
   b. The size of the store scared him.
6. What is the writer's purpose for writing this paragraph? Telling a childhood story when he was scared.

Narrative Paragraph 2

The paragraph on the next page deals with an embarrassing moment in the writer's life.

Preview Questions

1. Think of an embarrassing moment in your life. What happened? What was the result?
2. Imagine that you are a server in a restaurant. What do you think is the most embarrassing thing that could happen to you in this job?

Example Paragraph 72

Talent Show Disaster

My most **embarrassing** moment happened during a talent show at my high school. Many other students chose to play a musical instrument, do a magic trick, or tell a joke, but I decided to sing my favorite song. I had practiced the song for many weeks and could sing it perfectly. However, this day did not go as I had planned. When my name was called, I walked on the **stage** and the curtains opened. All of a sudden, 300 people were watching me. I held the microphone in my hand, but my hands were shaking. Then the music came on. When it was time for me to sing, I forgot the song **lyrics** and missed the entire first part. Then I sang the **chorus** horribly. The **audience** tried not to laugh, but I was so embarrassed! When the song ended, I did not look at the audience and ran off the stage in **tears**.

a disaster: a complete failure

embarrassing: causing someone to feel uncomfortable

the stage: a raised area in a building or a room where people make speeches or perform

the lyrics: the words of a song

the chorus: the part of a song that repeats

the audience: a group of people who watch a show or other public event

a tear: water from your eyes when you cry

1. What is the topic sentence? My most embarrassing moment happened during a talent show at my high school.

2. Why was the writer embarrassed? She forgot the song lyrics and missed the entire first part of the song she was supposed to sing

3. What is the beginning of the story? (*Circle one.*)

   a. She was embarrassed. **b.** She chose to do a song.

4. What is the middle of the story? (*Circle one.*)

   a. She could not remember the words. **b.** She wanted to change the words.

5. What is the end of the story? (*Circle one.*)

   a. She left the room quickly. **b.** She helped some of the audience.

6. What is the writer's purpose for writing this story? She tells an embarrassing moment in her life

Narrative Paragraph 3

The example narrative on the next page tells about a time in a boy's life when he was unhappy. He learned an important lesson from his unhappiness.

Preview Questions

1. Think of your best friend. How long have you been best friends?
2. What are the most important qualities in a friend? Different from 1st Q. – in general
3. Have you ever moved away and had to make new friends? Describe the situation. Was it easy? If not, how did you overcome this situation?

Example Paragraph 73

A Lesson in Friendship

I learned the hard way how to make friends in a new school. At my old school in Toronto, I was on the football and track teams, so I was very popular and had lots of friends. Everything changed when I was 16 years old because my parents decided to move to Florida. Going to a new school was not easy for me. The first few days in my new school were extremely difficult. The class schedule was different, and the teachers were more informal than in my old school. All the students dressed **casually** in shorts and T-shirts instead of a school uniform. Some kids tried to be nice to me, but I did not want to talk to them. To me, they looked and acted **funny**! After a few weeks, I realized that no one even tried to talk to me anymore. I began to feel lonely. Two months passed before I got the courage to talk to a few classmates. Finally, I realized that they were normal people, just like me. I began to develop some **relationships** and eventually some good friendships. I learned a **valuable** lesson about making friends that year.

casually: informally

funny: strange

a relationship: a friendship

valuable: important

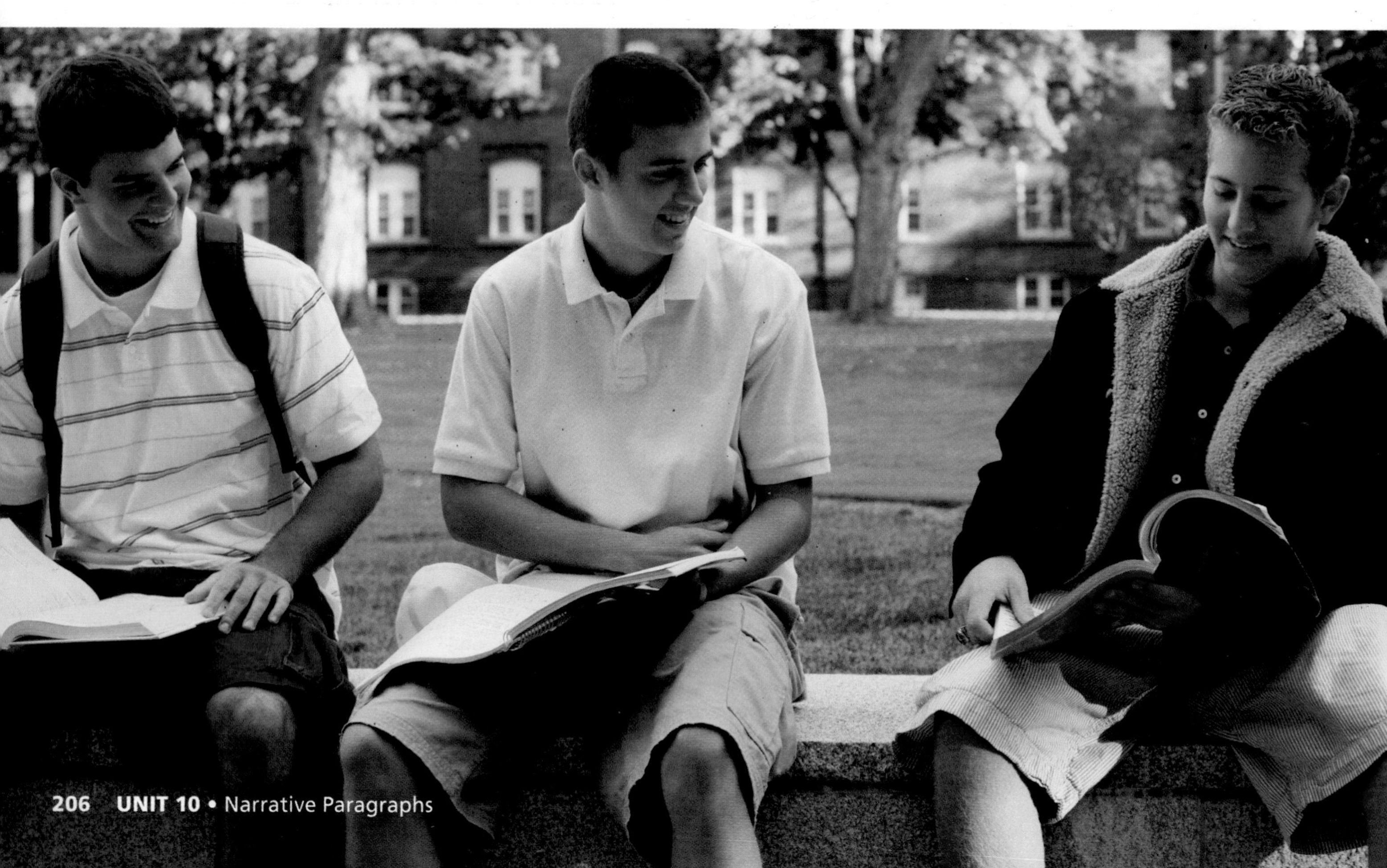

Post-Reading

1. What is the general topic of this paragraph? A lesson in friendship.

2. What is the topic sentence? I learned the hard way how to make friends in a new school.

3. In your own words, what is the beginning of the story?

   A 16-year-old boy who used to be very popular in his old school had to move to a new place and started a new school.

4. In your own words, what is the middle of the story?

   He had a hard time in the new school. Everything was different and he didn't want to talk to anyone.

5. In your own words, what is the end of the story?

   Finally, he got the courage to talk to a few classmates and made new friends.

6. What lesson did the writer learn from this experience?

   He learned that he needed to be active in making friends.

Working with Ideas for Narrative Paragraphs

You can find stories from your own memories and experiences. Many times, the best narrative stories are about real events that actually happened to someone. In fact, there is an expression in English that "truth is stranger than fiction," which means that it is sometimes more difficult to invent a story ("fiction") than to tell about something that actually happened ("truth").

ACTIVITY 2 Recognizing Good Topics for Narrative Paragraphs

Read the following paragraph titles. Put a check (✓) next to the titles that you think would make good narrative paragraphs. Be prepared to explain your choices.

___✓___ My Best Friend, Luke ________ Natural Disasters

________ How to Become a Doctor ________ Bears

___✓___ The Day I Almost Died ___✓___ A Wonderful Day in the Mountains

Compare your choices with a classmate. Do you agree on which titles would make the best narrative paragraphs? Explain why or why not.

Using Descriptive Language to Help Readers See Your Story

In narrative writing, you want the readers to be able to imagine that they are actually in the story with you. In order to accomplish this goal, you need to describe your story and your experiences as carefully as possible. Use specific vocabulary to help your readers imagine that they are actually there with you in your story. Your goal is to make your readers understand why this event is so special or significant for you.

Sentence	General Vocabulary	More Descriptive Vocabulary
The movie was ________.	nice	interesting, thrilling, inspiring, heart-warming, superb
These essays are ________.	bad	boring, horrible, empty, dull, shocking, violent
I felt ________.	good	marvelous, fantastic, elated, wonderful, relaxed
We were ________.	afraid	terrified, anxious, alarmed, scared, petrified

ACTIVITY 3 Describing a Moment

Think about a moment in your life where something interesting or unusual happened, or look at the photograph for ideas. What was happening before that moment, during that moment, and right after that moment? Write some details about that moment, including the place, things that happened, your feelings, and how you feel today. Use descriptive language.

Moment: ____

Where were you? ____

What happened? Before: ____

____

During: ____

____

After: ____

____

What were you feeling? Before: ____

____

During: ____

____

After: ____

____

Your overall impression or feeling: ____

ACTIVITY 4 Sequencing Sentences in a Paragraph

These sentences form a narrative of a personal experience with death. Read the sentences and number them from 1 to 7 to indicate the best order.

______ **a.** At 7:18 the next morning, a severe earthquake measuring 8.1 on the Richter scale hit Mexico City. I was asleep, but the violent side-to-side movement of my bed woke me up. Then I could hear the rumble of the building as it was shaking.

______ **b.** As I was trying to stand up, I could hear the walls of the building cracking. I was on the third floor of a six-story building, and I thought the building was going to collapse. I really believed that I was going to die.

______ **c.** I flew to Mexico City on September 17. The first two days were uneventful.

______ **d.** My trip to Mexico City in September 1985 was not my first visit there, but this unforgettable trip helped me realize something about life.

______ **e.** I visited a few friends and did a little sightseeing. On the evening of the eighteenth, I had a late dinner with some friends that I had not seen in several years. After a very peaceful evening, I returned to my hotel and quickly fell asleep.

______ **f.** In the end, approximately 5,000 people died in this terrible tragedy, but I was lucky enough not to be among them. This unexpected disaster taught me that life can be over at any minute, so it is important for us to live every day as if it is our last.

______ **g.** When I looked at my room, I could see that the floor was moving up and down like water in the ocean. Because the doorway is often the strongest part of a building, I tried to stand up in the doorway of the bathroom.

ACTIVITY 5 Copying a Paragraph

Now copy the sentences from Activity 4 in the best order for a narrative paragraph. Add a title of your choice.

Example Paragraph 74

Title ______________________________

Background information (topic sentence) ______________________________

____

____

Beginning of story ______________________________

____

____

____

____

Middle of story ______________________________

____

____

____

____

____

____

____

End of story ______________________________

____

____

____

____

For further practice with the sentences and paragraphs in this part of the unit, go to Practice 19 on pages 297–298 in Appendix 1.

Grammar for Writing

Maintaining Verb Tense Consistency

When writers tell a story, they usually use the simple past tense and perhaps the past progressive tense. Be careful to keep the verb tense consistent, or the same. For example, if your story begins with the simple past tense, do not suddenly switch to the simple present tense and then go back to the simple past tense.

Explanation	Examples
Use the **present tense** to show a general truth or activity.	My friends **live** in Mexico.
Use the **present progressive tense** to show an action that is in progress at this moment.	My friends **are living** in Mexico now.
Use the **simple past tense** to show that something happened in the past.	My friends **lived** in Mexico in 1985.
Use the **past progressive tense** to show that something was in progress at a specific time.	My friends **were living** in Mexico when the earthquake happened.

ACTIVITY 6 Identifying Verb Tenses

Read this narrative paragraph. Circle the verbs. The verbs in the first two sentences have been done for you. Then answer the questions that follow.

Example Paragraph 75

Ali's Surprise

Ali knew how difficult it was to get a student visa for the United States. However, he gathered all the important paperwork, including his I–20 document, passport, bank statements, and even a letter from his doctor. On the cold morning of his interview, he jumped on a bus to the capital. For five long hours, he rode in silence, looked out the window at the gray landscape, and wondered about the interview. When he arrived at the embassy, he saw a line of more than 100 people. He patiently waited until a guard gave him a number to enter the warm building. The faces of the embassy personnel frightened him, except for an older woman who reminded him of his grandmother. She was working at window number 4. He hoped that she would be the one to look at his paperwork. When it was his turn, he looked up quickly. A baby-faced worker at window number 3 was calling him to

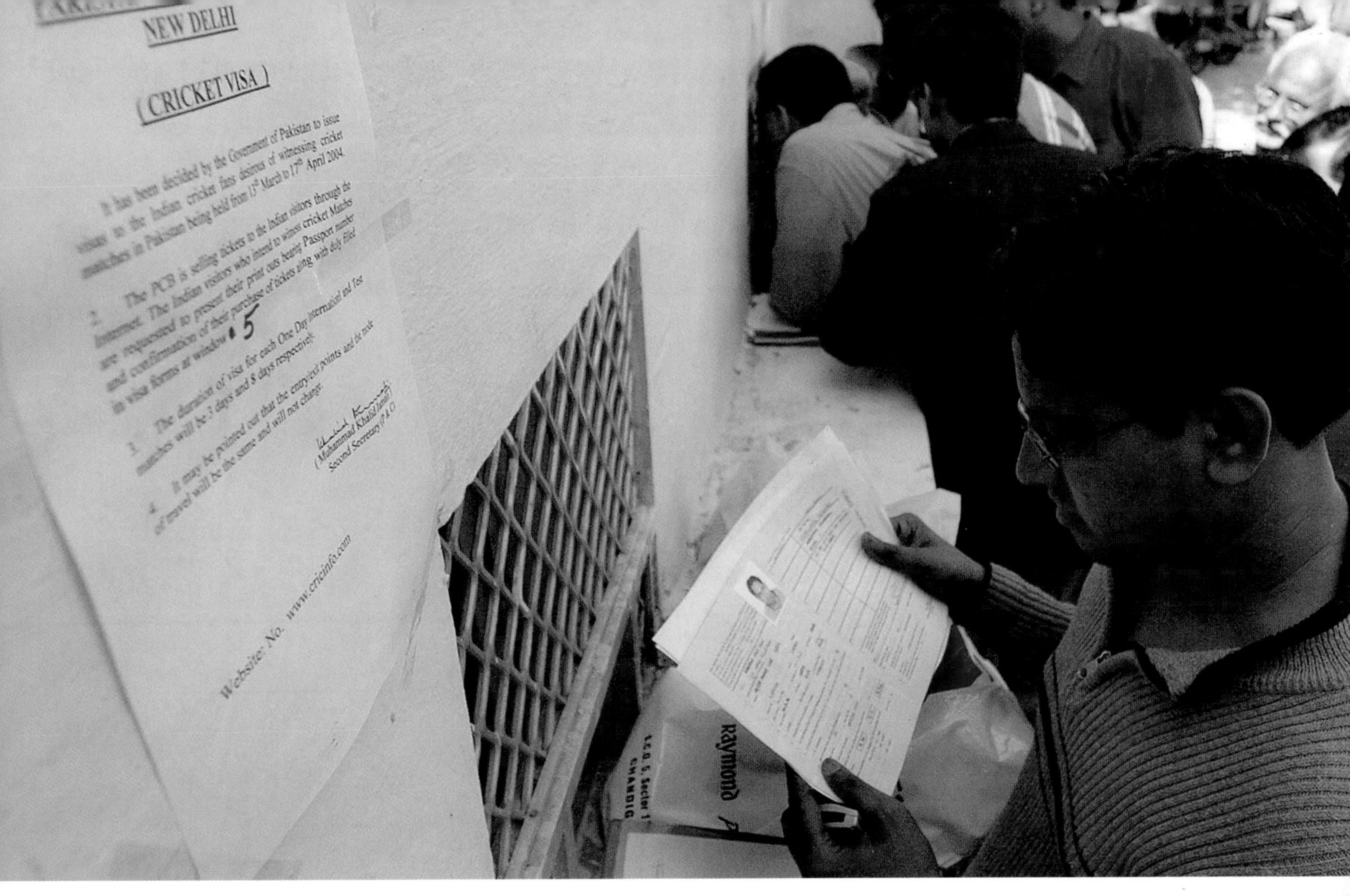

come up. Ali stepped up to the window and gave all his documents to the young embassy employee. He glanced at "Grandma" and thought his chance was gone. Then he heard her message to another man, "You will not get a visa in a thousand years! Next in line, please." Ali was shocked. He turned to the embassy worker in front of him. The worker said, "Here you are, sir. Your student visa is valid for one year." Ali could not believe it. The impossible had happened. Happily, he took his passport and left the building.

1. What tense is used for most of the verbs in this paragraph? ____________________

2. A few of the verbs are not in this tense. Can you explain this ? ____________________

____

____

____

____

ACTIVITY 7 Using Correct Verb Tenses

Read the following narrative paragraph. Circle all the verbs. Then make corrections so that all the verbs are in a tense that expresses past time—either the simple past tense or the past progressive tense.

Example Paragraph 76

My First Job

The happiest day of my life is when I get my first job last year. After college, I try and try for six months to get a job with an advertising firm, but my luck is bad. Finally, one day while I am eating a sandwich in a downtown coffee shop, my luck will begin to change. A young woman who is sitting next to me asks if she could read my newspaper. I say OK, and we start talking. She begins to tell me that she is an executive in a huge advertising company and is looking for an assistant. I will tell her that I am very interested in mass communications and study it for four years at the university. She gives me her business card, and within one week, I am her administrative assistant. It is the best lunch of my life!

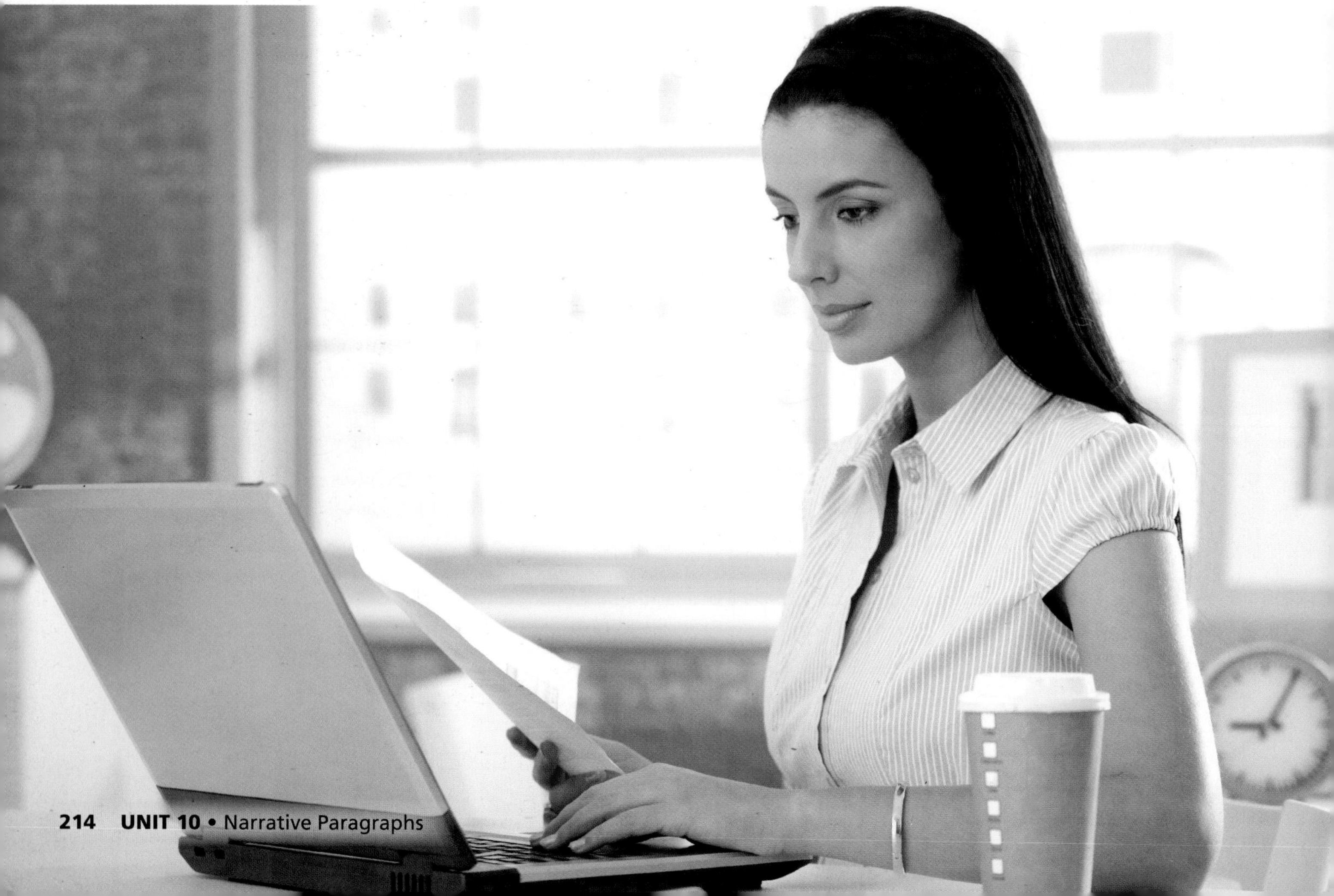

ACTIVITY 8 Editing Narrative Paragraphs

Read the teacher's four comments below and the four narrative paragraphs on pages 216–218. Match each teacher comment to the correction needed in each paragraph. Write the number on the line at the end of the paragraph.

Teacher Comments

1. *Your first sentence is too specific to be a topic sentence. Who is "her"? Your topic sentence should tell the reader what the paragraph is going to be about.*
2. *Be careful with verbs. The verbs you used jump from the simple present to the simple past tense.*
3. *Your paragraph is good. However, you didn't indent the first line of your paragraph. Be careful with correct paragraph form.*
4. *This isn't a narrative paragraph—it is a descriptive one. Follow directions more carefully.*

Example Paragraph 77

A Problem with My Creation

I took pottery lessons with her for many years, but this one time her advice led to a disaster. I made a **vase** from clay that weighed about five pounds. The clay was very wet when I finished, and it needed to dry before I could put the vase in the oven. I asked her how long I had to wait, and she told me about one week. Because it was my first time making such a large vase, I did **not think twice about** her advice. However, one week later, my vase was still wet. She put it in the oven anyway. Not long after, we heard a loud popping noise. It scared both of us, and we ran to the oven to see what was wrong. When she finally opened the oven, pieces of clay were everywhere. Because there were too many air bubbles in the wet clay, my vase exploded. It was the most terrible incident ever! After we cleaned up the mess, my pottery teacher **apologized** and said she would help me make another vase.

a vase: a container for flowers and water

to not think twice about something: do something without thinking

to apologize: say you are sorry

Teacher Comment: 1

Example Paragraph 78

My Favorite Place

My bedroom is small but comfortable. The walls are covered with posters and banners of my favorite sports teams. On the left side, there is a small bed that I have had since I was ten years old. Next to the bed is my dresser. It is blue and white with gold **knobs**. Beside the dresser is my bookshelf, which holds most of my schoolbooks, dictionaries, and novels. Across from the bookshelf, you can see my closet. It is too small to hold all my clothes, so I hang some of my stuff on my chair. The clothes get **wrinkled** there, but I do not mind. My mom does not like it that my room is so messy, so one of these days I am going to clean it up and make her happy.

a knob: a small round handle on a drawer or door

wrinkled: not smooth, with lines

Teacher Comment: 4

Example Paragraph 79

A Travel Nightmare

When I decided to travel across Europe with a backpack, I did not think I would meet the local police. My best friend and I were sitting in Frankfurt on a train bound for Paris when the nightmare began. A young man comes to the window of the train and asks me what time the train leaves. It took us only ten seconds to open the window and answer him. When we turned away from the window and sat down in our seats, we noticed that our backpacks were missing. Quickly, we got off the train and went to the police headquarters inside the station. We explained what happened. The police officers did not look surprised. They say it is a common way of stealing bags. One person stays outside the train and asks a passenger for help or information. While the passenger is talking to this person, someone else comes quietly into the train car and steals bags, purses, or other valuables. The team players are so good at it that they can steal what they want in less than three seconds. The police officers tell us that there is really nothing we can do, but they suggest that we look through the garbage cans and hope that the robbers took only our money and threw our passports and bags away. We look and look but we never found our bags. The next morning, we are not in Paris; we are at our embassy in Frankfurt, waiting for new passports.

Teacher Comment: 2

Example Paragraph 80

The Trick That Failed

Twin brothers Freddie and Felix often played tricks at school, but one day they went too far. On that day they decided to try to cheat on a French exam. Freddie was very good at learning languages and was always the best student in both Spanish and French. Felix, however, excelled in mathematics. He was not interested in languages at all. When Felix discovered that he had to take a standardized exam in French, he asked his brother for help. The day of Felix's test, they met in the boys' restroom during lunch and switched clothes. Freddie went to his brother's French class and took the test for him. Meanwhile, Felix followed Freddie's schedule. After school, the twins laughed about their trick and headed home. As they entered the house, their mother called them into the kitchen. She was furious! She had received a phone call from the school principal. The French teacher had found out about the trick! "How did he know?" cried Felix. "Easily," replied his mother. "Everyone at the school knows that one obvious difference between you and your brother is that you are right-handed and Freddie is left-handed. While the French teacher was grading the tests, he noticed that the check marks on the test were

made by a left-handed person." Felix and Freddie got into a lot of trouble that day, but they learned a valuable lesson—and they never cheated again.

Teacher Comment: 3

Building Better Sentences: For further practice with the sentences and paragraphs in this part of the unit, go to Practice 20 on page 298 in Appendix 1.

Building Better Vocabulary

ACTIVITY 9 Word Associations

Circle the word or phrase that is most closely related to the word or phrase on the left. If necessary, use a dictionary to check the meaning of words you do not know.

	A	B
1. heart-warming	a bad feeling	a good feeling
2. valuable	important	not important
3. grief	negative	positive
4. a rumble	a noise	a smell
5. to flow	to move	to seem
6. applauded	negative	positive
7. came up to me	approached me	persuaded me
8. to switch	to appreciate	to change
9. class is over at 9	it begins at 9	it ends at 9
10. to witness	to see	to think
11. to collapse*	to cancel	to fall
12. scary	afraid	necessary
13. casually	formal	not formal
14. a tragedy	a bad event	a good event
15. to hug	to embrace	to prosper

*Words that are part of the Academic Word List. See pages 275–276 for a complete list.

ACTIVITY 10 Using Collocations

Fill in each blank with the word on the left that most naturally completes the phrase on the right. If necessary, use a dictionary to check the meaning of words you do not know.

1. chance / task	a difficult ___task___
2. at / up	to set ___up___
3. deep / hard	to take a ___deep___ breath
4. lesson / nightmare	a valuable ___lesson___
5. of / on	What's going ___on___ ?
6. hear / see	___Hear___ the rumble
7. natural / tense	a ___natural___ disaster
8. shirt / truck	a wrinkled ___shirt___
9. ears / lungs	screamed at the top of her ___lungs___
10. against / without	___without___ any hesitation at all

Original Writing Practice: Narrative Paragraph

ACTIVITY 11 Original Writing Practice

Write a narrative paragraph about an experience that you have had. Follow these guidelines:

- Choose a topic such as your first time driving a car, your graduation day, or a special event in your life.
- Brainstorm the events in your story.
- Write a topic sentence with controlling ideas.
- Give enough background information to help your readers understand the setting.
- Write supporting sentences for the middle of your narrative.
- Check for consistency in simple past and past progressive verbs.
- Use descriptive vocabulary words.
- Write the end of the story.
- Use at least two of the vocabulary words or phrases presented in Activity 9 and Activity 10. Underline these words and phrases in your paragraph.

If you need ideas for words and phrases, see the Useful Vocabulary for Better Writing on pages 277–281.

ACTIVITY 12 Peer Editing

Exchange papers from Activity 11 with a partner. Read your partner's paragraph. Then use Peer Editing Sheet 10 on NGL.Cengage.com/GW2 to help you comment on your partner's paragraph. Be sure to offer positive suggestions and comments that will help your partner improve his or her writing. Consider your partner's comments as you revise your own paragraph.

Additional Topics for Writing

Here are some ideas for narrative paragraphs. When you write your paragraph, follow the guidelines in Activity 11.

PHOTO TOPIC: Look at the photo on pages 198–199. Write about a surprising, frightening, happy, or funny experience you have had.

TOPIC 2: Create a short story using an animal as the main character. What happens to this animal? You can tell a story from your own country or culture that you think foreigners would not know.

TOPIC 3: Write about how someone you know got in trouble. What happened?

TOPIC 4: Write about an important lesson that you have learned from a real experience.

TOPIC 5: Write about the most memorable movie you have seen. Briefly explain the plot (story) of the film.

Timed Writing

How quickly can you write in English? There are many times when you must write quickly, such as on a test. It is important to feel comfortable during those times. Timed-writing practice can make you feel better about writing quickly in English.

1. Take out a piece of paper.
2. Read the writing prompt.
3. Brainstorm ideas for five minutes.
4. Write a short narrative paragraph (six to ten sentences).
5. You have 25 minutes to write.

Choose a specific event from your childhood that you consider special or significant. Why do you still remember this event? You might decide to write about your first day of school, a particularly difficult class or exam, a time when you were called to the principal's office for something you had done, or one of your early birthday parties. Describe the people and places that are related to the event. Use descriptive language to help your readers imagine that they were actually there with you at the event. Your goal is to make your readers clearly understand why this event is so special or significant to you.

Unit

11 Paragraphs in an Essay: Putting It All Together

Two Mongolian men talking on a cellphone in Xilingol Grassland, Inner Mongolia, China.

OBJECTIVES To understand how paragraphs and essays are related
To understand the basic steps in composing an essay
To write an essay

Can you write an essay about the effect of technology in rural places?

From Paragraphs to Essays

In this book, you have studied many different aspects of writing a good paragraph, including these five features:

✓ **INDENTED LINE**	The first line of a paragraph is indented.
✓ **ONLY ONE TOPIC**	All of the sentences in the paragraph are about one topic.
✓ **TOPIC SENTENCE**	A paragraph has a topic sentence that states the main idea.
✓ **SUPPORTING DETAILS**	The writer gives supporting details about the ideas in the topic sentence.
✓ **CONCLUDING SENTENCE**	The last sentence, or concluding sentence, brings the paragraph to a logical conclusion.

The steps in the process of writing a paragraph are:

- developing ideas (brainstorming)
- narrowing down the topic
- creating the topic sentence and controlling idea(s)
- writing supporting sentences (developing the ideas)
- writing concluding sentences (ending the paragraph)
- editing and revising your writing

Now that you have reviewed some facts about paragraphs, it is time to study how paragraphs work together to form an essay.

ACTIVITY 1 What Do You Know about Essays?

Answer these questions. Then work in small groups to compare answers.

1. What do you think an essay is? ______________________________

____

____

2. Have you ever written an essay? ❑ yes ❑ no If yes, what was the topic of one of your essays?

____

How long was that essay? ______________________________

3. What do you think the differences between a paragraph and an essay are? ______________________________

____

____

____

Getting to Know Essays

What Is an Essay?

An **essay** is a collection of paragraphs that presents facts, opinions, and ideas on a topic. An essay can be as short as three or four paragraphs or as long as ten or more typed pages that include many paragraphs.

People write essays for many possible reasons.

- An essay is a common assignment for students in an English composition class. Students write essays on various topics to practice their writing skills.
- Students also write essays for other classes, such as literature, history, or science classes. In these classes, the essays are about topics in the subject matter of the course. A research paper is a longer kind of essay.
- For students who want to enter a college or university, it is often necessary to take a standardized exam such as the American College Test (ACT), Scholastic Aptitude Test (SAT), Graduate Record Exam (GRE), or the Test of English as a Foreign Language (TOEFL). All of these exams have a writing section that requires student to write an essay.

How Are Essays and Paragraphs Similar?

Essays are similar to paragraphs in a number of ways. The following chart shows the main elements that paragraphs and essays have in common.

Comparison of Paragraphs and Essays

Purpose of Parts	Paragraph	Essay
Introduction • Gets readers interested. • Gives the main idea.	Topic sentence	Hook Thesis statement
Body • Organizes the main points. • Gives supporting information.	Supporting sentences	Supporting paragraphs Topic sentences
Conclusion • Signals the end of the writing.	Concluding sentence	Concluding paragraph

How Are Essays and Paragraphs Different?

much more

The main difference between an essay and a paragraph is the length and, therefore, the scope of the information. Remember that the length depends on the topic and on the purpose of the writing. For example, imagine that your teacher gives you the general topic of university education. You are asked to write a *paragraph* about something related to university education. A paragraph usually has five to ten sentences, so you must narrow down your subject to include the most important information in these few sentences. Your paragraph topic could be the tuition costs at the university.

On the other hand, your teacher might ask you to write an *essay* about university education. Your essay will need to include several paragraphs about a larger topic, such as a comparison of university and community college education. In this case, your five paragraphs could be 1. a thesis about the trends in higher education costs, 2. university costs, 3. community college costs, 4. the costs vs. economic conditions, and finally, 5. a concluding paragraph. In general, the topic of each paragraph is very specific while the essay topic must cover a wider scope.

ACTIVITY 2 Topics for Paragraphs and Essay

Each pair of sentences is about one topic. Decide which sentence is the topic sentence for a paragraph (P) and which is the thesis statement for an essay (E). (Hint: The thesis statements cover more information.)

1. Topic: Japanese customs

a. ________ If you travel to Japan, you should first find out about Japanese customs, taboos, and people.

b. ________ The worst mistake that a foreigner can make with Japanese customs is standing up chopsticks in a bowl of rice.

2. Topic: Education in Taiwan and the United States

a. ________ One difference between the educational systems in Taiwan and the United States is the role of sports programs in the curriculum.

b. ________ Because I have studied in both countries, I have seen several areas in which education in Taiwan and education in the United States are different.

3. Topic: Household chores

a. ________ Ironing clothes is my most dreaded household task because it cannot be completed quickly or thoughtlessly.

b. ________ The three most dreaded household tasks include ironing clothes, washing dishes, and cleaning the bathroom.

4. Topic: School uniforms

a. ________ Wearing school uniforms is a good choice for public school students for a number of reasons.

b. ________ Wearing school uniforms would make students' morning routines much simpler.

5. Topic: Sports in society

a. ________ In my opinion, there is too much emphasis on sports in our society, and this emphasis has many negative effects on all of us.

b. ________ One serious effect of society's love of sports is that our children learn that winning is the most important part of any sport.

What Does an Essay Look Like?

There are many different kinds of essays just as there are many different kinds of paragraphs. The following example essay is simple, clearly organized, and easy to understand. It was written by a student in an English composition class. This was the assignment:

> Many inventions in the past 100 years have changed people's lives. In your opinion, which invention has been the most important and why? Use specific examples and details in your essay.

As you read the essay, notice the thesis statement that states the main idea of the essay, the topic sentence in each paragraph, and the transition words that help connect ideas.

Example Essay 1

The Most Important Invention in the Last Century

1 When you woke up today, you turned on the lights, ran the hot water in the shower, put on mass-produced clothing, watched television, drove to work in your car, and checked your e-mail on your computer or phone. Every day we are surrounded by thousands of useful things that were invented only a relatively short time ago. *In fact,* we depend on these things for the good quality of life that we have now. All of these inventions have been very important to humans, but the one that has been the most important in improving people's health over the centuries is the discovery of antibiotics.

Transition Phrase → *In fact*

Thesis Statement → All of these inventions have been very important to humans, but the one that has been the most important in improving people's health over the centuries is the discovery of antibiotics.

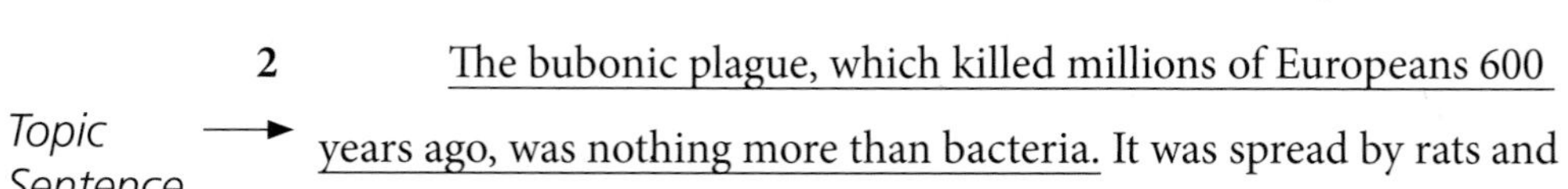

2 The bubonic plague, which killed millions of Europeans 600 years ago, was nothing more than bacteria. It was spread by rats and

Topic Sentence → The bubonic plague, which killed millions of Europeans 600 years ago, was nothing more than bacteria.

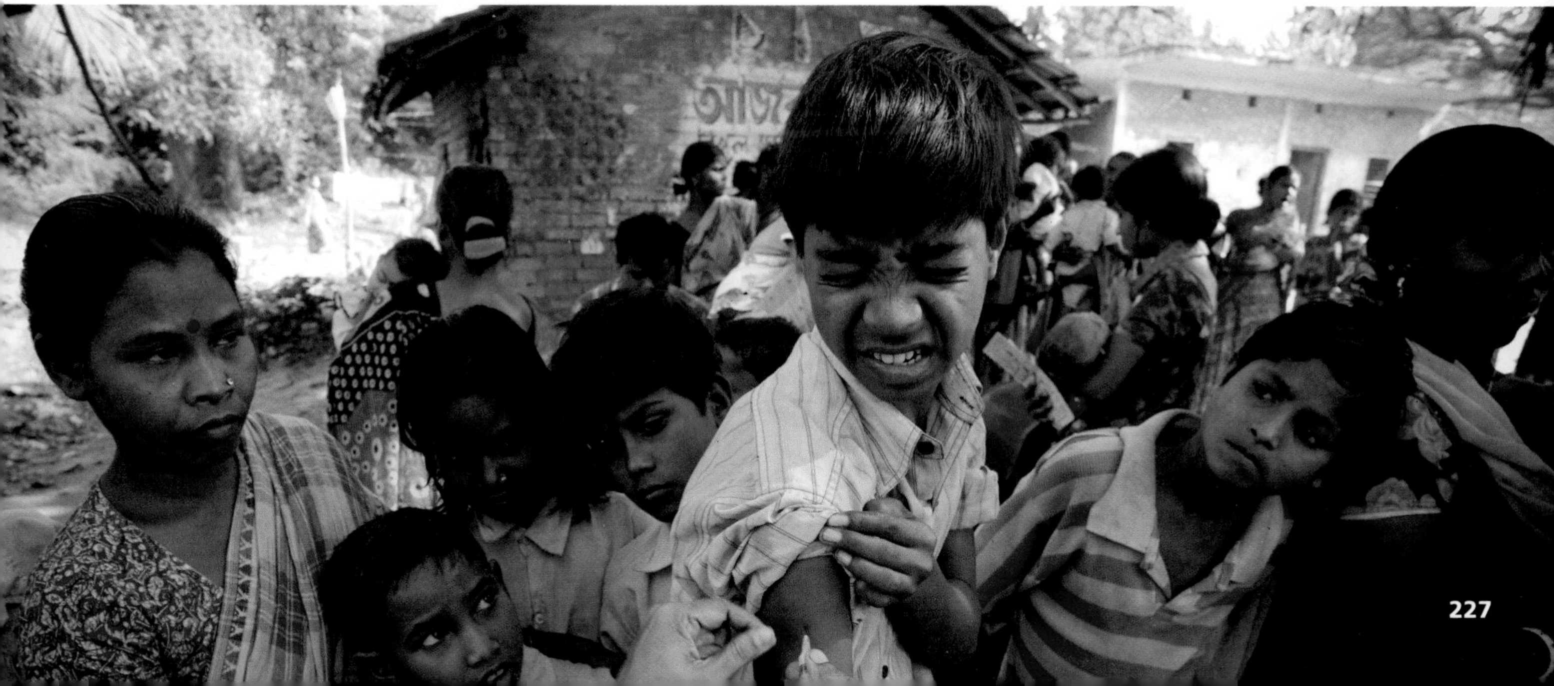

fleas. This disease was also called the Black Death because when a person **contracted** the disease, his or her neck and face would swell up and turn black. Back then, no one was aware that this plague could have easily been treated with penicillin. The Black Plague eventually retreated, but people were still in danger of dying from simple bacteria.

3 Even as recently as 100 years ago, medical knowledge was much more limited than it is now. Something as **trivial** as a simple cut could sometimes result in an **amputation** or even death if it became **infected.** Medical professionals knew what was happening; *however,* there was simply no way to stop the infection from spreading or causing more harm. The discovery of penicillin in the early part of the twentieth century changed all of that. Antibiotics finally enabled humans to maintain their good health and continue their lives for many more years.

← *Topic Sentence*

← *Transition Word*

Transition Phrase → 4 *In fact*, antibiotics are an inexpensive and effective treatment for a number of **ailments**. When we have an infection nowadays, we do not think about it too much. We go to the doctor, who will prescribe some kind of medicine. We take this medicine as directed, and *then,* after a few days, we are healthy again. The medicine is probably a form of antibiotics. *In addition,* these antibiotics are painless and fast acting. Without them, countless people would suffer through painful and life-threatening ailments.

← *Topic Sentence*

← *Transition Word*

Transition Phrase →

5 When people think of the most important invention in the past 100 years, most people think about electricity, cars, airplanes, or computers. While all of these are certainly extremely important, the invention of antibiotics promoted good health and longer lives. People tend to take antibiotics and other medicine for granted, but they should not do this. If antibiotics had not been invented in the past century, millions of people would have died much earlier, and human beings would not be able to enjoy the quality of life that we have today.

← *Restated Thesis*

a flea: a small insect that lives on animals; it jumps very quickly

to contract: to get something, such as a disease

trivial: not important

an amputation: the removal of an exterior body part, such as a leg or an arm

to be infected: to have disease-producing bacteria (or similar substances) in the body

an ailment: a sickness, an illness

An Essay Outline

The steps in writing an essay are similar to the steps in writing a good paragraph. After you brainstorm a suitable topic for an essay or paragraph, you think about an introduction, supporting ideas, and a conclusion. For an essay, an important step is to make an **outline.** Here is an outline of "The Most Important Invention in the Last Century" that you just read. Reread the essay before you read the outline. Then compare the essay information with the outline to help you understand its organization better.

I. Introduction (Paragraph 1)—Many important things have been invented in the last century, but the most important was the discovery of antibiotics.

II. Body (Paragraph 2)—Hundreds of years ago, millions of Europeans died from bubonic plague.

III. Body (Paragraph 3)—Medicine was limited until the invention of penicillin in the early twentieth century.

IV. Body (Paragraph 4)—Antibiotics are currently used for a variety of ailments.

V. Conclusion (Paragraph 5)—The invention of antibiotics promoted good health and longer lives.

The Hook

The very first thing that good writers do is get their readers' attention with an interesting sentence, which is called a **hook** because it hooks, or catches, the readers. There are several kinds of hooks, and all of them are good tools.

Type of Hook	Examples
A Question	Have you ever wondered how a jet with 300 passengers can lift off from the earth?
A Comparison	My bedroom is like an art museum in any large city.
A Problem	When I won an air ticket to any place that I wanted to visit, I had a hard time selecting my destination city.
A Quotation or Proverb	They say that "the grass always looks greener on the other side of the fence," and there is good reason for people to believe this statement.

The Thesis Statement

We learned that the most important part of any paragraph is the topic sentence. The first paragraph of an essay has a similar sentence that is called a **thesis statement.** It tells the reader what the essay is about. The thesis statement also indicates what the organization of the essay will be. The thesis statement is usually the last sentence in the introduction paragraph. Find and reread the thesis statement in "The Most Important Invention in the Last Century." (Answer: "All of these inventions have been very important to humans, but the one that has been the most important in improving people's health over the centuries is the discovery of antibiotics.")

Now read these examples of thesis statements.

1. Three things make traveling to Southeast Asia an unforgettable experience.
2. Serving in the military offers not only professional advantages but also personal benefits.
3. The person I most respect and admire is my Aunt Josephine.

As you can see, the topics for the essays with these thesis statements range from serious subjects to personal stories. The thesis statement that you write will depend on the assignment that your teacher gives you.

Supporting Ideas

Essays need **supporting ideas** just like paragraphs. Writers should have two or three ideas that support the thesis statement. Each of these ideas will eventually become a separate paragraph. Asking a question about the thesis statement is a good way to come up with material for supporting paragraphs. Remember that it is important to provide specific examples and details within the paragraph.

Here are some questions to ask and ideas to develop about the thesis statements you read on page 229.

1. Three things make traveling to Southeast Asia an unforgettable experience.

Question: Why is it an unforgettable experience?

Possible ideas to develop: The people are very friendly; there are beautiful places to see; the food is incredibly delicious.

2. Serving in the military offers not only professional advantages but also personal benefits.

Question: What are these advantages and benefits?

Possible ideas to develop: Professional advantages: a full-time job with good benefits, vocational training. Personal benefits: a sense of pride in serving one's country, developing maturity

3. The person I most respect and admire is my Aunt Josephine.

Question: Why do you admire her so much?

Possible ideas to develop: She taught me about hard work; she loved me unconditionally; she always gave me excellent advice.

Different Kinds of Essay Organization

Once you write a thesis statement, you can develop your essay in different ways. In the following activity, you will work with some possibilities for essay organization.

ACTIVITY 3 Working with Essay Organization

Read the thesis statements of four essays and the outlines of the first two essays. For the last two, write a brief outline that shows how you might organize the essay. Follow the first two examples.

1. Thesis Statement: Prisoner education has succeeded by providing various programs that help inmates be successful when they are released.

   I. Introduction (Paragraph 1)
   II. Body (Paragraph 2): *Program 1*
   III. Body (Paragraph 3): *Program 2*
   IV. Body (Paragraph 4): *Program 3*
   V. Body (Paragraph 5): *One or more examples of a prison that uses all three of these programs*
   VI. Conclusion (Paragraph 6)

2. Thesis Statement: Three things make traveling to Southeast Asia an unforgettable experience.

   I. Introduction (Paragraph 1)
   II. Body (Paragraph 2): *Friendly people*
   III. Body (Paragraph 3): *Beautiful sights*
   IV. Body (Paragraph 4): *Incredibly tasty food*
   V. Conclusion (Paragraph 5)

3. Thesis Statement: Computer literacy is important for children for many reasons.

____

____

____

____

____

____

4. Thesis Statement: The person I most respect and admire is my Aunt Josephine.

____

____

____

____

____

____

ACTIVITY 4 Comparing Outlines

Now work in groups to compare your outlines from Activity 3. Discuss how you would develop the ideas in the essays in items 3 and 4 based on your outline.

ACTIVITY 5 Working with a Sample Essay

Read and study the essay on pages 232–233.

Example Essay 2

The Benefits of Being Bilingual

1 The Vieira family moved to the United States in 2001. At that time, they made a decision. They decided to stop speaking Portuguese at home and only communicate in English. They were, in fact, living in an English-speaking country. The Vieira children are adults now, and from time to time they travel to Portugal to visit old family and friends. There is a problem, however. Mr. and Mrs. Vieira's children cannot communicate with their relatives. This particular event happens frequently all over the world. When people immigrate to new lands, many of them begin to disregard not only their cultural traditions but also their native language. Over time, they lose the many benefits to being bilingual.

2 One of the most basic advantages of being bilingual is being able to communicate with more people around the world. People do not have to rely on others to automatically know their own language or use an interpreter to get their message across. These bilingual people are independent and self-reliant. In contrast, people who are monolingual must put all their trust in others in order to make communication happen. Bilinguals are masters of their own words and ideas.

3 Speaking a second language also allows people to experience another culture. Even if these people have never visited another country, bilingualism enhances cultural and social awareness of another group of people. Idiomatic expressions, vocabulary, and even jokes can have a powerful impact on a person's understanding of another culture. For example, a person who speaks American English knows the expression "to put your John Hancock*" on something, which means to sign your name. However, only people who know about John Hancock's role in the signing of the Declaration of Independence can fully understand the literal meaning and historical significance of this expression. Thus, becoming bilingual clearly increases knowledge of a new culture.

4 Finally, widespread bilingualism can contribute to global awareness. If everyone in the world spoke a second or third language, people could better communicate and perhaps have a better global understanding of others' ideas, values, and behaviors. Being able to speak another country's language makes people more understanding of the problems and situations in that country. Conversely, not knowing the language of a potential enemy can only increase miscommunication and suspicion.

Body Paragraph 3

5 The benefits of bilingualism are clear. In fact, there is no single disadvantage to speaking more than one language. The real tragedy, however, is not that people do not make the effort to study and learn a second language. The problem is that people who already have the gift of speaking another language forget it and lose the ability to communicate in that language because they do not use it.

Conclusion

Cultural Note: This expression has a much larger historical context. When the American colonists wrote the Declaration of Independence, some people were afraid to sign their name because this action put their lives in danger. However, John Hancock was not afraid and wrote his name first on the list and in very big letters so the king would have no trouble seeing it. From this part of American history and culture, we have the modern expression "to put your John Hancock" on a document.

Post-Reading

Circle the best answer.

1. How does the essay begin?

   a. a fact **b.** an opinion **c.** a story

2. Reread the concluding paragraph. Which word best describes it?

   a. suggestion **b.** opinion **c.** prediction

3. Which paragraph discusses the cultural benefits of speaking a second language?

   a. Paragraph 1 **b.** Paragraph 3 **c.** Paragraph 5

4. Which paragraph discusses the global benefits of bilingualism?

   a. Paragraph 1 **b.** Paragraph 2 **c.** Paragraph 4

5. Which paragraph gives the author's opinion about people who have lost a language?

   a. Paragraph 2 **b.** Paragraph 3 **c.** Paragraph 5

ACTIVITY 6 Working with an Outline

Reread "The Benefits of Being Bilingual" and complete the outline.

I. Introduction (Paragraph 1)

A. Hook: *Story of Vieira children*

B. Thesis Statement: Over time, they lose the many benefits to being bilingual.

II. Body

A. Paragraph 2: Topic Sentence: One of the most basic advantages of being bilingual is being able to communicate w/ more people around the world

1. Supporting Idea: *They can communicate with more people.*

2. Supporting Idea: *They do not need an interpreter.*

3. Supporting Idea: *They are in charge of their own ideas.*

4. Supporting Idea: *Monolingual people cannot speak on their own.*

B. Paragraph 3: Topic Sentence: *Speaking a second language also allows people to experience another culture.*

1. Supporting Idea: *Bilinguals have more cultural and social awareness of another group of people.*

2. Supporting Idea: *Idiomatic expressions, vocabulary, and jokes help people understand a different culture.*

3. Supporting Idea (example): "To put your John Hancock" on something = to sign your name.

C. Paragraph 4: Topic Sentence: Widespread bilingualism can contribute to global awareness.

1. Supporting Idea: *Countries could become closer.*

2. Supporting Idea: People can more understand the problems and situations in that country.

3. Supporting Idea: *Not knowing an enemy's language can increase miscommunication.*

III. Concluding paragraph (Paragraph 5)

A. Restatement of Thesis: *Bilingualism has only positive effects.*

B. Opinion: The problem is that people who already speak a foreign language forget it or do not use it.

In class

Putting an Essay Together

Now that you have learned some of the basics of an essay, it is time to practice writing one. In the following activities, you will work with your classmates to produce an essay.

ACTIVITY 7 Brainstorming

In this activity, you will brainstorm ideas for an essay that you will write in Activity 8. Read the following essay topic. Then follow the steps below to brainstorm ideas about this topic.

Topic: Living in a big city is better than living in a small town.

1. Form three groups. Each group must brainstorm and come up with as many reasons as possible why living in a large city is better than living in a small town.

Your group's reasons: ______________________________

____

____

____

2. Write all your ideas on the board. As a class, vote for the three best reasons. (These reasons will become the topic sentences for the essay you will write in Activity 8.) Each group will brainstorm examples for one reason. Decide which reason each group will write about. Write them below.

Group 1 reason: ______________________________

____

Group 2 reason: ______________________________

____

Group 3 reason: ______________________________

____

3. Brainstorm some examples that support your topic sentence (reason).

____

____

____

____

4. Share your group's examples with the rest of the class. Fill in the list below.

Group 1 reason: ______________________________

Examples: ______________________________

____

Group 2 reason: ______________________________

Examples: ______________________________

____

Group 3 reason: ______________________________

Examples: ______________________________

____

ACTIVITY 8 Writing an Essay Draft

You are now ready to complete an essay. Read the following partial essay and fill in the blanks with the information you gathered. Use additional paper if necessary.

The Advantages of City Life

1 The population of Small Hills is 2,500. Everyone knows everyone else. The mayor of the city is also the owner of the sporting goods store. There is only one school in Small Hills, and all the students know each other, from age six to age eighteen. On weekends, many residents of Small Hills go to the only restaurant in town, and perhaps after dinner, they go to the only movie theater. This routine continues. On the other hand, the population of Los Angeles is approximately 4 million. It is a city that is so culturally diverse that at any given time one can go to any type of restaurant, watch any type of movie, and see countless exhibits and museums. Which type of life is better? It seems obvious that living in a large city full of diversity is much better than living in a small, rural community.

2 First, living in a large city is better because ______________________________

____

____

____

____

____

____

____

3 In addition, city life can ______________________________

____

____

____

____

____

____

____

4 Finally, large cities give people the opportunity to ________________________________

____

____

____

____

____

____

____

5 In conclusion, there are many benefits to living in a large city. While some people might be afraid of existing among such a large group of people, the benefits that a large city can afford its citizens are well worth it. Besides, there is always a quiet, relaxed place, even in busy metropolitan areas.

ACTIVITY 9 Peer Editing

Exchange books with a partner and look at Activity 8. Read your partner's essay. Then use Peer Editing Sheet 11 on NGL.Cengage.com/GW2 to help you comment on your partner's essay. Be sure to offer positive suggestions and comments that will help your partner improve his or her writing. Consider your partner's comments as you revise your own essay.

Building Better Vocabulary

ACTIVITY 10 Word Associations

Circle the word or phrase that is most closely related to the word or phrase on the left. If necessary, use a dictionary to check the meaning of words you do not know.

	A	B
1. to narrow down	to become general	to become specific
2. aware*	you realize	you do not realize
3. threatening	negative	positive
4. trivial	important	not important
5. widespread*	common	rare
6. dreaded	negative	positive

7. the mayor	one person	most people
8. obvious*	easy to recognize	hard to recognize
9. a routine	usual	unusual
10. disregard	ignore	multiple
11. enhance*	approach	improve
12. enable*	allow	occur
13. potential*	possible	powerful
14. countless	a few	a lot
15. an infection	a health benefit	a health problem

*Words that are part of the Academic Word List. See pages 275–276 for a complete list.

ACTIVITY 11 Using Collocations

Fill in each blank with the word on the left that most naturally completes the phrase on the right. If necessary, use a dictionary to check the meaning of words you do not know.

1. of / on — the scope ___of___ a report
2. make / take — to ___take___ something for granted
3. come / know — to ___come___ up with a good example
4. car / job — a full-time ___job___
5. of / on — the role ___of___ education
6. friendly / specific — a ___specific___ example
7. give / show — to ___give___ a person some advice
8. in / on — an emphasis ___on___ sports
9. on / to — X has an impact ___on___ Y
10. danger / tragedy — to put their lives in great ___danger___

Original Student Writing: Essay

ACTIVITY 12 Essay Writing Practice

Write an essay about one of the topics in this list.

Narrative Essay:	Tell a story about a time in your life when you learned a valuable lesson.
Comparison Essay:	What are the differences between being an entrepreneur and working for a company?
Cause-Effect Essay:	Why do some people prefer to take classes online rather than in a traditional classroom setting?
Argumentative Essay:	Should high schools include physical education in their curriculum or devote their time to teaching only academic subjects?

- Use at least two of the vocabulary words or phrases presented in Activity 10 and Activity 11. Underline these words and phrases in your essay.
- Be sure to follow the steps of the writing process in the *Brief Writer's Handbook with Activities* (see Understanding the Writing Process: The Seven Steps on pages 244–250). The most important steps for both paragraphs and essays are:

    1. choosing a good topic
    2. brainstorming ideas
    3. outlining / organizing ideas
    4. writing the first draft
    5. getting feedback from a peer
    6. revising
    7. proofreading the final draft

If you need ideas for words and phrases, see the Useful Vocabulary for Better Writing on pages 277–281.

Additional Topics for Writing

Here are some ideas for essays. When you write your essay, follow the guidelines in Activity 12.

PHOTO TOPIC: Look at the photo on pages 222–223. Write about the effect of technology in rural places.

TOPIC 2: Write about the daily life of a taxi driver. What do you think happens during a typical day? What are some of the joys and challenges?

TOPIC 3: Write about why you think people are getting married at an older age. What are some of the reasons? What are some of the benefits?

TOPIC 4: Write about ways and techniques you use to prepare for a big exam. How do you plan your time? What are your best strategies?

TOPIC 5: Write about the value of competition. What does it provide? How is it beneficial?

Timed Writing

In many classes, you will be asked to write short essays within a limited amount of time. Good writers use their time wisely by reading the writing prompt two or three times, spending a few minutes brainstorming the topic, and outlining their ideas before they begin writing their draft. By doing these steps, they often have time to review their writing before they turn it in. In this assignment, your instructor will give you a time limit for writing a basic essay in class.

Read the essay guidelines and writing prompt below. On a piece of paper, write a basic outline for this writing prompt (include the thesis statement and your three main points). When you have completed your outline (try to use no more than five minutes), write a five-paragraph essay. The total time for all your writing is 40 minutes.

Essay Guidelines

- Remember to give your essay a title.
- Double-space your writing.
- Write as legibly as possible (if you are not using a computer).
- Include a short introduction (with a thesis statement), three body paragraphs, and a conclusion.

What should happen to students who are caught cheating on an exam? Why?

Brief Writer's Handbook with Activities

Understanding the Writing Process: The Seven Steps

This section can be studied at any time during the course. You will want to refer to the seven steps many times as you write your paragraphs.

The Assignment

Imagine that you have been given the following assignment: *Write a definition paragraph about an everyday item.*

What should you do first? What should you do second, third, and so on? There are many ways to write, but most good writers follow certain general steps in the writing process.

Look at this list of steps. Which ones do you usually do? Which ones have you never done?

STEP 1: Choose a topic.

STEP 2: Brainstorm.

STEP 3: Outline.

STEP 4: Write the first draft.

STEP 5: Get feedback from a peer.

STEP 6: Revise the first draft.

STEP 7: Proofread the final draft.

Now you will see how one student went through all the steps to do the assignment. First, read the final paragraph that Susan gave her teacher. Read the teacher's comments as well.

Example Paragraph 44

Gumbo

The dictionary definition of *gumbo* does not make gumbo sound as delicious as it really is. The dictionary defines gumbo as a "thick soup made in south Louisiana." However, anyone who has tasted this delicious dish knows that this definition is too bland to describe gumbo. It is true that gumbo is a thick soup, but it is much more than that. Gumbo, one of the most popular of all Cajun dishes, is made with different kinds of seafood or meat mixed with vegetables, such as green peppers and onions. For example, seafood gumbo contains shrimp and crab. Other kinds of gumbo include chicken, sausage, or turkey. Regardless of the ingredients in gumbo, this regional delicacy is very delicious.

Teacher comments:

100/A+ Excellent paragraph!

I enjoyed reading about gumbo. Your paragraph is very well written. All the sentences relate to one single topic. I really like the fact that you used so many connectors—however, such as.

Now look at the steps that Susan went through to compose the paragraph that you just read.

Steps in the Writing Process

Step 1: Choose a Topic

Susan chose gumbo as her topic. This is what she wrote about her choice.

When I first saw the assignment, I did not know what to write about. I did not think I was going to be able to find a good topic.

First, I tried to think of something that I could define. It could not be something that was really simple like television or a car. Everyone already knows what they are. I thought that I should choose something that most people might not know.

I tried to think of general areas like sports, machines, and inventions. However, I chose food as my general area. Everyone likes food.

Then I had to find one kind of food that not everyone knows. For me, that was not too difficult. My family is from Louisiana, and the food in Louisiana is special. It is not the usual food that most Americans eat. One of the dishes we eat a lot in Louisiana is gumbo, which is a kind of thick soup. I thought gumbo would be a good topic for a definition paragraph because not many people know it, and it is sort of easy for me to write a definition for this food.

Another reason that gumbo is a good choice for a definition paragraph is that I know a lot about this kind of food. I know how to make it, I know what the ingredients are, and I know what it tastes like. It is much easier to write about something that I know than about something that I do not know about.

After I was sure that gumbo was going to be my topic, I went on to the next step, which is brainstorming.

Susan's notes about choosing her topic

Step 2: Brainstorm

The next step for Susan was to brainstorm ideas about her topic.

In this step, you write down every idea that pops into your head about your topic. Some of these ideas will be good, and some will be bad—write them all down. The main purpose of brainstorming is to write down as many ideas as you can think of. If one idea looks especially good, you might circle that idea or put a check mark next to it. If you write down an idea and you know right away that you are not going to use it, you can cross it out.

Look at Susan's brainstorming diagram on the topic of gumbo.

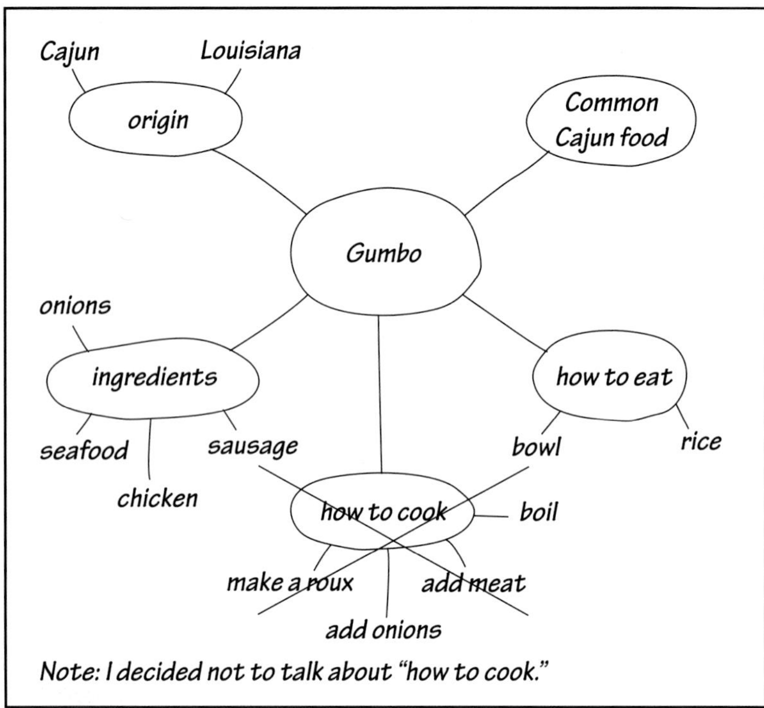

Susan's brainstorming diagram

Step 3: Outline

At this point, some writers want to start writing, but that is not the best plan. After you brainstorm your ideas, the next step is to make an outline. An outline helps you organize how you will present your information. It helps you see which areas of the paragraph are strong and which are weak.

After brainstorming, Susan studied her list of ideas. She then made a simple outline of what her paragraph might look like. Some writers prepare very detailed outlines, but many writers just make a list of the main points and some of the details for each main point.

Read the outline that Susan wrote.

What is gumbo?

1. A simple definition of gumbo.

2. A longer definition of gumbo.

3. A list of the different ingredients of gumbo.

- *A. seafood or meat*
- *B. with vegetables (onions)*
- *C. seafood gumbo*

4. How gumbo is served.

Susan's outline

As you can see, this outline is very basic. There are also some problems. For example, Susan repeats some items in different parts of the outline. In addition, she does not have a concluding sentence. These errors will probably be corrected at the first draft step, the peer editing step, or the final draft step.

Step 4: Write the First Draft

Next, Susan wrote a first draft. In this step, you use the information from your outline and from your brainstorming session to write a first draft. This first draft may contain many errors, such as misspellings, incomplete ideas, and incorrect punctuation. At this point, do not worry about correcting the errors. The main goal is to put your ideas into sentences.

You may feel that you do not know what you think about the topic yet. In this case, it may be difficult for you to write, but it is important to start the process of writing. Sometimes writing helps you think, and as soon as you form a new thought, you can write it down.

Read Susan's first draft, including her notes to herself.

(Rough draft)
Susan Mims

Introduction is weak ??? Use dictionary!

Do you know what gumbo is. It's a seafood soup. However, gumbo is really more than a kind of soup, it's special. ???

Gumbo is one of the most popular of all Cajun dish. es

Combine: It's made with various kind of seafood or meet. s meat
This is mixed with vegetables such as onions. + green peppers

Combine: Seafood Gumbo is made with shrimp and crab. g
Also chicken, sausage, and turkey, etc. Regardless ok ???
of what is in Gumbo, it's usually served in bowl g a
over the rice.
Is this correct? Ask teacher!

Susan's first draft

What do you notice about this first draft? Here are a few things that a good writer should pay attention to:

- First of all, remember that this paper is not the final draft. Even native speakers who are good writers usually write more than one draft. You will have a chance to revise the paper and make it better.
- Look at the circles, question marks, and writing in the margin. These are notes that Susan made to herself about what to change, add, or reconsider.
- Remember that the paper will go through the peer-editing process later. Another reader will help you make your meaning clear and will look for errors.

In addition to the language errors that writers often make in the first draft, the handwriting is usually not neat. Sometimes it is so messy that only the writer can read it!

Step 5: Get Feedback from a Peer

Peer editing a draft is a critical step toward the final goal of excellent writing. Sometimes it is difficult for writers to see the weaknesses in their own writing, so receiving advice from another writer can be very helpful.

Ask a colleague, friend, or classmate to read your writing and to offer suggestions about how to improve it. Some people do not like criticism, but constructive criticism is always helpful for writers. Remember that even professional writers have editors, so do not be embarrassed to receive help.

Susan exchanged papers with another student, Jim, in her class. On the next page is the peer editing sheet that Jim completed about Susan's paragraph. Read the questions and answers.

Peer Editing Sheet

Writer: Susan Date: 2-14

Peer Editor: Jim

1. What is the general topic of the paper? gumbo

2. What is the writer's purpose? (in 15 words or less)

to define gumbo

3. Is the paragraph indented? ☑ yes ❑ no

4. How many sentences are there? 6

5. Is the first word of every sentence capitalized? ☑ yes ❑ no
If you answered *no,* circle the problem(s) on the paper.

6. Does every sentence end with correct punctuation? ❑ yes ☑ no
If you answered *no,* circle the problem(s) on the paper.

7. Are there any other capitalization or punctuation errors? ☑ yes ❑ no
If you answered *yes,* circle the problem(s) on the paper.

8. Write the topic sentence here.

You have two sentences: Do you know what gumbo is. It is a seafood soup.

9. Do you think the topic sentence is good for this paragraph? Comments?

No, you need one sentence that introduces your topic and purpose better.

10. Does the paragraph talk about just one topic? ☑ yes ❑ no

If you answered *no*, what is the extra topic? ______

In what sentence is this extra topic introduced? ______

11. Does every sentence have a verb? ☐ yes ☑ no

If you answered *no,* circle the error(s)on the paper.

12. Write any mistakes that you found. Add appropriate corrections.

Error 1: it's-don't use contractions in formal writing

Correction: it is

Error 2: etc.-don't use this

Correction: You should list all the kinds.

Error 3: ______

Correction: ______

13. Did you have any trouble understanding this paragraph? ☐ yes ☑ no

If you answered *yes,* tell where and/or why.

______

14. What questions do you have about the content? What other information should be in this paragraph?

How do you make gumbo? Is it easy to cook? Why do you think people started making gumbo?

15. What is your opinion of the writing of this paragraph?

It is good, but the concluding sentence gives new information. It does not conclude! Also, do not repeat the word "gumbo" so much. Do not use "is" so much! Use other verbs.

16. What is your opinion of the content of this paragraph?

I like the topic. I think I ate gumbo at a restaurant once.

Step 6: Revise the First Draft

In this step, you will see how Susan used the suggestions and information to revise her paragraph. This step consists of three parts:

1. React to the comments on the peer editing sheet.
2. Reread the paragraph and make changes.
3. Rewrite the paragraph one more time.

Here is what Susan wrote about the changes she decided to make.

I read my paragraph again several times. Each time I read it, I found things that I wanted to change in some way. Sometimes I corrected an obvious error. Other times I added words to make my writing clear to the reader. Based on Jim's suggestion, I used "this delicious dish" and other expressions instead of repeating "gumbo" so many times.

I used some of Jim's suggestions, but I did not use all of them. I thought that some of his questions were interesting, but the answers were not really part of the purpose of this paragraph, which was to define gumbo.

I was happy that the peer editor was able to understand all my ideas fully. To me, this means that my writing is good enough.

Susan's notes about changes she decided to make

Step 7: Proofread the Final Draft

Most of the hard work should be over by now. In this step, the writer pretends to be a brand-new reader who has never seen the paper before. The writer reads the paper to see if the sentences and ideas flow smoothly.

Read Susan's final paper again on page 244. Notice any changes in vocabulary, grammar, spelling, or punctuation that she made at this stage.

Of course, the very last step is to turn the paper in to your teacher and hope that you get a good grade!

Editing Your Writing

While you must be comfortable writing quickly, you also need to be comfortable with improving your work. Writing an assignment is never a one-step process. For even the most gifted writers, it is often a multiple-step process. When you were completing your assignments in this book, you probably made some changes to your work to make it better. However, you may not have fixed all of the errors. The paper that you turned in to your teacher is called a **first draft,** which is sometimes referred to as a **rough draft.**

A first draft can almost always be improved. One way to improve your writing is to ask a classmate, friend, or teacher to read it and make suggestions. Your reader may discover that one of your paragraphs is missing a topic sentence, that you have made grammar mistakes, or that your essay needs different vocabulary choices. You may not always like or agree with the comments from a reader, but being open to changes will make you a better writer.

This section will help you become more familiar with how to identify and correct errors in your writing.

Step 1

Below is a student's first draft for a timed writing. The writing prompt for this assignment, was "Many schools now offer classes online. Which do you prefer and why?" As you read the first draft, look for areas that need improvement and write your comments. For example, does every sentence have a subject and a verb? Does the writer always use the correct verb tense and punctuation? Does the paragraph have a topic sentence with controlling ideas? Is the vocabulary suitable for the intended audience? What do you think of the content?

The Online Courses

Online courses are very popular at my university. I prefered traditional face-to-face classes. At my university, students have a choice between courses that are taught online in a virtual classroom and the regular kind of classroom. I know that many students prefer online classes, but I cannot adjust to that style of educate. For me, is important to have a professor who explains the material to everyone "live" and then answer any questions that we have. Sometimes students might think they understand the material until the professor questions, and then we realize that we did not understand everything. At that moment, the professor then offers other explanation to help bridge the gap. I do not see this kind of spontaneous learning and teaching can take place online. I have never taken an online course until now. Some of my friends like online courses because they can take the class at his own convenience instead of have to assist class at a set time. However, these supposed conveniences are not outweigh the educational advantages that traditional face-to-face classes offer.

Step 2

Read the teacher comments on the first draft of "The Online Courses." Are these the same things that you noticed?

Your title is OK. Any other ideas?

The Online Courses

Combine first two sentences.

Online courses are very popular at my university. I prefered traditional face-to-face classes. At my university, students have a choice between courses that are taught online in a virtual classroom and the regular kind of classroom, I know that many students prefer online classes, but I cannot adjust to that style of educate. For me, is important to have a professor who explains the material to everyone "live" and then answer any questions that we have. Sometimes students might think they understand the material until the professor questions, and then we realize that we did not understand everything. At that moment, the professor then offers other explanation to help bridge the gap. I do not see this kind of spontaneous learning and teaching can take place online. I have never taken an online course until now. Some of my friends like online courses because they can take the class at his own convenience instead of have to assist class at a set time. However, these supposed conveniences are not outweigh the educational advantages that traditional face-to-face classes offer.

Give more details about CLASSROOM. Describe it.

WORD FORM SUBJ?

POSES A QUESTION

Which gap??? HOW?

Purpose of this sentence? Connected to the topic?

Add more reasons here!

You have some very good ideas in this paragraph. Your topic sentence and concluding sentence are good. Your title is OK, but can you spice it up? It's rather plain right now. Check to make sure that all of your sentences are relevant. Also, I've circled several grammar errors. You need to change these. I also recommend adding some info in a few places. All in all, it's a good paragraph. I understand why you don't like online courses. The more specific reasons you can provide, the better you can convince your readers.

Step 3

Now read the writer's second draft of the paragraph. How is it the same as the first draft? How is it different? Did the writer fix all the sentence mistakes?

Online Courses

Online courses are very popular at my university but I prefer traditional face-to-face classes. At my university students have a choice between courses that are taught online in a virtual classroom and the regular kind of classroom with a room, a professor, and students in chairs. I know that many students prefer online classes, but I cannot adjust to that style of education. For me, it is important to have a professor who explains the material to everyone "live" and then answers any questions that we might have. Sometimes students might think they understand the material until the professor poses a question, and then we realize that we did not understand everything. At that moment, the professor then offers another explanation to help bridge the gap between our knowledge and the truth. I do not see how this kind of spontaneous leaerning and teaching can take place online. Some of my friends like online courses because they can take the class at their own convenience instead of having to attend class at a set time. They also like to save transportation money and time. However, these supposed conveniences do not outweigh the many educational advantages that traditional face-to-face classes offer.

Capitalization Activities

Basic Capitalization Rules

1. Always capitalize the first word of a sentence.

> **T**oday is not Sunday.
>
> **I**t is not Saturday either.
>
> **D**o you know today's date?

2. Always capitalize the word *I* no matter where it is in a sentence.

> John brought the dessert, and **I** brought some drinks.
>
> **I** want some tea.
>
> The winners of the contest were Ned and **I**.

3. Capitalize proper nouns—the names of specific people, places, or things. Capitalize a person's title, including Mr., Mrs., Ms., and Dr. Compare these example pairs.

Proper nouns: When our teacher **M**r. **H**ill visited his home state of **A**rizona, he took a short trip to see the **G**rand **C**anyon.

Common nouns: When our teacher visited his home state, he saw many mountains and canyons.

Proper nouns: The **S**tatue of **L**iberty is located on **L**iberty **I**sland in **N**ew **Y**ork.

Common nouns: There is a famous statue on that island, isn't there?

4. Capitalize names of countries and other geographic areas. Capitalize the names of people from those areas. Capitalize the names of languages.

> People from **B**razil are called **B**razilians. They speak **P**ortuguese.
>
> People from **G**ermany are called **G**ermans. They speak **G**erman.

5. Capitalize titles of works, such as books, movies, and pieces of art. If you look at the example paragraphs in this book, you will notice that each of them begins with a title. In a title, pay attention to which words begin with a capital letter and which words do not.

*G*umbo | *A* ***L****esson in* ***F****riendship* | *An* ***I****mmigrant in the* ***F****amily*

The ***K****ing and I* | *The* ***T****ale of* ***P****inocchio* | *Love at* ***F****irst* ***S****ight*

The rules for capitalizing titles are easy.

- Always capitalize the first letter of a title.
- If the title has more than one word, capitalize all the words that have meaning (content words).
- Do not capitalize small (function) words, such as *a, an, and, the, in, with, on, for, to, above,* and *or.*

Capitalization Activities

ACTIVITY 1

Circle the words that have capitalization errors. Make the corrections above the errors.

1. the last day to sign up for the trip to sao paolo is this Thursday.
2. does jill live in west bay apartments, too?
3. the flight to Vancouver left late Saturday night and arrived early Sunday morning.
4. My sister has two daughters. Their names are rachel and rosalyn.
5. one of the most important sporting events is the world cup.

ACTIVITY 2

Complete these statements. Be sure to use correct capitalization.

1. *U.S.A.* stands for the United ________________ of ________________.
2. The seventh month of the year is ________________.
3. ________________ is the capital of Brazil.
4. One of the most popular brands of jeans is ________________.
5. The first person to walk on the moon was named ________________.
6. Parts of Europe were destroyed in ________________ (1914–18).
7. My favorite restaurant is ________________.
8. Beijing is the largest city in ________________.
9. The winter months are ________________, ________________, and ________________.
10. The last movie that I saw was ________________.

ACTIVITY 3

Read the following titles. Rewrite them with correct capitalization.

1. my favorite food ________________________________
2. living in montreal ________________________________
3. the best restaurant in town ________________________________
4. my best friend's new car ________________________________
5. a new trend in Hollywood ________________________________
6. why i left my country ________________________________
7. my side of the mountain ________________________________
8. no more room for a friend ________________________________

ACTIVITY 4

Read the following paragraph. Circle the capitalization errors and make corrections above the errors.

Example Paragraph 81

A visit to Cuba

according to an article in last week's issue of *time*, the prime minister of canada will visit cuba soon in order to establish better economic ties between the two countries. because the united states does not have a history of good relations with cuba, canada's recent decision may result in problems between washington and ottawa. In an interview, the canadian prime minister indicated that his country was ready to reestablish some sort of cooperation with cuba and that canada would do so as quickly as possible. there is no doubt that this new development will be discussed at the opening session of congress next tuesday.

ACTIVITY 5

Read the following paragraph. Circle the capitalization errors and make corrections above the errors.

Example Paragraph 82

crossing the atlantic from atlanta

it used to be difficult to travel directly from atlanta to europe, but this is certainly not the case nowadays. union airways offers several daily flights to london. jetwings express offers flights every day to frankfurt and twice a week to berlin. other european air carriers that offer direct flights from atlanta to europe are valuair and luxliner. However, the airline with the largest number of direct flights to any european city is not a european airline. smead airlines, which is a new and rising airline in the united states, offers 17 flights a day to 12 european cities, including paris, london, frankfurt, zurich, rome, and athens.

ACTIVITY 6

Read the following paragraph. Circle the capitalization errors and make corrections above the errors.

Example Paragraph 83

my beginnings in foreign languages

I have always loved foreign languages. When I was in tenth grade, I took my first foreign language class. It was french I. My teacher was named mrs. montluzin. She was a wonderful teacher who inspired me to develop my interest in foreign languages. Before I finished high school, I took a second year of french and one year of spanish. I wish my high school had offered latin or greek, but the small size of the school body prevented this. Over the years since I graduated from high school, I have lived and worked abroad. I studied arabic when I lived in saudi arabia, japanese in japan, and malay in malaysia. Two years ago, I took a german class in the united states. Because of recent travels to uzbekistan and kyrgyzstan, which are two republics from the former soviet union, I have a strong desire to study russian. I hope that my love of learning foreign languages will continue.

Punctuation Activities

End Punctuation

The three most common punctuation marks found at the end of English sentences are the **period**, the **question mark**, and the **exclamation point**. It is important to know how to use all three of them correctly. Of these three, however, the period is by far the most commonly used punctuation mark.

1. **period** (.) A period is used at the end of a declarative sentence.

   This sentence is a declarative sentence.

   This sentence is not a question.

   All three of these sentences end with a period.

2. **question mark** (?) A question mark is used at the end of a question.

   Is this idea difficult**?**

   Is it hard to remember the name of this mark**?**

   How many questions are in this group**?**

3. **exclamation point** (!) An exclamation point is used at the end of an exclamation. It is less common than the other two marks.

   I cannot believe you think this topic is difficult!

   This is the best writing book in the world!

   Now I understand all of these examples!

ACTIVITY 1

Add the correct end punctuation.

1. Congratulations
2. Do most people think that the governor was unaware of the theft
3. Do not open your test booklet until you are told to do so
4. Will the president attend the meeting
5. Jason put the dishes in the dishwasher and then watched TV

ACTIVITY 2

Look at an article in any English newspaper or magazine. Circle every end punctuation mark. Then answer these questions.

1. How many final periods are there? ______________ (or ______________ %)
2. How many final question marks are there? ______________ (or ______________ %)
3. How many final exclamation points are there? ______________ (or ______________ %)
4. What is the total number of sentences? ______________

Use this last number to calculate the percentages for each of the categories. Does the period occur most often?

Commas

The comma has several different functions in English. Here are some of the most common ones.

1. A comma separates a list of three or more things. There should be a comma between the items in a list.

   He speaks French and English. (No comma is needed because there are only two items.)

   She speaks French, English, and Chinese.

2. A comma separates two sentences when there is a combining word (coordinating conjunction) such as *and, but, or, so, for, nor,* and *yet.* The easy way to remember these conjunctions is *FANBOYS (for, and, nor, but, or, yet, so).*

   Six people took the course, but only five of them passed the test.

   Sammy bought the cake, and Paul paid for the ice cream.

   Students can register for classes in person, or they may submit their applications by mail.

3. A comma is used to separate an introductory word or phrase from the rest of the sentence.

   In conclusion, doctors are advising people to take more vitamins.

   First, you will need a pencil.

   Because of the heavy rains, many of the roads were flooded.

   Finally, add the nuts to the batter.

4. A comma is used to separate an appositive from the rest of the sentence. An appositive is a word or group of words that renames a noun before it. An appositive provides additional information about the noun.

   subject (noun) — appositive — verb

   Washington, the first president of the United States, was a clever military leader.

   In this sentence, the phrase *the first president of the United States* is an appositive. This phrase renames or explains the noun *Washington.*

5. A comma is sometimes used with adjective clauses. An adjective clause usually begins with a relative pronoun *(who, that, which, whom, whose, whoever,* or *whomever).* We use a comma when the information in the clause is unnecessary or extra. (This is also called a nonrestrictive clause.)

   The book that is on the teacher's desk is the main book for this class.

   (Here, when you say "the book," the reader does not know which book you are talking about, so the information in the adjective clause is necessary. In this case, do not set off the adjective clause with a comma.)

   The History of Korea, which is on the teacher's desk, is the main book for this class.

   (The name of the book is given, so the information in the adjective clause is not necessary to help the reader identify the book. In this case, you must use commas to show that the information in the adjective clause is extra, or nonrestrictive.)

ACTIVITY 3

Add commas as needed in these sentences. Some sentences may be correct, and others may need more than one comma.

1. For the past fifteen years Mary Parker has been both the director and producer of all the plays at this theater.
2. Despite all the problems we had on our vacation we managed to have a good time.
3. I believe the best countries to visit in Africa are Senegal Tunisia and Ghana.
4. She believes the best countries to visit in Africa are Senegal and Tunisia.
5. The third step in this process is to grate the carrots and the potatoes.
6. Third grate the carrots and the potatoes.
7. Blue green and red are strong colors. For this reason they are not appropriate for a living room wall.
8. Without anyone to teach foreign language classes next year the school will be unable to offer French Spanish or German.
9. The NEQ 7000 the very latest computer from Electron Technologies is not selling very well.
10. Because of injuries neither Carl nor Jamil two of the best players on the football team will be able to play in tomorrow's game.
11. The job interview is for a position at Mills Trust Company which is the largest company in this area.

12. The job interview is for a position at a large company that has more than 1,000 employees in this area.

13. Kevin's birthday is January 18 which is the same day that Laura and Greg have their birthdays.

14. Martina Navratilova whom most tennis fans refer to only as Martina dominated women's tennis for years.

15. My brother who lives in San Salvador has two children. (I have several brothers.)

16. My brother who lives in San Salvador has two children. (I have only one brother.)

17. This flight is leaving for La Paz which is the first of three stops that the plane will make.

18. No one knows the name of the person who will take over the committee in January so there have been many rumors about this.

19. Greenfield Central Bank the most recent bank to open a branch here in our area has tried to establish a branch here for years.

20. On the right side of the living room an antique radio sits on top of a glass table that also has a flowerpot a photo of a baby and a magazine.

Apostrophes

Apostrophes have two basic uses in English. They indicate either a contraction or possession.

Contractions: Use an apostrophe in a contraction in place of the letter or letters that have been deleted.

He's (he is *or* he has), they're (they are), I've (I have), we'd (we would *or* we had)

Possession: Use an apostrophe to indicate possession. Add an apostrophe and the letter *s* after the word. If a plural word already ends in *s*, then just add an apostrophe.

Gandhi's role in the history of India
Yesterday's paper
the boy's books (One boy has some books.)
the boys' books (Several boys have one or more books.)

ACTIVITY 4

Correct the apostrophe errors in these sentences.

1. I am going to Victors birthday party on Saturday.
2. My three cousins house is right next to Mr. Wilsons house.
3. Hardly anyone remembers Stalins drastic actions in the early part of the last century.
4. It goes without saying that wed be better off without so much poverty in this world.
5. The reasons that were given for the childrens bad behavior were unbelievable.

Quotation Marks

Below are three of the most common uses for quotation marks.

1. To mark the exact words that were spoken by someone:

   The king said, "I refuse to give up my throne." (The period is inside the quotation marks.)*

   "None of the solutions is correct," said the professor. (The comma is inside the quotation marks.)*

   The king said that he refuses to give up his throne. (No quotation marks are needed because the sentence does not include the king's exact words. This style is called indirect speech.)

   * Note that the comma separates the verb that tells the form of communications (*said, announced, wrote*) and the quotation.

2. To mark language that a writer has borrowed from another source:

   The dictionary defines gossip as an "informal conversation, often about other people's private affairs," but I would add that it is usually malicious.

   This research concludes that there was "no real reason to expect this computer software program to produce good results with high school students."

   According to an article in *The San Jose Times,* about half of the money was stolen. (No quotes are necessary here because it is a summary of information rather than exact words from the article.)

   NOTE: See pages 273–274 for more information on citing sources.

3. To indicate when a word or phrase is being used in a special way:

   The king believed himself to be the leader of a democracy, so he allowed the prisoner to choose his method of dying. According to the king, allowing this kind of "democracy" showed that he was indeed a good ruler.

ACTIVITY 5

Add quotation marks where necessary. Remember the rules for placing commas, periods, and question marks inside or outside the quotation marks.

1. As I was leaving the room, I heard the teacher say, Be sure to study Chapter 7.
2. It is impossible to say that using dictionaries is useless. However, according to research published in the latest issue of the *General Language Journal,* dictionary use is down. I found the article's statement that 18.3 percent of students do not own a dictionary and 37.2 percent never use their dictionary (p. 75) to be rather shocking.

   Source: Wendt, John "Dictionary Use by Language Students," *General Language Journal* 3 (2007): 72-101.
3. My fiancée says that if I buy her a huge diamond ring, this would be a sign that I love her. I would like to know if there is a less expensive sign that would be a sure sign of my love for her.
4. When my English friend speaks of a heat wave just because the temperature reaches over 80°, I have to laugh because I come from Thailand, where we have sunshine most of the year. The days when we have to dress warmly are certainly few, and some people wear shorts outside almost every month of the year.
5. The directions on the package read, Open carefully. Add contents to one glass of warm water. Drink just before bedtime.

Semicolons

The semicolon is used most often to combine two related sentences. Once you get used to using the semicolon, you will find that it is a very easy and useful punctuation tool to vary the sentences in your writing.

- Use a semicolon when you want to connect two simple sentences.
- The function of a semicolon is similar to that of a period. However, in order to use a semicolon, there must be a relationship between the sentences.

Joey loves to play tennis. He has been playing since he was ten years old.

Joey loves to play tennis; he has been playing since he was ten years old.

Both sentence pairs are correct. The main difference is that the semicolon in the second example signals the relationship between the ideas in the two sentences. Notice also that *he* is not capitalized in the second example.

ACTIVITY 6

The following sentences use periods for separation. Rewrite the sentences. Replace the periods with semicolons and make any other necessary changes.

1. Gretchen and Bob have been friends since elementary school. They are also next-door neighbors.

 ____

2. The test was complicated. No one passed it.

 ____

3. Tomatoes are necessary for a garden salad. Peas are not.

 ____

4. Mexico lies to the south of the United States. Canada lies to the north.

 ____

ACTIVITY 7

Look at a copy of an English newspaper or magazine. Circle all the semicolons on a page. The number should be relatively small.

NOTE: If the topic of the article is technical or complex, there is a greater chance of finding semicolons. Semicolons are not usually used in informal or friendly writing. Thus, you might see a semicolon in an article about heart surgery or educational research, but not in an ad for a household product or an e-mail or text message to a friend.

Editing for Errors

ACTIVITY 8

Find the 14 punctuation errors in this paragraph and make corrections above the errors.

Example Paragraph 84

An Unexpected Storm

Severe weather is a constant possibility all over the globe; but we never really expect our own area to be affected However last night was different At about ten o'clock a tornado hit Lucedale This violent weather destroyed nine homes near the downtown area In addition to these nine houses that were completely destroyed many others in the area had heavy damage Amazingly no one was injured in last nights terrible storm Because of the rapid reaction of state and local weather watchers most of the areas residents saw the warnings that were broadcast on television

ACTIVITY 9

Find the 15 punctuation errors in this paragraph and make corrections above the errors.

Example Paragraph 85

Deserts

Deserts are some of the most interesting places on earth A desert is not just a dry area it is an area that receives less than ten inches of rainfall a year About one-fifth of the earth is composed of deserts Although many people believe that deserts are nothing but hills of sand this is not true In reality deserts have large rocks mountains canyons and even lakes For instance only about ten percent of the Sahara Desert the largest desert on the earth is sand

ACTIVITY 10

Find the 15 punctuation errors in this paragraph and make corrections above the errors.

Example Paragraph 86

A Review

I Wish I Could Have Seen His Face Marilyn Kings latest novel is perhaps her greatest triumph In this book King tells the story of the Lamberts a poor family that struggles to survive despite numerous hardships. The Lambert family consists of five strong personalities. Michael Lambert has trouble keeping a job and Naomi earns very little as a maid at a hotel The three children range in age from nine to sixteen. Dan Melinda and Zeke are still in school This well-written novel allows us to step into the conflict that each of the children has to deal with. Only a writer as talented as King could develop five independent characters in such an outstanding manner The plot has many unexpected turns and the outcome of this story will not disappoint readers While King has written several novels that won international praise *I Wish I Could Have Seen His Face* is in many ways better than any of her previous works.

Additional Grammar Activities

Verb Tense

ACTIVITY 1

Fill in the blanks with the verb that best completes the sentence. Be sure to use the correct form of the verb. Use the following verbs: *like, cut, break, stir,* and *spread.*

Example Paragraph 87

A Simple Sandwich

Making a tuna salad sandwich is not difficult. Put two cans of flaked tuna in a medium-sized bowl. With a fork, ________________ the fish apart. ________________ up a large white onion or two small yellow onions. ________________ in one-third cup of mayonnaise. Then add salt and pepper to taste. Some people ________________ to mix pieces of boiled eggs into their salad. Once you finish making the salad, ________________ it between two slices of bread. Now you are ready to eat your easy-to-make treat.

ACTIVITY 2

Fill in the blanks with the correct form of any appropriate verb.

Example Paragraph 88

Who Killed Kennedy?

One of the most infamous moments in U.S. history ________________ in 1963. In that year, President John F. Kennedy ________________ assassinated in Dallas, Texas. Since this event, there ________________ many theories about what ________________ on that fateful day. According to the official U.S. government report, only one man ________________ the bullets that ________________ President Kennedy. However, even today many people ________________ that there ________________ several assassins.

ACTIVITY 3

Fill in the blanks with the correct form of any appropriate verb.

Example Paragraph 89

A Routine Routine

I have one of the most boring daily routines of anyone I ________________. Every morning, I ________________ at 7:15. I ________________ a shower and ________________ dressed. After that, I ________________ breakfast and ________________ to the office. I ________________ from 8:30 to 4:30. Then I ________________ home. This ________________ five days a week without fail. Just for once, I wish something different would happen!

ACTIVITY 4

Fill in the blanks with the correct form of the verbs in parentheses.

Example Paragraph 90

The Shortest Term in the White House

William Henry Harrison (be) ________________ the ninth president of the United States. His presidency was extremely brief. In fact, Harrison (be) ________________ president for only one month. He (take) ________________ office on March 4,1841. Unfortunately he (catch) ________________ a cold that (become) ________________ pneumonia. On April 4, Harrison (die) ________________. He (become) ________________ the first American president to die while in office. Before becoming president, Harrison (study) ________________ to become a doctor and later (serve) ________________ in the army.

ACTIVITY 5

Fill in the blanks with the correct form of the verbs in parentheses.

Example Paragraph 91

The History of Brownsville

Brownsville, Texas, is a city with an interesting history. Brownsville (be) ________________ originally a fort during the Mexican-American War. During that war, American and Mexican soldiers (fight) ________________ several battles in the area around the city. As a matter of fact, the city (get) ________________ its name from Major Jacob Brown, an American soldier who was killed in a battle near the old fort. However, Brownsville's history (be) ________________ not only connected to war. After the war, the city was best known for farming. The area's rich soil (help) ________________ it become a thriving agriculture center. Over time, the agricultural industry (grow) ________________, and today Brownsville farmers (be) ________________ well-known for growing cotton and citrus. In sum, both the Mexican-American War and farming have played important historical roles in making Brownsville such an interesting city.

Articles

ACTIVITY 6

Fill in the blanks with the correct article. If no article is required, write an X in the blank.

Example Paragraph 92

______ Simple Math Problem

There is ______ interesting mathematics brainteaser that always amazes ______ people when they first hear it. First, pick ______ number from ______ 1 to ______ 9. Subtract ______ 5. (You may have a negative number.) Multiply this answer by ______ 3. Now square ______ number. Then add ______ digits of ______ number. For ______ example, if your number is 81, add 8 and 1 to get an answer of ______ 9. If ______ number is less than ______ 5, add ______ 5. If ______ number is not less than ______ 5, subtract ______ 4. Now multiply this number by ______ 2. Finally, subtract ______ 6. If you have followed ______ steps correctly, ______ your answer is ______ 4.

ACTIVITY 7

Fill in the blanks with the correct article. If no article is required, write an X in the blank.

Example Paragraph 93

______ Geography Problems among ______ American Students

Are ______ American high school students ______ less educated in ______ geography than high school students in ______ other countries? According to ______ recent survey of ______ high school students all over ______ globe, ______ U.S. students do not know very much about ________ geography. For ________ example, ________ surprisingly large number did not know ________ capital of ________ state in which they live. Many could not find ________ Mexico on a map even though Mexico is one of ________ two countries that share ________ border with ________ United States. Some ________ educators blame this lack of ________ geographical knowledge on the move away from memorization of material that has taken ________ place in ________ recent years in American schools. Regardless of ________ cause, the unfortunate fact appears to be that American ________ high school students are not learning enough about this subject area.

ACTIVITY 8

Fill in the blanks with the correct article. If no article is required, write an X in the blank.

Example Paragraph 94

________ Homeowners Saving ________ Money with a New Free Service

People who are concerned that their monthly electricity bill is too high can now take ________ advantage of ________ special free service offered by the local electricity company. ________ company will do ________ home energy audit on any house to find out if ________ house is wasting ________ valuable energy. Homeowners can call ________ power company to schedule ________ convenient time for ________ energy analyst to visit their home. The audit takes only about ________ hour. ________ analyst will inspect ________ home and identify potential energy-saving ________ improvements. For ________ example, he or she will check ________ thermostat, the air-conditioning, and ________ seals around doors and windows. The major energy-use ________ problems will be identified, and ________ analyst will recommend ________ ways to use ________ energy more efficiently.

ACTIVITY 9

Fill in the blanks with the correct article. If no article is required, write an X in the blank.

Example Paragraph 95

__________ Great Teacher

To this day, I am completely convinced that __________ main reason that I did so well in my French class in __________ high school was the incredible teacher that I had, __________ Mrs. Montluzin. I had not studied __________ foreign language before I started __________ Mrs. Montluzin's French class. __________ idea of being able to communicate in a foreign language, especially __________ French, intrigued me, but __________ idea also scared me. __________ French seemed so difficult at first. We had so much __________ vocabulary to memorize, and we had to do __________ exercises to improve our grammar. While it is true that there was __________ great deal of work to do, __________ Mrs. Montluzin always tried her best to make French class very interesting. She also gave us __________ suggestions for learning __________ French, and these helped me a lot. Since this French class, I have studied a few other languages, and my interest in __________ foreign languages today is due to __________ success I had in French class with __________ Mrs. Montluzin.

ACTIVITY 10

Fill in the blanks with the correct article. If no article is required, write an X in the blank.

Example Paragraph 96

__________ Surprising Statistics on __________ Higher Education in __________ United States

Although __________ United States is a leader in many areas, it is surprising that __________ number of Americans with __________ college degree is not as high as it is in some ________ other countries. Only about 22 percent of ________ Americans have attended college for four or more years. To ________ most people, this rather low ratio of one in five is shocking. Slightly more than ________ 60 percent of ________ Americans between ________ ages of 25 and 40 have taken some ________ college classes. Though these numbers are far from what ________ many people would expect in ________ United States, these statistics are ________ huge improvement over figures at ________ turn of ________ last century. In ________ 1900, only about ________ 8 percent of all Americans even entered ________ college. At ________ present time, there are about 21 million students attending ________ college.

Editing for Errors

ACTIVITY 11

This paragraph contains eight errors. They are in word choice (one), article (one), modal* (one), verb tense (one), subject-verb agreement (three), and word order (one). Mark these errors and write the corrections above the errors.

Example Paragraph 97

A Dangerous Driving Problem

Imagine that you are driving your car home from mall or the library. You come to a bend in the road. You decide that you need to slow down a little, so you tap the brake pedal. Much to your surprise, the car does not begin to slow down. You push the brake pedal all the way down to the floor, but still anything happens. There are a few things you can do when your brakes does not work. One was to pump the brakes. If also this fails, you should to try the emergency brake. If this also fail, you should try to shift the car into a lower gear and rub the tires against the curb until the car come to a stop.

*Modals are *can, should, will, must, may,* and *might.* Modals appear before verbs. We do not use *to* between modals and verbs. (*Incorrect:* I should to go with him. *Correct:* I should go with him.) Modals do not have forms that take *-s, -ing,* or *-ed.*

ACTIVITY 12

This paragraph contains ten errors. They are in prepositions (three), word order (one), articles (two), and verb tense (four). Mark these errors and write the corrections above the errors.

Example Paragraph 98

The Start of My Love of Aquariums

My love of aquariums began a long time ago. Although I got my first fish when I am just seven years old, I can still remember the store, the fish, and salesclerk who waited on me that day. Because I made good grades on my report card, my uncle has rewarded me with a dollar. A few days later, I was finally able to go to the local dime store for spend my money. It was 1965, and dollar could buy a lot. I looked a lot of different things, but I finally chose to buy a fish. We had an old fishbowl at home, so it seems logical with me to get a fish. I must have spent 15 minutes pacing back and forth in front of all the aquariums before I finally choose my fish. It was a green swordtail, or rather, she was a green swordtail. A few weeks later, she gave birth to 20 or 30 baby swordtails. Years later, I can still remember the fish beautiful that got me so interested in aquariums.

ACTIVITY 13

This paragraph contains eight errors. They are in prepositions (one), articles (three), word forms (two), verb tense (one), and subject-verb agreement (one). Mark these errors and write the corrections above the errors.

Example Paragraph 99

An Effect of Cellphones on Drivers

Cellular phones, can be threat to safety. A recent study for Donald Redelmeier and Robert Tibshirani of the University of Toronto showed that cellular phones pose a risk to drivers. In fact, people who talk on the phone while driving are four time more likely to have an automobile accident than those who do not use the phone while drive. The Toronto researchers studied 699 drivers who had been in an automobile accident while they were using their cellular phones. The researchers concluded that the main reason for the accidents is not that people used one hand for the telephone and only one for driving. Rather, cause of the accidents was usually that the drivers became distracted, angry, or upset by the phone call. The drivers then lost concentration and was more prone to a car accident.

ACTIVITY 14

This paragraph contains seven errors. They are in verb tense (one), articles (two), word forms (three), and subject-verb agreement (one). Mark these errors and write the corrections.

Example Paragraph 100

Problems with American Coins

Many foreigners who come to the United States have very hard time getting used to America coins. The denominations of the coins are one, five, ten, 25, and 50 cents, and one dollar. However, people used only the first four regularly. The smallest coin in value is the penny, but it is not the smallest coin in size. The quarter is one-fourth the value of a dollar, but it is not one-fourth as big as a dollar. There is a dollar coin, but no one ever use it. In fact, perhaps the only place to find one is at a bank. All of the coins are silver-colored except for one, the penny. Finally, because value of each coin is not clearly written on the coin as it is in many country, foreigners often experience problems with monetarily transactions.

ACTIVITY 15

This paragraph contains seven errors. They are in word order (one), articles (two), preposition (one), subject-verb agreement (one), and verb tense (two). Mark these errors and write the corrections.

Example Paragraph 101

An Oasis of Silence

Life on this campus can be extremely hectic, so when I want the solitude, I go usually to the fourth floor of the library. The fourth floor has nothing but shelves and shelves of rare books and obscure periodicals. Because there are only a few small tables with some rather uncomfortable wooden chairs and no copy machines in this floor, few people are staying here very long. Students search for a book or periodical, found it, and then take it to a more sociable floor to photocopy the pages or simply browse through the articles. One of my best friends have told me that he does not like this floor that is so special to me. For him, it is a lonely place. For me, however, it is oasis of silence in a land of turmoil, a place where I can read, think, and write in peace.

Citations and Plagiarism

When writing a paragraph or an essay, writers should use their own words for the most part. Sometimes, however, writers want to use ideas that they have read in a book, an article, or on a website or even heard in a speech. It can make the paragraph or essay more interesting, more factual, or more relevant to the reader. For example, if a writer is working on a paragraph about a recent election, he or she may want to use a quotation from a famous politician. In this case, the writer must indicate that the words are not his or her own, but that they came from someone else. Indicating that a writer's words are not original is called **citing**. In academic writing, it is necessary for a writer to cite all sources of information that are not original.

If the information does not come from the writer's head, it must be cited.

Writers who do not—whether intentionally or unintentionally—give credit to the original author are **plagiarizing**, or stealing, someone else's words. **This is academic theft, and most institutions take this very seriously.**

To avoid plagiarism, it is important to use quotes or a paraphrase which includes an in-text citation, and add a reference or bibliography at the end of your writing.

Using Quotes

Quotations are used when a writer wants to keep the source's exact words. See the examples.

✓ The original reference is the source.

✓ The reference itself is the bibliographical reference.

✓ Use quotation marks " " for original words.

✓ The following verbs are often used to introduce quotes.

describes	points out	states
argues	finds	predicts
claims	insists	reports

Examples: Here are three different examples of quoting a sentence from a text.

Original: There is absolutely no empirical evidence – quantitative or qualitative – to support the familiar notion that monolingual dictionaries are better than bilingual dictionaries for understanding and learning L2.

Quote 1: According to Folse (2004), "There is absolutely no empirical evidence – quantitative or qualitative – to support the familiar notion that monolingual dictionaries are better than bilingual dictionaries for understanding and learning L2."

Quote 2: And while instructors continue to push for monolingual dictionaries, "there is absolutely no empirical evidence – quantitative or qualitative – to support the familiar notion that monolingual dictionaries are better than bilingual dictionaries for understanding and learning L2." (Folse, 2004).

Quote 3: As Folse points out, "There is absolutely no empirical evidence – quantitative or qualitative – to support the familiar notion that monolingual dictionaries are better than bilingual dictionaries for understanding and learning L2" (2004).

Reference/Bibliography

Folse, Keith. *Vocabulary Myths: Applying Second Language Research to Classroom Teaching*. Ann Arbor: University of Michigan Press, 2004.

Paraphrasing

Sometimes writers want to paraphrase or summarize outside information. In this case, the same rules still hold true. **If it is not from the writer's head, it must be cited.**

Original: Every year, the town of Vinci, Italy, receives as many as 500,000 visitors—people coming in search of its most famous son, Leonardo.

Paraphrase: Although a small town, Vinci is visited by many tourists because it is the birthplace of Leonardo da Vinci (Herrick, 2009).

Original: This quiet, unimposing hill town is relatively unchanged from the time of Leonardo.

Paraphrase: Herrick (2009) explains that even after 500 years, the town of Vinci has remained pretty much the same.

Reference/Bibliography

Herrick, T. (2009, January 1). Vinci: A Visit to Leonardo's Home Town. *Offbeat Travel*. Retrieved May 1, 2013, from www.offbeattravel.com/vinci-italy-davinci-home.html

Bibliography

At the end of your paragraph or essay, you must list the sources you used. There are several formats (APA, Chicago, or MLA) for documenting your sources. Always check with your instructor before turning in a paper or essay. This bibliography usually includes the author(s), the publication name, the city, the publisher, the publication year, the media type, and the page number or website.

Here are some guidelines for referencing different works:

Source	Include	Example
Book	Name of author, title of book, publication city: publisher, and year of publication	Folse, Keith. *Vocabulary Myths: Applying Second Language Research to Classroom Teaching.* Ann Arbor: University of Michigan Press, 2004.
Online Article	Name of author (if there is one), title of article, name of Web page, date of publication (if there is one), name of website, Accessed date from URL	"Great Website Design," *Website Design Basics*, http://www.websitedesignbasics.com, Accessed June 26, 2013
Website	Name of Web page, date, name of website. Accessed date, URL	"Global Warming 101." *Union of Concerned Scientists*. Accessed December 14, 2012, http://www.ucsusa.org/global_warming/global_warming_101/
Newspaper	Name of author, title of article, name of newspaper, section date, and page numbers	Smith, Steven, "What To Do in Case of Emergencies." *USA Today*, December 13, 2008, 2–3.
Speech/ Interview	Name of author, title of speech or interview, place or course, and date.	Vestri, Elena. Understanding Logical Fallacies. Lecture, ENGL 102, Khalifa University, Abu Dhabi. Feb. 21, 2013.

Academic Word List

Averil Coxhead (2000)

The following words are on the Academic Word List (AWL). The AWL is a list of the 570 highest-frequency academic word families that regularly appear in academic texts. The AWL was compiled by researcher Averil Coxhead based on her analysis of a 3.5 million word corpus.

abandon
abstract
academy
access
accommodate
accompany
accumulate
accurate
achieve
acknowledge
acquire
adapt
adequate
adjacent
adjust
administrate
adult
advocate
affect
aggregate
aid
albeit
allocate
alter
alternative
ambiguous
amend
analogy
analyze
annual
anticipate
apparent
append
appreciate
approach
appropriate
approximate
arbitrary
area
aspect
assemble
assess
assign
assist
assume
assure
attach
attain
attitude
attribute
author
authority
automate

available
aware
behalf
benefit
bias
bond
brief
bulk
capable
capacity
category
cease
challenge
channel
chapter
chart
chemical
circumstance
cite
civil
clarify
classic
clause
code
coherent
coincide
collapse
colleague
commence
comment
commission
commit
commodity
communicate
community
compatible
compensate
compile
complement
complex
component
compound
comprehensive
comprise
compute
conceive
concentrate
concept
conclude
concurrent
conduct
confer
confine

confirm
conflict
conform
consent
consequent
considerable
consist
constant
constitute
constrain
construct
consult
consume
contact
contemporary
context
contract
contradict
contrary
contrast
contribute
controversy
convene
converse
convert
convince
cooperate
coordinate
core
corporate
correspond
couple
create
credit
criteria
crucial
culture
currency
cycle
data
debate
decade
decline
deduce
define
definite
demonstrate
denote
deny
depress
derive
design
despite

detect
deviate
device
devote
differentiate
dimension
diminish
discrete
discriminate
displace
display
dispose
distinct
distort
distribute
diverse
document
domain
domestic
dominate
draft
drama
duration
dynamic
economy
edit
element
eliminate
emerge
emphasis
empirical
enable
encounter
energy
enforce
enhance
enormous
ensure
entity
environment
equate
equip
equivalent
erode
error
establish
estate
estimate
ethic
ethnic
evaluate
eventual
evident

evolve
exceed
exclude
exhibit
expand
expert
explicit
exploit
export
expose
external
extract
facilitate
factor
feature
federal
fee
file
final
finance
finite
flexible
fluctuate
focus
format
formula
forthcoming
found
foundation
framework
function
fund
fundamental
furthermore
gender
generate
generation
globe
goal
grade
grant
guarantee
guideline
hence
hierarchy
highlight
hypothesis
identical
identify
ideology
ignorant
illustrate
image

immigrate
impact
implement
implicate
implicit
imply
impose
incentive
incidence
incline
income
incorporate
index
indicate
individual
induce
inevitable
infer
infrastructure
inherent
inhibit
initial
initiate
injure
innovate
input
insert
insight
inspect
instance
institute
instruct
integral
integrate
integrity
intelligent
intense
interact
intermediate
internal
interpret
interval
intervene
intrinsic
invest
investigate
invoke
involve
isolate
issue
item
job
journal
justify
label
labor
layer
lecture
legal
legislate
levy

liberal
license
likewise
link
locate
logic
maintain
major
manipulate
manual
margin
mature
maximize
mechanism
media
mediate
medical
medium
mental
method
migrate
military
minimal
minimize
minimum
ministry
minor
mode
modify
monitor
motive
mutual
negate
network
neutral
nevertheless
nonetheless
norm
normal
notion
notwithstanding
nuclear
objective
obtain
obvious
occupy
occur
odd
offset
ongoing
option
orient
outcome
output
overall
overlap
overseas
panel
paradigm
paragraph
parallel

parameter
participate
partner
passive
perceive
percent
period
persist
perspective
phase
phenomenon
philosophy
physical
plus
policy
portion
pose
positive
potential
practitioner
precede
precise
predict
predominant
preliminary
presume
previous
primary
prime
principal
principle
prior
priority
proceed
process
professional
prohibit
project
promote
proportion
prospect
protocol
psychology
publication
publish
purchase
pursue
qualitative
quote
radical
random
range
ratio
rational
react
recover
refine
regime
region
register
regulate

reinforce
reject
relax
release
relevant
reluctance
rely
remove
require
research
reside
resolve
resource
respond
restore
restrain
restrict
retain
reveal
revenue
reverse
revise
revolution
rigid
role
route
scenario
schedule
scheme
scope
section
sector
secure
seek
select
sequence
series
sex
shift
significant
similar
simulate
site
so-called
sole
somewhat
source
specific
specify
sphere
stable
statistic
status
straightforward
strategy
stress
structure
style
submit
subordinate
subsequent

subsidy
substitute
successor
sufficient
sum
summary
supplement
survey
survive
suspend
sustain
symbol
tape
target
task
team
technical
technique
technology
temporary
tense
terminate
text
theme
theory
thereby
thesis
topic
trace
tradition
transfer
transform
transit
transmit
transport
trend
trigger
ultimate
undergo
underlie
undertake
uniform
unify
unique
utilize
valid
vary
vehicle
version
via
violate
virtual
visible
vision
visual
volume
voluntary
welfare
whereas
whereby
widespread

Useful Vocabulary for Better Writing

These useful words and phrases can help you write better sentences and paragraphs. Many are found in the *Great Writing 2: Great Paragraphs* model paragraphs, and they can make your writing sound more academic, natural, and fluent.

Giving and Adding Examples

Words and Phrases	Examples
For example, S + V / *For instance,* S + V	Our reading teacher assigns a lot of homework. *For example,* last night we had to read ten pages and write an essay.
The first reason + VERB	The article we read in class gave three reasons that our planet is in trouble. *The first reason* is about the increasing population.

Concluding Sentences

Words and Phrases	Examples
In conclusion, S + V	*In conclusion,* I believe everyone should vote in every election.
By doing all of these things, S + V	*By doing all of these things,* we can improve education in our country.
Because of this, S + V	*Because of this,* many people will have better health care.
As a result, S + V	*As a result,* I chose to go to college in France instead of my country.
For these reasons, S + V	*For these reasons,* I prefer to eat at home instead of a restaurant.
In sum, S + V / *In summary,* S + V / *To summarize ,* S + V	*In sum,* World War II was a very complicated war with many countries fighting for very different reasons, but in many ways, it was a continuation of World War I.
In other words, S + V	*In other words,* the judge made an incorrect decision.
From the information given, we can conclude that S + V	*From the information given, we can conclude that* Mark Johnson is certainly the best soccer player in this decade.
It is clear that S + V	*It is clear that* exercising every day improved your health.

Comparing

Words and Phrases	Examples
NOUN *is* COMPARATIVE ADJECTIVE *than* NOUN	New York *is larger than* Rhode Island.
S + V + COMPARATIVE ADVERB *than* Y.	The cats ran *faster than* the dogs.
S + V. *In comparison,* S + V.	Canada has provinces. *In comparison,* Brazil has states.
Although NOUN *and* NOUN *are similar in* NOUN, S + V	*Although* France *and* Spain *are similar in* size, they are different in many ways.
NOUN *and* NOUN *are similar.*	Brazil *and* the United States *are* surprisingly *similar.*
NOUN *is the same*	Our house *is the same* size as your house.
...*as* ADJECTIVE *as*...	Our house is *as big as* your house.
Like NOUN, NOUN *also*	*Like* Brazil, Mexico *also* has states.
both NOUN *and* NOUN...	*In both* German *and* Japanese, the verb appears at the end of a sentence.

Likewise, S + V / *Also*, S + V	The blooms on the red roses last longer than most other flowers. *Likewise*, the blooms for the pink rose are long-lasting.
Similarly, S + V .../ *Similar to* NOUN	Economists believe India has a bright future. *Similarly*, Brazil's future is on a very positive track.

Contrasting

Words and Phrases	Examples
S + V. *In contrast*, S + V.	*Algeria* is a very large country. *In contrast*, the UAE is very small.
Contrasted with / In contrast to NOUN	*In contrast to* last year, our company has doubled its profits this year.
Although / Even though / Though S + V	*Although* Spain and France are similar in size, they are different in many other ways.
Unlike NOUN,	*Unlike* the pink roses, the red roses are very expensive.
However, S + V	Canada has provinces. *However*, Brazil has states.
One the one hand, S + V *On the other hand*, S + V	*On the one hand*, Maggie loved to travel. *On the other hand*, she hated to be away from her home.
The opposite S + V	Most of the small towns in my state are experiencing a boom in tourism. In my hometown, *the opposite* is true.
NOUN *and* NOUN *are different*.	My older brother *and* my younger brother *are very different*.

Telling a Story / Narrating

Words and Phrases	Examples
When I was X, I would VERB	*When I was* a child, *I would* go fishing every weekend.
I have never felt so ADJ *in my life*.	*I have never felt so* anxious *in my life*.
I will never forget NOUN	*I will never forget* the day I took my first international flight.
I can still remember NOUN / *I will always remember* NOUN	*I can still remember* the day I started my first job.
NOUN *was the best / worst day of my life*.	My wedding was *the best day of my life*.
Every time X happened, Y happened.	*Every time* I used that computer, I had a problem.
This was my first ...	*This was my first* job after graduating from college.

Describing a Process

Words and Phrases	Examples
First (Second, Third, etc.), ... *Next, ... After that, ... Then, ...* *Finally, ...*	*First*, I cut the apples into small pieces. *Next*, I added some mayonnaise. *After that*, I added some salt. *Finally*, I mixed everything together well.
The first thing you should do is VERB	*The first thing you should do is* turn on the computer.
VERB+*-ing requires you to follow (number) of steps*.	*Saving* a file on a computer *requires you to follow several simple steps*.
Before you VERB, *you should* VERB.	*Before you* write a paragraph, *you should* brainstorm for ideas.
After (When)...	*After* you brainstorm your ideas, you can select the best ones to write about in your essay.

After that, …	*After that,* you can select the best ones to write about in your essay.
The last step is… / Finally, …	*Finally,* you should cook all of the ingredients for an hour.
If you follow these important steps in VERB + *-ing,…*	*If you follow these important steps in* applying for a passport, you will have your new document in a very short time.

Defining

Words and Phrases	Examples
The NOUN, *which is a/an* NOUN + ADJECTIVE CLAUSE, MAIN VERB	An owl, *which is* a bird that has huge round eyes, is awake most of the night.
According to the dictionary…	*According to* The Collins Cobuild Dictionary of American English, gossip is "an informal conversation, often about people's private affairs."
The dictionary definition of NOUN	*The dictionary definition of* gumbo is not very good.
X released a report stating that S + V	*The president's office released a report stating that* the new law will require all adults between the ages of 18 and 30 to serve at least one year of active military duty.
In other words, S + V	*In other words,* we have to redo everything we have done so far.
,…which means…	The paper is due tomorrow, *which means* if you want to get a good grade, you need to finish it today.
NOUN *means…*	Gossip *means* talking or writing about other people's private affairs.

Showing Cause and Effect

Words and Phrases	Examples
Because of NOUN, S + V. *Because* S + V, S + V.	*Because of* the traffic problems, it is easy to see why the city is building a new tunnel.
NOUN *can trigger* NOUN. NOUN *can cause* NOUN.	An earthquake *can trigger* tidal waves and *can cause* massive destruction.
Due to NOUN, …	*Due to* the snowstorm, all schools will be closed tomorrow.
As a result of NOUN…	*As a result of* his efforts, he got a better job.
Therefore,…/ As a result,…/ For this reason,…/ Consequently,…	It suddenly began to rain. *Therefore,* we all got wet.
NOUN *will bring about …*	The use of the Internet *will bring about a* change in education.
NOUN *has had a good / bad effect on…*	Computer technology *has had both positive and negative effects* on society.
The correlation is clear / evident.	*The correlation* between junk food and obesity *is clear.*

ribing

rds and Phrases	Examples
ositions of location: *above, across, around, in* *dark, near, under…*	The children raced their bikes *around* the school.
scriptive adjectives: *wonderful, delightful, dangerous, informative, rusty…*	The *bent, rusty* bike squeaked when I rode it.
SUBJECT *is* ADJECTIVE.	This dictionary *is informative.*
X is the most ADJECTIVE + NOUN.	To me, Germany *is the most interesting* country in Europe.
X tastes / looks / smells / feels like NOUN.	My ID card *looks like* a credit card.
X is known / famous for its NOUN.	France *is known for* its cheese.

Stating an Opinion

Words and Phrases	Examples
Without a doubt, VERB *is* ADJECTIVE *idea / method / decision / way.*	*Without a doubt,* walking to work each day *is* an excellent *way* to lose weight.
Personally, I believe/think/feel/agree/ disagree/ suppose S + V.	*Personally, I believe that* smoking on a bus should not be allowed.
VERB+*-ing should not be allowed.*	Smoking in public *should not be allowed.*
In my opinion/ view/ experience, NOUN	*In my opinion,* smoking is rude.
For this reason, S + V. / *That is why I think…*	I do not have a car. *For this reason,* I do not care about rising gasoline prices.
There are many benefits / advantages to NOUN.	*There are many benefits* to swimming every day.
There are many drawbacks / disadvantages to NOUN.	*There are many drawbacks to* eating your meals at a restaurant.
I am convinced that S + V	*I am convinced that* education at a university should be free to all citizens.
NOUN *should be required / mandatory.*	College *should be required.*
I prefer NOUN *to* NOUN.	*I prefer* soccer to football.
To me, banning / prohibiting NOUN *makes (perfect) sense.*	*To me, banning* cell phones while driving *makes perfect sense.*
For all of these important reasons, I think / believe / feel (that) S + V	*For all of these important reasons, I think* smoking *should be* banned in public.
Based on X, I have come to the conclusion that S + V	*Based on* two books that I read recently, *I have come to the conclusion that* global warming is the most serious problem that my generation faces.

Arguing and Persuading

Words and Phrases	Examples
It is important to remember that S + V	*It is important to remember* that school uniforms would only be worn during school hours.
According to a recent survey, S + V	*According to a recent survey,* 85 percent of high school students felt they had too much homework.
Even more important, S + V	*Even more important,* statistics show the positive effects that school uniforms have on behavior.
Despite this, S + V	The report says this particular kind of airplane is dangerous. *Despite this,* the government has not banned this airplane.
SUBJECT *must / should / ought to* VERB	Researchers *must* stop unethical animal testing.
The reason for S + V	*The reason for* people's support of this plan is that it provides equal treatment for all citizens.
To emphasize, S + V	*To emphasize,* I support a lower age for voting but only for those who already have a high school diploma.
For these reasons, S + V	*For these reasons,* public schools should require uniforms.
Obviously, S + V	*Obviously,* there are many people who would disagree with what I have just said.
Without a doubt, S + V	*Without a doubt,* students ought to learn a foreign language.
I agree that S + V. *However* S + V	*I agree that* a college degree is important. *However,* getting a practical technical license can also be very useful.

Reacting/Responding

Words and Phrases	Examples
TITLE *by* AUTHOR *is a / an…*	*Harry Potter and the Goblet of Fire by* J.K. Rowling *is an* entertaining book to read.
My first reaction to the prompt / news / article was / is NOUN.	*My first reaction to the article was* fear.
When I read / look at / think about NOUN, *I was amazed / shocked / surprised …*	*When I read* the article, *I was surprised* to learn of his athletic ability.

Appendices

Appendix 1

Building Better Sentences

Being a good writer involves many skills, such as being able to write with correct grammar, use variety in vocabulary selection, and state ideas concisely. A good writer also learns to create longer, more detailed sentences from simple ideas. Study the short sentences below.

The time was yesterday.

It was afternoon.

There was a storm.

The storm was strong.

The movement of the storm was quick.

The storm moved toward the coast.

The coast was in North Carolina.

Notice that every sentence has an important piece of information. A good writer would not write all these sentences separately. Instead, the most important information from each sentence can be used to create ONE longer, coherent sentence.

Read the sentences again; this time, the important information has been circled.

The time was yesterday.

It was afternoon.

There was a storm.

The movement of the storm was quick.

The storm moved toward the coast.

The coast was in North Carolina.

Here are some strategies for taking the circled information and creating a new sentence.

1. Create time phrases to introduce or end a sentence: yesterday + afternoon
2. Find the key noun: storm
3. Find key adjectives: strong
4. Create noun phrases: a strong + storm
5. Change word forms: movement = move; quick = quickly

   moved + quickly
6. Create prepositional phrases: toward the coast,

   toward the coast (of North Carolina)

   or

   toward the North Carolina coast

Now read this improved, longer sentence:

Yesterday afternoon, a strong storm moved quickly toward the North Carolina coast.

Here are some additional strategies for building better sentences:

7. Use coordinating conjunctions *(and, but, or, nor, yet, for, so)* to connect two sets of ideas.
8. Use subordinating conjunctions, such as *after, while, since,* and *because,* to connect related ideas.
9. Use clauses with relative pronouns, such as *who, which, that,* and *whose,* to describe or define a noun or noun phrase.
10. Use pronouns to refer to previously mentioned information.
11. Use possessive adjectives and pronouns, such as *my, her, his, ours,* and *theirs.* These words can make your writing flow more smoothly.

Study the following example.

> Susan went somewhere. That place was the mall. Susan wanted to buy new shoes. The shoes were for Susan's mother.

Now read the improved, longer sentence:

> Susan went to the mall because she wanted to buy new shoes for her mother.

Practices

This section contains practices for the example paragraphs in Units 1–10. Follow these steps for each practice:

1. Read the sentences. Circle the most important information in each sentence.
2. Write an original sentence from the information you circled. Use the strategies listed above.

Practice 1 Unit 1

X **A.**

1. An egg salad sandwich is one of the easiest foods to make.
2. An egg salad sandwich is one of the most delicious foods to make.
3. This is for lunch.

An egg salad sandwich is one of the easiest and most delicious foods to make for lunch.

X **B.**

1. Brazil is near Chile.
2. Chile is near Brazil.
3. Brazil and Chile are different in geography.
4. Brazil and Chile are different in population.
5. Brazil and Chile are different in language.

While Chile and Brazil are near each other, they have different geographies, populations, and languages.

X **C.**

1. First, boil eggs.
2. There are two eggs.
3. Do this for five minutes.

First, boil two eggs for five minutes.

Practice 2 Unit 1

A.

1. I was 23 years old at the time.
2. I had just graduated.
3. The graduation was from college.

I was 23 years old when I graduated from college.

B.

1. Chile and Brazil are two countries.
2. Chile is important.
3. Brazil is important.
4. They are in South America.

Chile and Brazil are two important countries in South America.

C.

1. Jim Thorpe won medals.
2. The medals were Olympic medals.
3. They were gold medals.
4. He won them in 1912.
5. He was not allowed to keep the medals.

Jim Thorpe won Olympic gold medals in 1912, but he was not allowed to keep them.

Practice 3 Unit 2

A.

1. Mimi is a teacher.
2. She teaches kindergarten.
3. She is a teacher at a school.
4. The school is King Elementary School.

Mimi teaches kindergarten at King Elementary School.
(is a kindergarten teacher)

B.

1. She teaches children.
2. The children are very young.
3. There are 22 children.

She teaches 22 very young children.

C.

1. Mimi must attend meetings.
2. Mimi must create lessons.
3. The lessons are new.
4. Mimi must do this after school.

After school, she must attend meetings and create new lessons.

Practice 4 Unit 3

A.

1. The season is winter.
2. This season is the best.
3. This season is for kids.

The best season for kids is winter.

B.

1. This dictionary contains words.
2. The dictionary is monolingual.
3. There are more than 42,000 words.

This monolingual dictionary contains more than 42,000 words.

C.

1. The crash of a jet baffled investigators.
2. The crash was shocking.
3. The jet was a 747 jumbo jet.
4. The crash was off the coast of New York.

The shocking crash of a 747 jumbo jet off the coast of New York baffled investigators.

Practice 5 Unit 3

A.

1. Research has confirmed that eating vegetables, such as broccoli, may reduce the risk of some types of cancer.
2. The research is recent.
3. The vegetables are dark green ones.
4. The vegetables are leafy vegetables.
5. Another example of this is cabbage.

Recent research has confirmed that eating dark green and leafy vegetables, such as broccoli and cabbage, may reduce . . . .

B.

1. Research suggests that studying music can improve a person's brain function.
2. Research suggests that studying music can improve a person's intelligence.
3. There is a great deal of the research.

A great deal of research suggests that studying music can improve a person's brain function and intelligence

C.

1. A heart is necessary for life.
2. The heart is good.
3. The heart is strong.
4. The life is long.
5. The life is healthy.

A good + strong heart is necessary for a long, healthy life.

Practice 6 Unit 3

A.

1. Malaysia is a country.
2. Thailand is a country.
3. These two countries are in Asia.
4. They are in Southeast Asia.

Malaysia and Thailand are two countries in Southeast Asia.

B.

1. Malaysia has beaches.
2. There are miles of beaches.
3. The beaches are beautiful.
4. These beaches attract tourists.
5. This is true about Thailand, too.

Malaysia and Thailand have miles of beautiful beaches that attract tourists.

C.

1. Students can choose to major in art.
2. They are at a university.
3. Only a small number choose to major in this subject.
4. This number is low for a reason.
5. The reason is that they are concerned about job possibilities.
6. The job possibilities are in the future.

Only a small number of univ. students choose to major in art because they are concerned about future job possibilities.

Practice 7 Unit 4

A.

1. One of the cities to visit is Washington, D.C.
2. It is one of the best cities.
3. It is on a coast of the United States.
4. The coast is in the east.

One of the best cities to visit on the east coast of the U.S is Washington, D.C.

B.

1. The area consists of over two million square feet.
2. The area belongs to the Grand Palace.
3. The wall is more than 6,000 feet long.
4. This wall surrounds the palace.

The area of the Grand Palace is over two million square feet and is surrounded by a wall that is more than 6,000 feet long

C.

1. Texas is home to snakes.
2. There are several kinds of snakes.
3. These snakes are poisonous.

Texas is home to several kinds of poisonous snakes

Practice 8 Unit 4

A.

1. Music is popular.
2. The music is soft.
3. It is popular because it helps students.
4. It helps students sleep better.

Soft music is popular because it helps students sleep better.

B.

1. Giraffes have eyelashes to protect their eyes.
2. The eyelashes are thick.
3. They protect their eyes from dust.
4. The dust is in their habitat.
5. Their habitat is dry.

Giraffes have thick eyelashes to protect their eyes from dust in their dry habitat

C.

1. Students learn that North America and South America are one continent.
2. They call this the Americas.

Students learn that North America and South America are one continent called the Americas.

11/26/18

Practice 9 Unit 5

A.

1. Only tourists attempt to cross the bridge.
2. The tourists are adventure-seeking.
3. The bridge is narrow and swinging.
4. This happens today.

(Today) Only adventure-seeking tourists attempt to cross the narrow, swinging bridge today.

B.

1. Hockey is a sport.
2. It is a popular sport.
3. It is popular in Canada.
4. It is popular in the United States.

Hockey is a popular sport in Canada and the U.S

C.

1. Teh tarikh is a beverage.
2. Teh tarikh is popular.
3. Teh tarikh is served in restaurants.
4. Teh tarikh is served in markets.
5. These restaurants and markets are in Southeast Asian countries.
6. Examples of these countries are Malaysia and Singapore.

Teh tarikh is a popular beverage served in restaurants + markets in Southeast Asian countries, such as Malaysia and Singapore.

Practice 10 Unit 5

A.

1. Coins were left under the mast.
2. The mast was part of the ship.
3. There were a small number of coins.
4. This happened when a new ship was built.

When a new ship was built, a small number of coins were left under the mast of the ship.

B.

1. Scientists find evidence of this tradition.
2. The evidence is in a variety of locations.
3. The tradition is long-standing.
4. This happens today.

Today scientists find evidence of a long-standing tradition in a variety of locations.

C.

1. Floods provided the marsh with water to support its plants and animals.
2. These floods always did this.
3. The water was new.
4. The marsh had a wide variety of plants and animals.

These floods always provided the marsh with new water to support a wide variety of plants and animals.

Practice 11 Unit 6

A.

1. The pretzel became popular.
2. This event happened rapidly.
3. This event happened throughout Europe.

The pretzel rapidly became popular throughout Europe.

B.

1. Pretzels were made in a monastery.
2. They were the first pretzels made.
3. It was an Italian monastery.
4. This happened in A.D. 610.

(In A.D. 610) the first pretzel were made in an Italian monastery.

C.

1. The pretzel is a snack.
2. It is especially popular.
3. This is true in Germany.
4. This is true in Austria.
5. This is true in the United States.
6. It is true today.

Today the pretzel is an especially popular snack in Germany, Austria, and the U.S.

Practice 12 Unit 6

A.

1. A hurricane is a storm.
2. The storm is dangerous.
3. The storm features winds and rain.
4. The winds are high.
5. The rains are heavy.

B.

1. A hurricane resulted in thousands of deaths.
2. The hurricane surprised the residents of Galveston, Texas.
3. This happened in 1900.

C.

1. A folly is an action.
2. This action is costly.
3. The action has a result.
4. The result is bad or absurd.

Practice 13 Unit 7

A.

1. Keeping a vocabulary notebook is not complicated to do.
2. The notebook is for learning words.
3. The words are English.
4. The words are new.
5. This statement is true if you follow a few steps.
6. The steps are easy.

____

____

B.

1. You should follow these directions.
2. The directions are simple.
3. Eating a taco can be an experience.
4. The experience is less messy.

____

____

C.

1. I am going to explain the steps.
2. The steps are to do a math trick.
3. The math trick is really interesting.
4. I learned the trick yesterday.
5. The trick will amaze your friends.

____

____

Practice 14 Unit 7

A.

1. Hit the ball into the box.
2. The box is small.
3. It is on the opposite side of the net.

____

____

B.

1. The racket should be near your knee.
2. The racket is yours.
3. It is the knee on the left.
4. Do this after you have completed your serve.

____

____

C.

1. You will need a quart jar.
2. The jar must be clean.
3. The jar must have a tight lid.
4. You will need some tape.
5. You will need a goldfish.
6. You will need some water.
7. You will need a few plants.
8. The plants need to be green.
9. You need all this for the experiment.

____

____

Practice 15 Unit 8

A.

1. A mother is standing.
2. She is to your left.
3. Her child is standing.
4. The child is crying.

____

____

B.

1. The tornado used its power to uproot trees.
2. The tornado used its power to toss cars around.
3. The trees were huge.
4. The cars were tossed around as if they were toys.

____

____

C.

1. Mother also trimmed the flowers.
2. She did this to make room for their replacements.
3. The flowers were old.
4. Their replacements were bright.

____

____

Practice 16 Unit 8

A.

1. The trees are gray.
2. The trees are brittle.
3. The trees are old.
4. The trees are near the river.

____

____

B.

1. A cat is curled up in a ball.
2. The cat is fat.
3. The cat is striped.
4. The cat has whiskers.
5. The whiskers are long.
6. The cat is on the right side of the sofa.

____

____

C.

1. The Statue of Liberty has a crown on her head.
2. The crown has seven spikes.
3. These spikes symbolize the oceans and the continents.
4. There are seven oceans.
5. There are seven continents.

____

____

Practice 17 Unit 9

A.

1. I am in favor of a ban.
2. The ban is on cell phone use.
3. This use is by drivers.
4. I am in favor of a ban because cell phones and driving are a deadly mix.

____

____

B.

1. Texting is certainly very common.
2. This fact is true now.
3. This is because texting is convenient.
4. This is because texting is fast.

____

____

C.

1. School uniforms should be mandatory.
2. This should be for all students.
3. This is for a number of reasons.

____

____

Practice 18 Unit 9

A.

1. Too much time can cause damage.
2. The time is in the sun.
3. The damage is to the skin.
4. The damage is severe.
5. This occurs especially in young children.

____

____

B.

1. She parked a car.
2. It was her car.
3. She parked illegally.
4. She got a ticket.
5. The ticket was for $50.

____

____

C.

1. One source is the newspaper.
2. The source is good.
3. It is for topics.
4. The topics are for paragraphs.
5. The paragraphs are opinion paragraphs.

____

____

Practice 19 Unit 10

A.

1. I practiced my speech.
2. I did this with my notes.
3. I did this in front of a mirror.
4. I did this in front of my cat.
5. I did this in front of my husband.

____

____

B.

1. Everything changed.
2. This happened when I was 16 years old.
3. This happened because my parents decided to move.
4. The move was to Florida.

____

____

C.

1. I was in a building.
2. I was on the third floor.
3. It was a six-story building.
4. I thought the building was going to collapse.

____

____

Practice 20 Unit 10

A.

1. The man waited until a guard gave him a number.
2. He did this patiently.
3. The number was to enter the building.
4. The building was warm.

____

____

B.

1. He gathered the paperwork.
2. The paperwork was important.
3. The paperwork included his I-20 document.
4. The paperwork included his passport.
5. The paperwork included his bank statements.
6. The paperwork included even a letter.
7. The letter was from his doctor.

____

____

____

C.

1. My best friend was sitting on a train.
2. I was sitting on a train.
3. The train was in Frankfurt.
4. The train was bound for Paris.
5. This is when the nightmare began.

____

____

Appendix 2

Peer Editing Sheet Sample

This is an example of the Peer Editing Sheets available for ***Great Writing 2: Great Paragraphs***. To print them out, go to NGL.Cengage.com/GW2.

Unit 1

Writer: ______________________________ Date: ______________

Peer Editor: ______________________________

1. What is the general topic of the paragraph? ______________________________

Does the title relate to this general topic? ❑ yes ❑ no

2. What is the more specific topic? ______________________________

____

3. If you can find the topic sentence, write it here. ______________________________

____

4. How many sentences does the paragraph have? __________ Do all the sentences relate to the same topic? ❑ yes ❑ no If any sentence is not about the topic, write it here.

____

____

5. Can you understand the meaning of every sentence? ❑ yes ❑ no If you answered *no*, write the unclear sentence(s) here.

____

____

6. Does every sentence have a verb? ❑ yes ❑ no If any sentence does not have a verb, write that sentence here and add a verb.

____

____

____

7. Is the paragraph indented? ❑ yes ❑ no If you answered *no*, circle the area where it should be indented.

8. Are any key nouns repeated? ❑ yes ❑ no If so, give an example.

____

____

9. If you have ideas or suggestions for making the paragraph better, write them here.

____

____

____

Index